Parsing Natural Language

Proceedings of the Second Lugano Tutorial, July 6–11 1981,
Lugano, Switzerland

Parsing Natural Language

Edited by

MARGARET KING

*Dalle Molle Institute for Semantic
and Cognitive Studies,
University of Geneva, Switzerland*

1983

ACADEMIC PRESS

A Subsidiary of Harcourt Brace Jovanovich, Publishers

London   New York
Paris   San Diego   San Francisco
São Paulo   Sydney   Tokyo   Toronto

ACADEMIC PRESS INC. (LONDON) LTD.
24/28 Oval Road
London NW1

United States Edition published by
ACADEMIC PRESS INC.
111 Fifth Avenue
New York, New York 10003

British Library Cataloguing in Publication Data
Parsing natural language.
1. Language and languages
I. King, M.
425   P123

ISBN 0-12-408280-7

Printed in Great Britain

pd
2-8-84

CONTRIBUTORS

Eugene Charniak *Department of Computer Science, Brown University, Box 1910, Providence, Rhode Island 02912, U.S.A.*

Anne De Roeck *Dalle Molle Institute for Semantic and Cognitive Studies, 54 route des Acacias, 1227 Geneva, Switzerland*

Roderick Johnson *Centre for Computational Linguistics, UMIST, P.O. Box 88, Sackville Street, Manchester M60 1QD, England*

Margaret King *Dalle Molle Institute for Semantic and Cognitive Studies, 54 route des Acacias, 1227 Geneva, Switzerland*

Steve Pulman *School of English and American Studies, University of East Anglia, University Plain, Norwich NR4 7TJ, England*

Graeme Ritchie *Department of Computer Science, Herriot-Watt University, 79 Grassmarket, Edinburgh EH1 2HJ, Scotland*

Michael Rosner *Dalle Molle Institute for Semantic and Cognitive Studies, 54 route des Acacias, 1227 Geneva, Switzerland*

Geoffrey Sampson *University of Lancaster, Department of Linguistics and Modern English Language, School of English, Lancaster LA1 4YT, England*

Steven Small *Department of Computer Science, University of Rochester, Rochester, NY 14627, U.S.A.*

Giovanni B. Varile *Commission for the European Communities, DG XIII, Jean Monnet Building, Plateau du Kirchberg, Luxembourg*

Yorick Wilks *University of Essex, Department of Language and Linguistics, Wivenhoe Park, Colchester CO4 35Q, England*

ACKNOWLEDGEMENTS

The initial work on this book was done in preparation for a Tutorial on Parsing Natural Language, organised by the Dalle Molle Institute for Semantic and Cognitive Studies of the University of Geneva, the second in a series of tutorials held in Lugano under the general title of the Lugano Tutorials. The authors and the organisers would like to thank the Commune of Lugano for their continuing kindness in providing us with a very beautiful setting for an intensive week's work, and for all their help with the organisation of the tutorial. We should also like to thank Signor Angelo Dalle Molle, from whose original creation of a forum for interdisciplinary and cross-national discussion so much has sprung, and Martine Vermeire without whose constant support and help we should have been left with nothing more than random pieces of paper. Finally, the editor would like to add special thanks to Franco Boschetti, without whom nothing would ever have been possible, and to Anneke De Roeck, who took over far more than was reasonable of the editorial work.

PREFACE

This book is a product of the rather odd relationship between artificial intelligence and theoretical linguistics. The area of artificial intelligence represented here is that of work designed to produce computer programs capable of analysing natural language, usually for some practical purpose such as the construction of question answering or of machine translation systems. Theoretical linguistics takes the study of language as an end in itself, and is mainly interested in giving a coherent account of how language works. Clearly, each field ought to be able to make use of the other. The theoretical linguist may regard a computer program as a valid way of demonstrating that the theory is in fact consistent: the artificial intelligence worker may make use of the linguists' theoretical proposals as alternatives to his own in the construction of his programs. This book is the result of a week long tutorial intended to facilitate and encourage the dialogue between the two disciplines. One central theme, that of parsing, was chosen as the chief topic of the tutorial, on the grounds that parsing is currently proving of great interest to both parties. In order to facilitate discussion, introductory material was included to give those from one of the disciplines with little or no knowledge of the other some basic background. Recent work on parsing was then reported and examined, with the aim of describing the current state of the art and of stimulating new research.

The pattern of the book reflects these aims. A preliminary Section tries to establish a common starting point for those not expert in the area. The first chapter covers some basic terminology and defines concepts from the theory of formal languages which are used extensively by later chapters. The second chapter is ·essentially historical, covering early attempts at the computational application of the 1960s version of transformational grammar. The importance of these attempts derives chiefly from the nature of the problems encountered there. Much of the work discussed in Sections 2 and 3 was directly or indirectly stimulated by a desire to overcome them. The remaining chapters of the introductory Section cover established techniques which are frequently used as a starting point for discussion of new ideas, and can therefore be considered essential background. In all of these chapters, the approach taken has been to give the basic outline and some critical evaluation, rather than to concentrate on detailed discussion.

The second Section concerns recent developments in the field of syntax and their application to parsing. The developments discussed fall within the field of transformational grammar and are described in those terms. Nonetheless, where the ideas have been used within a computational framework, the basic mechanisms of the parser involved are given. The current revival of interest in syntactic methods is clearly demonstrated in this Section.

The final Section, on parsing and semantics, consists mainly of a discussion on the role of semantics within parsing, and an evaluation of the different ways in which semantic information can be incorporated into a parser. Its position at the end of the book reflects the history of parsing over the last few years. An initial concentration on syntactic parsers led to the realisation that syntax alone was not enough. The reaction took the form of parsers aimed at minimising the use of explicit syntactic information, relying instead on semantics. This period in the history of parsing is by now well covered in the literature, except for recent attempts to develop lexicon based semantic parsers, as described in the final chapter.

The authors come from a variety of backgrounds within the gamut of linguistics and artificial intelligence. Although the same material is sometimes touched on by more than one author, the difference of viewpoint of the authors concerned is in itself illuminating.

A final remark should be made about content. For many workers, both in artificial intelligence and in linguistics, one of the most important aspects of their work is in its psychological implications. Thus, they use their work as the basis for the construction of psychological theories, and also regard evidence that their theories represent psychological reality as critical. This aspect of work on parsing has been for the most part deliberately avoided, on the grounds that to discuss it properly would demand a radically different approach and would justify a book by itself. The exceptions to this are where psychological considerations have had a direct effect on the design of the parser being discussed.

Margaret King   January 1983

CONTENTS

Contributors   v

Acknowledgements   vi

Preface   vii

Section I   Introductory   1

1   An Underview of Parsing   3
    A. De Roeck

2   Transformational Parsing   19
    M. King

3   Production Systems   35
    M. Rosner

4   Parsing with Transition Networks   59
    R. Johnson

5   Charts: a Data Structure for Parsing   73
    N. Varile

Section II   Developments in Syntactic Parsing   89

6   Deterministic Parsing   91
    G. Sampson

7   A Parser with Something for Everyone   117
    E. Charniak

8   Context-free Parsing and the Adequacy of Context-free
    Grammars   151
    G. Sampson

9   Trace Theory, Parsing and Constraints   171
    S. Pulman

Section III   Parsing Semantics   197

10 Semantics in Parsing   199
    G. Ritchie

11 Deep and Superficial Parsing   219
    Y. Wilks

12 Parsing as Co-operative Distributional Inference.
    Understanding through Memory Interactions   247
    S. Small

Bibliography   277

Index   301

SECTION I

INTRODUCTORY

Apart from the first chapter which presents some basic terminology which will be used throughout the rest of the book, this first Section is primarily concerned with setting the stage for the two later Sections and in picking out themes which will recur throughout the book.

It starts with a discussion of transformational parsing, where transformational refers to the theory of transformational grammar as it was presented between, say 1965 and 1972. It is not just historical curiosity which motivates this discussion. Many of the early computational parsers were based on, or derived from, the then current theories of transformational grammar. Work on these parsers proved seminal in many ways, not least in that they raised a whole series of problems which later work aimed at resolving. Thus, one of the reasons for the development of augmented transition networks (chapter 4), for example, was to find an efficient way of finding a correct path through a grammar, whilst preserving the power of a transformational grammar.

The proposal of charts (chapter 5) as a way of representing intermediate and final results during a parse can be seen as a proposal to solve the problem of non-determinism posed by a transformational parser. At a certain point during the parse, more than one continuation is possible, with no way of knowing which is the correct one. At this point, the parser may opt for one of the possibilities and then be prepared to come back on its tracks and try another if the choice leads to a dead end, or it may try to follow both paths simultaneously and risk finishing up carrying around a large number of competing possibilities. (If each of two possibilities has in its turn two possibilities for further development then there are four possibilities – very large numbers are very rapidly reached this way.) Chart structures offer a way of keeping all the alternatives alive whilst minimising the amount of structure being carried around.

The connection with production systems (chapter 3) is less direct in terms of historical development, but none the less strong. A transformational grammar is a special case of a production system, with all the associated problems of modularity and control. The production system model allows 'chunks' of knowledge to be expressed individually and independently, just as a transformational rule expresses items of linguistic knowledge. But when these individual rules are combined into a system of rules in order to do something with them, they necessarily interact. The problem then becomes how to ensure that they interact in the right way at the right time, which is precisely the central problem of production systems.

So far we have picked out the themes of control, of representation and of non-determinism. The first two of these themes are implicitly present throughout the rest of this book. The third will receive special attention in the next Section.

1

An Underview of Parsing

A. De Roeck

1. INTRODUCTION

A notion that should become clear at an early stage in a book like this is the one of *parsing* in the context of language applications. Clearly the answer to the question 'what is parsing?' should at least fulfill two goals. First, it should be simple enough to contribute to a general understanding of the issue. Second, it should be general enough to be applicable to all instances. At the same time over-simplification is to be avoided lest the information become irrelevant to any practical purpose.

The only way I see of respecting these criteria consists of taking recourse to what has already been established in the disciplines of mathematical linguistics and compiling theory. Talking about *grammars* seems a reasonable starting point.

2. GRAMMARS

2.1 Generative grammar

We all speak a language. Only physical limitations like tiredness, etc. can stop us from inventing sentences in that language. Each of those sentences may be different from all the ones thought of before and we can go on expressing new sentences quasi-forever. All this means is that in a language there are infinitely numerous different sentences.

The task the linguist has set himself is to describe human languages, i.e. infinitely large sets of sentences, and to do so in a manner that enables him to make the difference between those utterances that are part of the language described and those that are not. There are essentially two ways he can go about his job. One consists of listing all the sentences in a particular language. Any possible fragment is then bound to be included in the enumeration and can be checked against it. Nevertheless this method has some severe disadvantages. First of all, having established that the number of sentences in a language is infinitely numerous it becomes easy to deduce that one would never be able to finish the list. Also, although putting a large number of sentences down on paper may in some sense be equivalent to describing them, the technique does not allow for the explicit expresion of what those sentences have in common – i.e. some generalities and characteristics of the language. For instance, listing 20,000 random English sentences does not explicitly specify that most of them have a verb. Clearly, this way of doing the job is hardly satisfactory.

There is, however, another possibility for describing all sentences that make up a language; one that takes less time and does allow for the expression of some generalities. It is based on the idea that humans, who are after all beings with a *limited* memory, can decide when hearing a sentence whether it belongs to a language they speak. This suggests that, per language, there exist a *finite* number of criteria which each sentence has to fulfill and of which humans have an *implicit* knowledge they can use when making linguistic judgements. Linguists set about trying to discover what those criteria may look like and formulate them *explicitly* in a *grammar*.

So, a *grammar* contains a limited number of *rules* that describe a language. If the rules only tell you what the sentences can look like the grammar is said to have *weak generative capacity*; if they also predict what structure will underly the sentences they describe, the grammar has *strong generative capacity*. The term 'generative' refers to the fact that the grammar *explicitly describes* or *predicts* 'all and only' the sentences in a language: a generative grammar is an *explicit definition* of a language, and the word 'generative' is in this context in no way equivalent to 'produce' or 'output'.

2.2 Formal Grammars

The point has come to translate all this into more formal terms. A language can be seen as an infinitely large set of sentences. Each sentence is characterised as a *wellformed string* over a finite vocabulary of *symbols*. For the sake of simplicity, you can think of those symbols as words, though this view is not quite correct. *Wellformed* means that the form of the string – i.e. the way the symbols are put together – does not violate certain criteria specified in *rules of formation* which are contained in a *grammar*

At this level it no longer suffices to say that a grammar describes a language. The notion of *formal grammar* surfaces here, still serving the same purpose of describing a language, but in a form which is very rigidly defined.

A formal grammar G is a quadruple $\langle V_N, V_T, P, S \rangle$, where:

V_T is a finite set of *terminal symbols*. If the grammar generates human language these symbols coincide more or less with the words of the language

V_N is a finite set of *non-terminal* symbols. Sometimes they are also referred to as *variables* (Hopcroft and Ullman 1969: 10). In linguistic applications they correspond to categories. It is their presence in the rules that allows a grammar to express general wellformedness conditions.

P   is a finite set of rules called *productions*. They are of the form '$\alpha \rightarrow \beta$' (α rewrites as β) where both α and β stand for strings of elements of V_N and V_T.

S   is the *starting symbol* or *root*. S is an element of V_N and has to occur at least once on the left hand side of the rewrite arrow in the productions (in the place of α).

A grammar G generates a language $L(G)$. There exist several different types of grammar, depending on the form of the strings α and β in the rules (i.e. exactly what elements of V_T and V_N occur in α and β). The type of G determines the type of $L(G)$: grammars of a certain type generate languages of a corresponding type.

2.3 Context-free grammars

Maybe an example is called for to make all this a bit clearer. Of the different types of grammar I pick out one, namely the kind of grammar that is called *context-free* (hereafter *CFG*). The choice is motivated by practical considerations. CFGs are relatively transparent and their nature is well understood thanks to multiple applications in computer science. On top of that they are claimed to generate a subset, arguably all, of English and of some other languages, which should make them useful in the context of this volume.

In a CFG the productions have to be of the form '$A \rightarrow \alpha$' where 'A' is one symbol belonging to V_N (the set of non-terminal symbols) and 'α' is a string of terminals and/or non-terminals. Here is an example of a CFG:

1. V_N = {S, NP, VP, N, ART, V}
   V_T = { cat, mouse, eats, the}
   P = {S → NP VP
         NP → Art N
         VP → V NP
         VP → V
         V → eats
         N → cat
         N → mouse
         Art → the}
   S

The symbols in V_N respectively stand for the categories 'Sentence', 'Noun Phrase', 'Verb Phrase', 'Noun', 'ARTicle' and 'Verb'. The symbols in V_T correspond to words occuring in everyday English. The form of the productions corresponds to the definition stipulated and 'S', the root or *axiom* is present and occurs, in this case only once, on the left hand side of a production.

The language this CFG generates consists of the following six sentences, which happen also to be wellformed strings of English:

2. The cat eats the mouse.
3. The mouse eats the cat.
4. The cat eats the cat.
5. The mouse eats the mouse.
6. The cat eats.
7. The mouse eats.

True enough, it was suggested earlier that the advantage, for linguists, of using a grammar for describing language lies in its capacity of describing *infinite* sets of sentences with finite means. Clearly the CFG in the example does not exploit that possibility. The reason for this lies in the absence of *recursion* in the rules – i.e. there is no rule or sequence of rules according to which a non-terminal symbol can be rewritten as itself. An example of such a rule would be 'S → S NP', where in one single rule 'S' can be rewritten as itself. Recursion can also be spread over several productions, e.g. as in the sequence 'VP → V NP', 'V → VP', where 'VP' rewrites as itself over two rules distance. Nevertheless, the lack of recursion in the CFG in 1 will be of no consequence for the utility of the example in this chapter.

Apart from generating the strings 2-7, the CFG in 1 also predicts their underlying structures. The structure it generates for sentence 2, for instance, is represented below under two different forms; first as a *bracketed string* as in 8

8. $(_S (_{NP} (_{Art}$ The $) (_N$ cat $)) (_{VP} (_V$ eats $) (_{NP} (_{Art}$ the $) (_N$ mouse $))))$

and as a *tree*, as in 9

9.

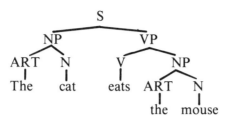

As a consequence it can be said that this grammar has strong generative capacity.

3. RECOGNISERS

In section 2 grammars have been defined as generating schemes, finite specifications for languages. There exists another way of specifying a language in a finite way, namely by means of *recognisers* – *abstract machines* which, when presented with a string of symbols will give a yes/no answer to the question '*Is this string a sentence of the language I [the recogniser] know about?* ' (For more details see also chapter 4 of this volume.)

A recogniser is often described as an *abstract* device which performs *operations* on an input string, according to a given finite set of *instructions*. Each of those instructions has to be *mechanically executable* using a *fixed* amount of time and energy. This comes down to saying that the set of instructions to a recogniser are a *procedure*.

An important point should be made here about the comparison between grammars and recognisers. A grammar and a recogniser are said to be *equivalent* if they respectively generate and recognise the same language, and for each type of grammar there exists a corresponding type of recogniser. But to say they are equivalent does not imply they have the same characteristics. A grammar offers a *static* description of a language, contained in a set of productions. Those productions though are not mechanically executable, and they are not ordered with respect to one another. They only give information about a language and give no clue about how that information gets used.

The instructions to a recogniser may *reflect* the same linguistic information as contained in a grammar but the machine will use it in a *dynamic* way, deciding which operation to perform next when confronted with some input at a given moment. This implies that the actual execution of the instructions is to some extent *ordered* as dictated by the input and by the instructions that were executed before. The set of rules to a recogniser is a procedure; the set of productions in a grammar is not.

4. PARSING

Consider again the sentence in 2 and its underlying structure (in 8 and 9). Although the CFG in 1 generates both, it doesn't offer any indication on how the link between the sentence and the structure gets established. The sample grammar defines six sentences and six structures but in order to decide which structure underlies example 2 the grammar is not enough. What is needed is a *procedure* that will, this time, not just recognise the sentence but also discover how it is built. The execution of that procedure is called *parsing* and the thing that executes it is called a *parser*.

So, parsers do essentially two things. On the one hand, when presented with a string, they have to recognise it as a sentence of the language they can parse. In this respect, parsers have built-in recognisers. On the other hand they have to assign to that sentence a structure which they have to *output*. This implies that parsers must rely on linguistic information as contained in a grammar with at least strong generative capacity, whereas recognisers, because they do not output structure, can be built referring to grammars with weak generative capacity.

Parsers belong to the type of objects called *transducers* – i.e. in simple terms a recogniser augmented with output facilities. Just as for recognisers, it is important to see that grammars and parsers have a different nature, since a parser has a set of instructions which constitute a procedure (but which can, nevertheless, use the same linguistic information as expressed in a grammar). For the sake of both simplicity and perspicuity, though, I will assume for the rest of this chapter that the parsers described have access to exactly the linguistic knowledge as expressed in the CFG of 1, and that each instruction corresponds to what is expressed in a single grammar rule (see 13 below). In other words, a rule 'X → YZ' is no longer to be read as a production but as an abbreviation of a more complex instruction to a parser that will use it to output a fragment of structure:

10.

$$X$$
$$\overset{\frown}{Y \quad Z}$$

A parser usually proceeds by taking a string of symbols (the input sentence) and applying a rule to it, which mostly comes down to rewriting a bit of the string. For example, the string 'ABC' is rewritten into the string 'ADC' by applying the rule 'B → D' (rewrite 'B' as 'D') and 'ADC' into 'AdC' according to a rule 'D → d'. The strings

'ABC', 'ADC' and 'AdC' are called *sentential forms* or *derivations*. The string 'ADC' is *directly derived* from 'ABC' since it is the result of the application of a single rule to 'ABC'. 'AdC' is *indirectly derived* from 'ABC' as more than one rule has to be executed to link up both strings. At each step the parser can output some structure. A sentence has been parsed when we know all the structures that can be assigned to it according to the set of rules available.

5. PARSING STRATEGIES

5.1 Criteria for a classification

Let us assume that a parser works by referring to rules which reflect linguistic knowledge (such as could also be contained in a grammar). Dissociated from a parser that uses them, such a set of rules can potentially be executed in surprisingly many different *orders* when assigning a structure to a sentence. Each different order corresponds to a different *parsing strategy* and parsers are classified according to the strategy to which they adhere.

Two criteria for looking at parsing strategies are considered standard and occur frequently in the literature. The first one focusses on the *linguistic structure* the parser outputs for the string it parses and takes into consideration whether that structure gets built starting from the input string (the *data*) – in this case the parser works *bottom-up* – or from the starting symbol (the symbol corresponding to the *axiom* of the grammar and which always *has* to be present as the *root* of the tree in any linguistic structure built; in 9 the symbol 'S') – in which case the parser works *top-down*.

The other criterion for classifying parsing strategies can be better explained by means of an example. Consider a set of rewrite instructions:

11a.	S	→	AB
b.	S	→	CD
c.	A	→	a
d.	B	→	b
e.	C	→	c
f.	D	→	d

For a given set of rules, it is possible to construct a scheme of all possible derivations those rules can yield. Considering that the beginning symbol, 'S' , is present two of the rules listed under 11 can be executed: rule 11a resulting in the derivation 'AB' and rule 11b yielding 'CD'. If rule 11a gets executed, a similar situation arises. To the string 'AB' rules 11c and 11d apply, respectively returning the strings 'aB' and 'Ab'; etc. Following this reasoning, all possible sequences of derivations that a given set of rewrite instructions allows can be discovered. The result is usually represented in the form of a tree as in 12.

12.

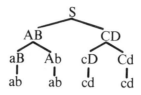

The tree in 12 pictures all possible sequences of derivations that can result from the rules in 11. Each node in the tree represents a point in the procedure where a choice presents itself in terms of different rules potentially to be executed on the same sentential form. The *leaves* of the tree – i.e. the nodes at the bottom – represent the sentential forms to which no further rules apply. In this case their content corresponds to those strings which can be parsed according to the rewrite instructions in 11 ('ab' and 'cd').

But, this tree should *not* be confused with the tree which linguists use to represent *linguistic* structure, and which expresses how the parts of a sentence fit together. The tree in 12 gives all possible *sequences of derivations* by which such a linguistic structure can be constructed. The classification of parsing strategies on the axis '*depth-first*' versus '*breadth-first*' is based on this kind of tree.

The sections 5.2 and 5.3 give further details about these two basic criteria for characterising parsers (top-down versus bottom-up and depth-first versus breadth-first).

5.2 Top-down versus bottom-up parsing

The following two examples will explain, although in general terms, how a very simple and frugal top-down and bottom-up parser assigns a structure to sentence 2

2. The cat eats the mouse.

provided both have access to the same set of rewrite instructions listed in 13:

13a. S   → NP VP
   b. NP → Art N
   c. VP → V NP
   d. VP → V
   e. V   → eats
   f. N   → cat
   g. N   → mouse
   h. Art → the

5.2.1 Top-down parsing. Top-down parsers always start with the starting symbol ('S'), find rules that apply to it and expand it. In this example the only rule available to do so is 13a. The result of the execution of 13a is the structure in 14:

14.

```
        S
       / \
      NP  VP
```

Two new nodes appeared. The parser first looks whether any of these two nodes is *terminal* – i.e. whether they contains symbols that would belong to V_T in the corresponding grammar. If so, those symbols will be checked against the string that is being parsed (sentence 2). If not, as is the case here, the parser further expands the first non-terminal node – in the example the 'NP' node. Rule 13b applies and is executed, yielding the structure 15

15.

```
          S
         / \
        NP  VP
       / \
     ART  N
```

Again, none of the newly constructed nodes is a terminal, and again the left-most non-terminal gets expanded. This way of proceding is repeated and after the application of rules 13h, 13f, 13c, 13e, 13b, 13h and 13g the string to be parsed is actually met. No further rules apply and the parse, outputting the structure 9, suceeds.

But things do not always turn out to be as straightforward as that. Take some steps back and imagine the parser has applied, to begin from the starting symbol, rules 13a, 13b and 13h yielding the structure

16.

```
          S
         / \
        NP  VP
       / \
     ART  N
      |
     the
```

The next non-terminal to be expanded is the node labelled 'N'. Before it was happily assumed rule 13f applies next, but there is no reason why rule 13g should not be executed instead. The parser then builds 17

17.

```
           S
          / \
         NP  VP
        / \
      ART  N
       |   |
      the mouse
```

In that case, the parser will find out when checking the newly found terminal against the data that 'mouse' does not correspond to the symbol it finds in the appropriate position in the sentence. It discovers its mistake and now has to do two things. First, it has to remember that 13g was not the right rule to apply in the previous state (illustrated in 16); then it has to reestablish the situation occurring before the application of 13g and try and find another rule to rewrite 'N'. The jargon refers to this move backwards as *backtracking* or *back-up*. The necessity for backtracking follows from the fact that, during the execution of the rewrite rules, a situation arose in which more than one option was available as to what to do next. This is the simplest case of *non-determinism* in a procedure. The set of rewrite rules in 13 is non-deterministic because whenever either of the non-terminals 'VP' or 'N' are encountered in a derivation more than one rule presents itself as a candidate for execution (for 'VP' 13c and 13d, for 'N' 13f and 13g), each resulting in a different structure. It is worth observing that a *deterministic* set of rules (where a similar situation does not arise) referring to a CFG can parse one and only one sentence.

Top-down parsers are sometimes called 'hypothesis driven' because they explore a particular derivation in the belief that it is the right one until they meet failure or success.

5.2.2 Bottom-up parsing. As opposed to top-down parsers, a bottom-up parser starts to work on the input string itself and *reduces* it to the root 'S'. It takes a sentence, replaces the words (terminal symbols) by their categories, and strings of categories by other categories. In order to do so it must look at the symbols on the right hand side of the rewrite rules and *reduce* them to the category written on the left hand side. Again, sentence 2 will get a structure assigned to it according to the grammar expressed in 13a-h, for instance by first applying 13g, yielding

18.   N
                                                |
            The   cat   eats   the   mouse

No rule applies to an 'N' node, either alone or combined with a string of terminals, so the parser looks at the next terminal, 'the', and reduces it according to rule 13h resulting in

19.   ART   N
                                         | |
            The   cat   eats   the   mouse

At this point there is a rule available that combines the categories 'Art' and 'N' reducing them to an 'NP' (rule 13b), as illustrated in

20.

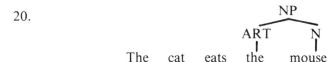

Then the terminal 'eats' is used by by rule 13e, after which 13c, 13f, 13h, 13b and 13a are executed.

With this strategy also, there is a need for backtracking. Imagine the intermediate structure after the execution of rule 13e in the above rule sequence, as pictured in 21:

21.

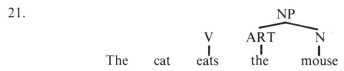

'V' can be reduced to 'VP' by rule 13d, thus leaving out the 'NP' and resulting, after the application of 13f, 13h, 13b and 13a in

22.

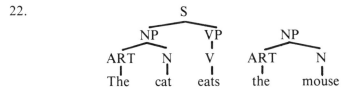

Structure 22 is illegal because, in spite of the fact that the root of the tree has been reached, there is a part of the structure that hangs loose (the rightmost 'NP'). In this case too the parser has to backtrack and remake a choice at an earlier stage.

It may seem odd that the parser just described parses a sentence starting from the right and working its way to the front of the string. Clearly language does not work like that, and this bottom-up parser can be argued to be psychologically not accurate on those grounds. Still, from the point of view of parsing and in terms of results obtained, a parser that starts from the left is equivalent to one that starts from the right if both refer to the same grammar, even if they follow different sequences of derivations. It may be useful to know that this right-to-left opposition has nothing to do with what is known in the literature as a *right* or *left parse*. A *right parse* is always the result of a bottom-up parser, which reduces sentential forms by referring to symbols found on the *right hand side of rules*. A top-down parser executes a *left parse*, deriving sentential forms by expanding the symbol found on the *left hand side of rules*.

Similarly, top-down and bottom-up parsers which refer to the same grammar, are also equivalent because they assign the same structures to the same sentences according to the same linguistic information – as shown by the examples. Their differences, besides the fact that they follow different sequences of derivations, have to be expressed in terms of memory needed and computing time involved. As the criteria for deciding which kind of parser to prefer in particular circumstances do not contribute to the aim of this chapter they will not be pursued here.

5.3 Depth-first versus breadth-first parsing

Let us have another look at the rewrite instructions in 11 and the corresponding *derivation tree* in 12. A similar tree can be drawn for all sets of rewrite instructions, picturing all possible sentential forms they allow to be constructed. Such a tree can be approached in two different ways: one concentrating on its vertical and the other on its horizontal aspect. These two distinct viewpoints result in a criterion for classifying parsing strategies.

5.3.1 Depth-first parsing. Let us consider the vertical aspect of the derivation tree in 12 and pick out one single vertical path linking the root with the sentence to be parsed. E.g. for sentence 'ab', contained in a leaf node, one could conceivably pick the path

23.

This path, like any other vertical path in the tree, gives a *sequence* of sentential forms. The word sequence has some importance here. It indicates that each sentential form is the result of the application of one single rule to the result of the execution of another single rule or to the root. If to a particular derivation several rules could potentially apply, only one rewriting possibility is retained. The other options are expressed in other paths of the tree and can not be traced along a single vertical path. Any parser that follows a sequence of sentential forms as can be represented on a single vertical path in a derivation tree is called a *depth-first* parser. Both the top-down and the bottom-up parser described in 5.2.1 and 5.2.2 belong to this type, the first starting the derivation at the top of the derivation tree, the other at the bottom.

12 shows clearly that more than one path may link a same sentence with the starting symbol 'S' (for each sentence – 'ab' and 'cd' – there

are two). Since a depth first parser explores only one path at the time it is possible that the path chosen from the beginning is not the right one. In those cases it becomes necessary that the parser be able to recover from its error by undoing the mistake (back-up: the parsers described in 5.2.1 and 5.2.2 illustrated this). For this reason depth-first parsers are usually implemented with backtracking facilities.

5.3.2 Breadth-first parsing. But one can also look at a derivation tree while stressing its horizontal dimension and taking into consideration all nodes at the same level in the tree. For instance, the root of the derivation tree consists of a node bearing the sentential form 'S'. Two daughter nodes hang off this node, containing, respectively, the sentential forms 'AB' and 'CD', each being the result of the application of alternative rules to 'S'. A parser which, in such a case, indeed does build both alternative derivations simultaneously and, in the next step, again applies all possible rules to both results, is called a *breadth-first* parser. An example can be found in chapter 5 on chart parsers.

Breadth first parsers apply all applicable rules to all sentential forms constructed; they explore the horizontal dimension of the derivation tree, exhausting all the choices which arise at the same time and taking them to their conclusion of either failure or success. This way of proceeding makes backtracking in case of failure superfluous: even if a derivation sequence resulting from a bad choice dies out, all successful alternatives being developed simultaneously will survive.

5.4 The classification

Two axes of classification have now been examined, namely the oppositions top-down versus bottom-up and depth-first versus breadth-first. The combination of these particular axes yields a total of four basic parsing strategies.

24.

	Depth-first	Breadth-first
Top-down	*top-down, depth-first*	*top-down, breadth-first*
Bottom-up	*bottom-up, depth-first*	*bottom-up, breadth-first*

Many more axes can be added, according to other classification criteria.
In practice few parsers conform to either of these strategies consistently,

and there is little reason why they should. After all, the scheme only presents a kind of abstraction, overlooking the host of practical considerations which do have some weight when it comes to actual applications. It is for instance quite common to find parsers which combine a bottom-up approach with some degree of top-down filtering. Still, for a lot of parsers it is possible to detect which of these strategies dominates. Standard ATNs, for example, can be characterised as top-down depth-first, whereas chartparsers usually work bottom-up breadth-first.

In principle, it is possible to make top-down parsers work bottom-up, and vice versa (be it with loss of efficiency) by altering the *content* of the rules (inverting left and right hand side) and interchanging the roles of starting symbol and data. This can be done because the linguistic information (the basis of this classification axis) in the rules is preserved. On the other hand, the distinction between breadth-first and depth-first parsers has to do with *how those rules get applied*. It is fixed through the application procedure, which in effect is the parser itself, rather than depending on the linguistic information encoded. As a consequence a similar inversion is harder to imagine.

6. DECIDABILITY

It was argued before that the set of rules to a recogniser or a parser constitute a procedure because each rule is executable mechanically using a fixed amount of space and time. An optimistic assumption has persisted throughout this chapter, that the procedure underlying any parser described could always cope with the input sentences, i.e. it always returned either a successful parse or a message that it could not proceed along the lines of a particular sequence of derivations. It should be said that this situation arises only in ideal cases and that not all procedures *halt* for any given input, but instead go on executing instructions forever, never stopping to return an answer of any kind, not even an indication of failure. This situation must clearly be avoided for practical reasons. Our interest is mainly in procedures that do stop, regardless of the input. A procedure that *always* halts is called an *algorithm*. Algorithms have many other definitions, but this is the most elementary one available.

Consider figure 25. The circle called 'P' is the set of all possibly imaginable strings over an alphabet of terminals. The small circle inside refers to all the strings in P which are wellformed according to the definition given in a grammar G: in short, all strings which belong to L(G). Whatever strings included in P but not in the set L(G) (i.e. the members of $\overline{L}(G)$, the complement of L(G)) are illformed with respect to the grammar G.

25.

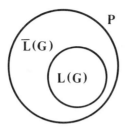

Imagine one wants to find out whether a certain string belongs to the language L(G), generated by grammar G, and the procedure for recognising which refers to that grammar is only guaranteed to halt if the input string indeed belongs to the language. In this case, the set of sentences making up L(G) is called *recursively enumerable* and the decision problem for L(G) – the problem of deciding whether a string belongs to the language – is called *recursively solvable*.

If, on the contrary the procedure will halt even if the string does not belong to L(G), the set of sentences L(G) is called *recursive* and the decision problem for L(G) is *decidable*. This last situation means that the procedure for recognising L(G) is an algorithm (according to the definition given above). As it will halt for all inputs, the algorithm recognises *both* members of L(G) and of $\overline{L}(G)$, in the first case returning 'yes' for an answer, in the second 'no'. This is another way of saying that a set is *recursive* or *decidable* if both itself and its complement are *recursively enumerable*.

7. CONCLUSION

This chapter has, I hope, contributed to some general understanding of 'parsing'. Nevertheless, the content of any of the concepts described can only become fully clear in the context of some application with respect to natural language. This aspect will be stressed in the next chapters of the first section.

2

Transformational Parsing

M. King

1. INTRODUCTION

Given that the theory of transformational grammar has changed so much since the version of it underlying the parsers described in this chapter, the reader may wonder why it is worthwhile to spend so much time on understanding the difficulties encountered by them. The reason is not only historical. Amongst parsers designed to do a practical job of work, tree-to-tree transducers are still very common. They inevitably encounter many of the problems described here as being specific to transformational parsers. Thus, the linguist writing rules for a working system is very likely to run up against problems of rule ordering, of unintended cycling, of 'ungrammatical' input causing the rule set to behave in an unforeseen fashion and so on. In a sense, then, the problems are more important than their context.

Many of the points made in the discussion in this chapter are drawn directly from the articles by Grishman (1976), Kay (1976), Petrick (1973), Walker (1966) and Zwicky, Friedman, Hall and Walker (1965). It would be unpracticable to try to give acknowledgment of each individual point, and sometimes invidious to do so, since the same point often occurs in one or more authors. I have however tried to state the source of examples where there is one.

A list of technical terms used, with rather informal definitions of them, are given in the appendix to the chapter.

2. WHAT COUNTS AS A TRANSFORMATIONAL PARSER ?

For the purposes of the present discussion, a parser counts as a transformational parser if it is based on a transformational generative grammar (of the type current in the late sixties and very early seventies), at least as far as its main components are concerned. That is, it is assumed to have a context-free or context-sensitive base component providing a mapping between a set of basic trees and a start symbol, as does the base component of a generative transformational grammar, and a transformational component providing a set of mappings between tree structures, as does the transformational component of a generative transformational grammar.

The difference, of course, is the use to which these components are put. Within the framework of generative grammar, the base component and the transformational component are seen only as defining the acceptable sentences of the language. When used as part of a generator, the grammar is viewed from the point of view of how sentences can be produced. In a parser containing the same two components, the aim is to analyse the sentence. In other words, the directionality is different. A generative grammar in itself is non-directional. A generator starts from the base component and produces surface strings, a parser starts from surface strings and tries to analyze by reconstructing the derivations which have produced that surface string. In parsing, the base component is used only as an acceptance device checking the validity of putative basic trees, since the base tree itself gives the supposed structural decomposition.

Parsers which are known to be equivalent in power to transformational parsers as defined above have not been counted here as transformational parsers, even if they assign structures very like basic trees. Only the components of the system have been allowed to count.

On the other hand no attempt is made here to distinguish between parsers designed to stick as closely as possible to the corresponding generative grammar, and those parsers where the corresponding generative grammar has served only as a starting point for manual construction of the rules to be used by the parser. In the latter case the transformational component produced for the parser may differ greatly from the generative transformational component: the two components are equivalent only in the coverage of structures obtained. Note that both ways of doing things are possible. Petrick's early systems (Petrick 1965, 1966) carried the attempt to stick to the generative grammar to the extreme of generating the parsing grammar automatically from the generative grammar. The MITRE system (Zwicky, Friedman, Hall and Walker 1965), on the other hand, from the beginning constructed the parsing grammar manually.

Both these systems are briefly described in the last section, where a further constraint has been imposed on the choice of systems used to exemplify transformational parsers, in that only implemented systems have been considered.

3. THE PROBLEMS OF TRANSFORMATIONAL PARSING

In this section an attempt is made to enumerate and explain the difficulties associated with transformational parsing. All of these problems are inherent in the transformational model, and must in some way be overcome by any transformational parser.

3.1 Getting started

Using transformational grammars for generation involves successive transformations of the basic tree input to the transformational component until the tree is finally decomposed and flattened to produce the surface string constituting a sentence defined by the grammar. Using a transformational grammar for parsing necessarily involves first constructing from the surface string a tree (or trees) on which the reverse transformations may operate.

Typically, this is done by a context free surface grammar, taking as input the potential grammatical categories assigned to the items of the surface string and producing a set of surface trees, which will serve as input to the transformational component and each of which must be considered a candidate for being the end point of a derivation.

In other words, the trees produced from the string of grammatical categories are meant to contain the tree that could be produced from the transformational component when generating which, when flattened, would give rise to this particular surface string.

The diagram below shows what point in the process the surface trees appear at.

1.

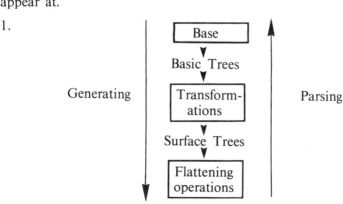

The construction of such a surface grammar must take into account all possible orderings of the surface string. Imagine, for example, that the base component contains a rule which produces

2. A → BC

If the transformational component then contains an optional transformation reversing the items 'BC', the surface grammar must foresee both possibilities, 'BC' and 'CB', in the surface string.

Similarly if an optional rule exists in the transformational component which rewrites one element by two, there are multiple paths to follow in the forward generation, each of which must be accounted for by the surface grammar. For example, if 'A' is optionally re-written 'BC', the derivation where 'A' is *not* re-written must be accounted for, as well as the derivations from 'B' and 'C' and from their combination.

More problems of this type can be found with no difficulty. But the implication is not that a surface grammar capable of accounting for them is difficult to construct. On the contrary, Petrick (1965) has shown that it can be done automatically from the base component and the transformations. Rather, the problem is that any surface grammar adequate to deal with all possible sentences (whether or not it is produced automatically), inevitably also produces a large number of spurious potential trees, with no way of selecting automatically from amongst them the genuine candidates for the end points of derivations.

Spurious here means that although the tree is legal in terms of the surface grammar, it is not, in terms of the transformational component, a tree which could possibly be generated in the generation of the surface string.

That this should be so follows inevitably from the fact that a context-free grammar is less powerful than a transformational grammar, and so less able to filter out unsuitable structures.

Unless some means is found of selecting among the surface trees, each one must be passed to the transformational component before it can be found to lead to a dead end (no basic tree yet produced, and no further reverse transformations applicable to the tree).

3.2 Finding the right sequence

Once the transformational component has been entered, it is not possible at any point to know, on the basis of the structure so far produced, what sequence of forward transformations might have produced that structure at some point during the derivation. Even if a reverse transformation matches, it is not certain that the corresponding forward transformation was involved in generating the sequence, since a different forward transformation may produce the same structure. Undoing the corresponding forward transformation could lead to a dead-end. To see this, imagine that the reverse transformations are in exact one to one correspondence with the forward transformations, and that in the forward grammar we have the following situation.

3.

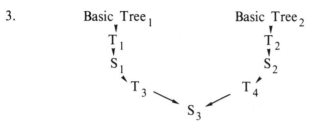

If the transformations are reversed, it is possible that S_3 'undone' by T_3 does not produce S_1, but a different structure, S_4, and that no further transformations can apply to S_4. In effect, a spurious path has been introduced:

4.

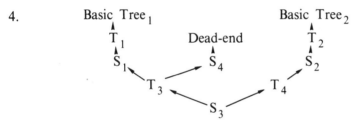

If T_4 is used, on the other hand, a basic tree would be reached. So both possibilities, applying the reverse transformation and not applying it must be considered. There is an important sense in which all reverse transformations are optional.

Unless further information, based on knowledge of the forward transformations, is used, all possible sequences must be pursued, and, clearly, the old spectre of combinatorial explosion raises its head.

Essentially, this type of information will be ordering information. For example, in the diagram above, it could be coded into T_3 that it should not operate on S_3 unless S_3 were produced by transformations which guaranteed that the structure produced by applying T_3 (in reverse) to it would be S_1 and not S_4.

This problem does not only occur if all transformations are considered to be optional (in the sense described above). Even if all transformations are made obligatory, and information on possible sequences included in the rules, the problem does not totally disappear unless the transformations are strictly ordered or unless there is never more than one transformation applicable at a time, since the same set of transformations applied in a different order may well produce different results, not necessarily all guaranteed to lead to a basic tree.

3.3 Optional transformations

This problem is really a special case of 3.2. When the grammar is used in generation, optional transformations pose no real difficulty: either the option is exercised or it is not, and with any particular derivation the choice has no consequences in terms of the number of possible structures to be considered: there is still only one.

When the transformations are used in reverse, during parsing, then the situation changes. In the last section we saw that no matter what transformation seemed to be applicable to a structure produced during the parsing process, the possibility must always be considered that, in *fact*, that particular transformation had not been responsible, during generation, for producing that structure. In that rather special sense we said that all reverse transformations had to be considered as optional, even those which in the generative use of the grammar had been obligatory. We saw too that the combinatorial explosion thus engendered could in practice sometimes be avoided by coding into the transformational rules information about possible sequences of transformations in the forward grammar.

If reverse transformations explicitly marked as optional are allowed, then the possibility of avoiding following two tracks – one where the transformation is applied and one where it is not – disappears: both tracks *must* be followed. The consequences are exactly those described in the last section.

3.4 Inter-dependence of transformations

A further fairly general problem should be mentioned before going on to discuss more detailed problems. A forward transformation cannot be considered as an independent entity, from which a reverse transformation can be produced, giving one reverse transformation for each forward transformation. Rather, the interaction of any individual transformation with all the rest of the grammar must be examined before a set of reverse transformations can be produced. To see this, consider a forward transformation which simply deletes an element (more will follow on deletions in the next section: here we shall simplify life considerably), e.g.

5. $A + C + D \Rightarrow A + D$

Now imagine that the only structure to which this transformation ever applies is

6.    , giving

A reverse transformation can be constructed undoing the effect of this forward transformation, but only because we *know* that it applies to one structure and to no more. If other forward transformations exist which produce

7.

e.g.

8. A + F + D ⇒ A + D

then we can no longer construct a reverse transformation restoring the deleted structure, simply because it is impossible to tell whether the deleted item was 'C' or 'F'. Yet it is impossible to tell from the forward transformation in isolation that this is the case: only a knowledge of the rest of the grammar can give us the relevant information (example based on Grishman 1976).

3.5 Deletions

Deletions are notorious for the problems they present; in fact, if a forward transformation straightforwardly deletes a portion of the tree, it is in principle impossible to re-construct that portion when working backwards; simply because no information is present in the structure to give a clue about what must be re-constructed or where.

Transformational grammarians often require that two or more copies of the same element occur in the tree before one copy can be deleted. (The identity condition.) This means that at least a copy is available if the deleted position must be re-constructed during parsing. Thus a forward transformation

9.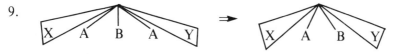

can effectively be undone during parsing by a reverse transformation

10.

(Note however that some means must be introduced to stop this transformation operating on its own output and thus cycling indefinitely: if it can be stipulated that the rule applies only once that presents no insuperable problem, but if it *could* apply more than once, the grammar writer has to hope that some further information is available in the context which can in practice be used to prevent cycling.)

The identity condition does not help a great deal however with transformations like the following, where a variable occurs between the two copies of the deletable element:

11.

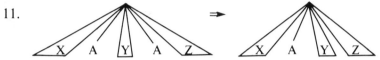

During parsing, not only is it impossible to know how many times the forward transformation might have applied, and therefore how many copies of 'A' should be inserted, it is also impossible to know *where* any new copies of 'A' should be inserted. The only information is that any new copy is somewhere to the right of the existing copy.

3.6 Ordering problems

The cycling problem in section 3.5 is essentially an ordering problem. The problem can be avoided by saying that a rule may only operate on the output of a rule which, in the ordering specified, comes before it.

It is interesting, though, to note that it is not sufficient, if the forward transformations are assumed to be linearly ordered, to assume that the order of the reverse transformations is the reverse linear order.

The following example, taken from Kay (1976), shows this. Assume a base component:

12. S → A (D) B C
    C → D E

and two obligatory and ordered forward transformations

13.

14.

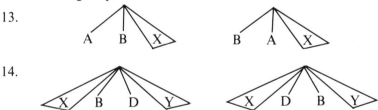

Now assume the (ungrammatical) input string 'A D B E', and that the reverse transformations are in reverse order. Transformation 2 applies to give

15. A B D E

Transformation 1 does not apply, so the base component is entered. The structure assigned is

16.

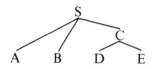

But, if this is a basic tree, transformation 2 could never have been used to produce the surface string, since, if we now enter the transformational component as a generator, with the above as a basic tree, then transformation 1 applies to give

17.

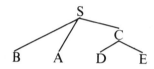

and transformation 2 no longer applies.

(During the application of rules applying to structures with embedded *Ss*, an additional element of order is required. Just as, when generating, lowest sentences are normally dealt with first in order to avoid premature destruction of sentence boundaries, so, when analysing, it is standard practice to deal first with highest sentences in the tree. This remark is not really presented as a problem, and is scarcely surprising.)

3.7 Cycling

A little has already been said about cycling and of the difficulty involved in avoiding it when a rule should be allowed to apply more than once on the same structure.

Kay (1976) points out that possible cycles are harder to detect than it might seem. The following is his example.

Take a context-sensitive grammar:

18a. S → ABC
 b. S → DE(S)
 c. B → D/A–
 d. B → F/–E
 e. D → G/A–
 f. D → B/–E

The grammar is well behaved in all respects. It is unambiguous and cycle-free. Now imagine that it is used as the basis for a parser, and is given the (ungrammatical) input string 'ADE'. Parsing proceeds as follows:

ADE
ABE (18c)
ADE (18f)
ABE (18c)
ADE (18f) and so on.

Of course, it might be argued that a parser should not be expected
to deal with ungrammatical input; but it is a rather rash assumption
to make that, in a realistic natural language parser, no ungrammatical
sentence will ever be input.

4. TRANSFORMATIONAL PARSING SYSTEMS

After a rather impressive list of problems to be dealt with, it seems
worth while to point out that transformational parsers do exist and
have given quite reasonable results over a restricted (sometimes highly
restricted) semantic domain.

The general pattern for their use is to use a phrase structure surface
grammar to produce the initial trees, and a reverse transformational
component to produce a putative basic tree. The base component is
then used as a recognizer, to check that the putative basic tree could
in fact be produced from the base component. The validity of the
derivation is then checked by generating from the basic tree via the
transformations to check that the surface sentence can in fact be
produced from that basic tree. This final step, which might seem at
first sight superfluous, is necessary because it is possible that a spurious
tree produced by the surface grammar may have led to spurious
matches of a transformation to the structure during the reverse
transformational analysis, and because the reverse transformations may
not incorporate all the constraints included in the forward transformations.

Variations on this basic scheme are possible. An early version of
Petrick's system (Petrick 1965) alternated the use of reversal rules and
phrase-structure rules, rather than applying all the surface grammar
rules before entering the reverse transformational component. A later
version allowed (optionally) a check on the validity of the inverse
transformational derivation at each point by testing the corresponding
forward transformation to make sure that if the transformation was
obligatory, it did *not* apply to the current tree if its inverse failed to
apply and that it did apply if the inverse applied, precisely undoing
the effect of applying the reverse transformation (Plath 1973). This
makes the final validation by synthesis step redundant, since it
accomplishes the same task.

Nonetheless, the basic scheme remains invariant in essentials.

5. RESOLVING PROBLEMS

In this section, each of the problems listed in section 3 will be taken in turn, and the attempts to solve those problems discussed.

5.1 The surface grammar

As noted, the primary problem with the surface grammar is that it produces too many spurious trees. One obvious way to cut down the problem is by using a more powerful mechanism than a context-free grammar, for example a context-sensitive grammar.

Another possibility is to produce the surface grammar manually rather than automatically, basing the rules on what actually occurs in text rather than what might theoretically occur. MITRE (Zwicky 1965) adopted this solution from the start, and Petrick, who in his early system (Petrick 1965, 1966) had used an automatically generated context-free grammar as a surface grammar, later (Petrick 1973) also constructed the surface grammar manually. He further introduced filtering transformations which function as restrictions on the surface grammar, but which act early in the transformation component. Others (e.g. Sager 1973) bring about the same effect by procedures operating during the surface analysis, using a context-free grammar augmented with restrictions.

5.2 Finding the right sequence

MITRE incorporated rejection rules into the reverse transformational process, in order to eliminate some trees as early as possible in the parsing (Walker 1966). These rejection rules incorporated some constraints which had previously only been in the forward transformational component.

Petrick, in the version of the REQUEST system reported in Rustin (1973), incorporated a number of control parameters attached to individual transformations, which help to direct the path through the reverse transformations. For example, one parameter is a proposition indicating a necessary condition for the transformation to be applied, e.g. that a particular S node must not be marked -QUESTION or that a particular NP node must have -WH. The conditions given can be any statable predicates over the trees picked out by the structural description part of the rule. Thus the application of transformations which would lead inevitably to dead ends can be avoided.

Another parameter blocks continuation down a false path. It is sometimes possible to state that only one way of applying a transformation should be possible. If this is so, Petrick marks the transformation with a flag. If multiple applicability does occur, an error message is sent and the transformation blocked.

Kay (1976) steers his parser down the right path by means of stringent ordering rules. We shall return to this when we discuss ordering below.

5.3 Optional transformations

For Petrick, all reverse transformations are optional, for MITRE, all reverse transformations are obligatory. There is obviously a trade-off here: MITRE has a larger number of input structures to consider at entry to the reverse transformational component, but it is better protected against explosion. On the other hand, MITRE must rely heavily on information coded into the rules to prevent wrong paths. (Note that MITRE is also obliged to insert a flag whenever a reverse transformation which would be optional as a forward transformation is applied, in order that the final validity check by synthesis can know when to use optional transformations. This is hardly a great disadvantage however).

5.4 Inter-dependence of transformations

The only practical way to solve this problem seems to be to construct the reverse transformations by hand.

Petrick's early system tried to avoid this, and relied on reverse transformations generated automatically from forward transformations. An immediate consequence of this was that it was impossible to include in the automatically generated transformations tests of the current analysis in order to determine what transformations could have applied to generate the tree. (Such tests were included in MITRE's manually constructed reverse transformations). Consequently if several reverse transformations could apply at some point in the analysis, the procedure had no information to help it to determine which would lead to a valid deep structure, so all possibilities had to be tried.

The problem was further aggravated by the fact that Petrick's early system did not construct a sentence tree. When a particular reverse transformation came up for consideration, just enough structure above the string was constructed (via a context-free grammar) to determine if the transformation was applicable. If it was, the transformation was applied and the structure was torn down again. Only a string of word categories was passed from one reverse transformation to another. The absence of a sentence tree meant that many sequences of reverse transformations were tried which did not correspond to any sequence of tree transformations and would therefore be eventually rejected.

Later versions of Petrick's system worked on a sentence tree during the reverse transformational stage, and used reverse transformations constructed by hand.

5.5 Deletions

To be brutal, deletions seem only to be dealable with in cases where the identity condition is met and where variables do not occur between the original and the copy.

5.6 Order

MITRE has the simplest ordering mechanism. Rules are linearly ordered, with the following refinements. A rule is specified as cyclical if it can be applied more than once before the next rule is applied. Otherwise it is marked as non-cyclical. As previously mentioned, rules dealing with embeddings work from the highest sentence down. This affects the order of application of rules to the extent that a rule may match a lower sentence, but not be applied because the higher sentence is still being dealt with.

The rules are also divided into sets: a set of reversed final singularies (rules not allowed to search for a match inside an embedded sentence), a set of reversed embeddings (allowed to search in an embedded sentence) and related singularies, and a set of reversed initial singularies. Rules are ordered inside each set, and the sets are applied in order.

The basic ordering of rules is much the same in Petrick's (1973) system, except that amongst the parameters attached to the rules is one which affects the order of rule application. Basically, the value of this parameter says what to do if a structure satisfies a transformation in more than one way. (It is assumed that two or more distinct applications of a transformation are independent.) The possible values cover *a)* ALL – all possible applications of the transformation are to be carried out independently without re-analysis of the sentence, *b)* ONE – any single way of applying the transformation is to be performed, *c)* SOME – some sub-set of the ways of applying the transformation is to be applied, *d)* REANALYZE – after performing one application of the transformation, the resulting structure is to be re-analyzed with respect to the same transformation, and again one instance is to be applied. This process is to be repeated until the transformation no longer applies. (The flag which prevents continuing down a wrong path mentioned earlier is a value of this parameter).

Kay (1976) offers facilities for much more rigid ordering. Each rule may be preceded by an expression taking one of the following forms:

$$n_1$$
$$n_1 / n_2 / n_3 \qquad \text{where } n_i \text{ is an integer}$$
$$n_1 // n_3$$

n_1 is a number assigned to the rule which defines its order relative to other rules. The same integer may be assigned to more than one rule, so the ordering is partial. If n_1 is empty, the system assigns 0.

n_2 and n_3 are used to specify where the input to the current rule (n_1) is to come from. They are to be interpreted as 'The input to the current rule must be the output from some rule numbered i, where $n_2 \leqslant i \leqslant n_3$.'

5.7 Cycling

Kay uses the ordering mechanism above to block some types of cycles. For example,

3, A → B
4//3, B → BC

will not cycle, since rule 4 is only allowed to operate on rules numbered 3 or less (and therefore not on its own output).

He includes also a special type of rule specifically designed to prevent cycling. Rules of this type contain only a left hand side. If any string matches the left hand side (Kay's descriptions of structure are all bracketed strings), from then onwards no rule is allowed to apply to the whole of that string.

For example, with the context-sensitive grammar given in section 3.7, which cycles with

ADE
ABE
ADE
ABE   and so on

a rule

ABE

would block the cycle.

In fairness to those who neglect this problem, it should be said that Kay himself remarks that in practice it is very rare.

6. CONCLUSION

This chapter has aimed at producing a general background knowledge of some of the problems associated with transformational parsers and of some solutions adopted in working systems. Later chapters in this book will describe other ways of tackling these same problems. In some cases, the solution adopted is purely computational, i.e. the problem remains, but a computational technique is developed to deal with it efficiently. In other cases, developments in linguistic theory make the problem disappear.

7. APPENDIX: TERMINOLOGY

A brief list of technical terms is given here, with very informal definitions.
a. *Base component.*   A context-free or context-sensitive phrase structure grammar, consisting of a set of production (reduction) rules. The 'end-points' of the base component are a special starting symbol and a set of basic trees.
b. *Transformational component.*   A set of transformational rules.
c. *Transformational rule.*   A rule mapping one tree onto another tree. Such a rule consists of a description against which particular input trees are mapped and a list of operations to be carried out if an input tree matches.
d. *Forward transformation.*   A transformational rule written on the assumption that the grammar is to be used in the generation of surface sentences.
e. *Reverse transformation.*   A transformational rule written on the assumption that the grammar describes the analysis of surface sentences.
f. *Cut.*   A subset *S* of the set of nodes *D* of a tree such that: *a)* No member of *S* is on a successor path from another member of *S* and *b)* No member of *D* could be added to *S* without violating a). Note that there can be more than one cut of the same tree. Thus, the dotted line in each of the trees below is a cut of the tree.

1.   2.

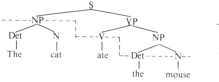
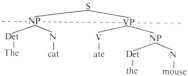

g. *Structural index / structural description.* A sequence of symbols such that each element is either the name of a node or a variable (matching any sequence of nodes). This sequence describes a family of trees, containing the sequence on a cut, and constitutes a structural description.

Either the position in the sequence is implicitly used as an identifier of the node or variable concerned or identifies are explicitly assigned. The identifiers are then attached to the matched nodes in a specific matching tree. This is the structural index.

h. *Structural change.* The list of operations to be carried out on the matched tree. This list normally makes use of the identifiers assigned to the nodes of the matched tree via the structural index.

i. *Proper analysis.* If the names of the nodes in a cut of the input tree, taken in left to right order and including sequences which match against variables where appropriate, match the structural description, then the cut is a proper analysis of the tree.

3

Production Systems

M. Rosner

1. INTRODUCTION

A Production System (hereafter, PS) is a particular kind of scheme for the specification of algorithms. PSs derive from a computational formalism proposed by Post (1943) that was based on string replacement rules. The closely related idea of a Markov algorithm (Markov 1954) involves imposing an order on these rules and using this order to decide which rule to apply next. Newell (1973) used the term to describe the organisation of some fairly simple list manipulation algorithms, which at the time were being used to build psychological models of human memory. Since then, they have achieved a reputation as the computational basis for 'expert' systems in a wide variety of different problem domains, including mass spectroscopy (Feigenbaum 1971), medical diagnosis (Shortliffe 1975), electronic circuit design (McDermott 1977), automated theory formation in mathematics (Lenat 1977), and others.

This article is not intended to be a review of existing systems, since many such already exist (e.g. Waterman and Hayes-Roth 1978, Rychener 1976, Stefik et al. 1982). Rather, it is an introduction to the principles according to which PSs are constructed (Sections 2, 3), the effect this has on the algorithms they compute (Sections 4, 5), and a comparison between PSs and procedural programming languages (Section 6).

Comparatively little use has been made of PSs for parsing – yet the basic architecture offers some very attractive features. In section 7, we discuss some aspects of PS design which are relevant to parsing viewed as a problem solving process, as well as some of the shortcomings inherent in the unadorned notion of a 'pure' PS.

2. ANATOMY

Although it is possible to organise PSs in many different ways, they all have certain features in common. Informally, we can consider these to be:

1) A *database*.
2) A *production set*.
3) An *interpreter*, which is a mechanism which employs 1) and 2) to perform computations.

Each production is essentially a pair consisting of a condition part and an action part. The condition part addresses some feature of the database, so that it is always possible to say whether the condition part of a given production is met at a given moment. The action part specifies what is to be done when the production is applied, and in principle there is no restriction on the nature of this action. It could, for example, call a subroutine, modify the data structure, halt the computer, invoke or disable other productions, and so on. However, for the sake of transparency, certain restrictions tend to be observed by designers of PSs to conform with the so-called 'spirit' of PSs (see Davis and King (1977) for further comments upon this concept).

Newell (1973) sums up the modus operandi of a PS in the following way:

> That production whose condition is true of the current data (assume there is only one) is executed, that is, the action is taken. The result is to modify the current data structures. This leads in the next instant to another (possibly the same) production being executed, leading to still further modification. So it goes, action after action being taken to carry out an entire program of processing, each evoked by its condition becoming true of the momentarily current collection of data structures. The entire process halts either when no condition is true (hence nothing is evoked), or when an action containing a stop operation occurs.

Newell himself admits that this description gives but a very rough sketch which needs a considerable amount of elaboration to yield a definite information processing system. This may not be obvious to the casual reader, so our aim, in what follows, is both to make it obvious, and to convey an idea of what choices are involved in constructing a working system.

2.1 The database

The database of a PS can be regarded as a kind of memory, whose chief characteristics are the number and nature of the items in it, the structure imposed upon them, and the way in which they are accessed. These vary widely from system to system. For example, in Newell's system described above, the number of such items was limited to 7 ± 2 in keeping with the then popular psychological investigations of Miller (1956), each one having a recursively defined list structure. The set of items was ordered, access for reading being defined in the sense of the ordering, and access for writing being limited to adding a new item at the 'front' of the database (whence the item at the 'back' was lost).

In contrast to this, the database of Colmerauer's (1970) Q-System contains an unlimited number of items, each of which consists of a string of trees. Two relationships between items, concatenation and alternation, are explicitly represented in the database using a directed graph, and access for both reading and writing is performed in a random fashion – i.e. anywhere on the graph.

2.2 The production set

An *uninterpreted* production, in its written form, consists of an ordered pair of symbol strings, separated by some delimiting symbol (we will use '➤'), e.g.

1. R1: ABC ➤ DEF

We normally distinguish the left and right hand sides (*lhs*; *rhs*) in the obvious way, so that the *lhs* of 1 is 'ABC', and the *rhs* is 'DEF'.

An *interpreted* production is a pair consisting of

A) a *condition* which is evaluable with respect to the database,
B) an executable *action* which in general changes the state of the database.

These two ways of regarding productions are often confused with each other. For example, one often hears locutions of the form: 'the lhs of production X is true at a given moment'. Strictly, this is inaccurate, for it is the interpreter (see below) which 'interprets' uninterpreted productions, thereby conferring upon the *lhs* and *rhs* the roles of condition and action. Now although it is frequently the case that the condition part of a production is derived from its *lhs*, and the action part from its *rhs*, it is possible in principle (although not always) for the lhs and rhs to serve opposite roles.

For a very simple example of this, let us suppose that R1 were to be interpreted in the conventional sense of a *rewrite rule*. This involves treating the lhs as a condition which is true when the database contains

'ABC', and the rhs as an action performed by replacing the item 'ABC' with the item 'DEF'. On the other hand, the rewrite interpretation of a production is clearly reversible – in the sense that it is possible to take the rhs as condition, and the lhs as action.

The rewrite interpretation of a production is an extremely simple example which is of particular interest in virtue of its reversibility and its extreme transparency. In the latter respect, it is characteristic of a 'pure' PS, a somewhat abstract concept which we hope the reader will grasp as we proceed. The reader should note, however, that there is an infinity of possible interpretations for productions, some of which are considerably less transparent than this. In Newell's (1973) system, for example, the first production mentioned is:

AA AND BB ⇒ (OLD *)
(Newell 1973: 8)

whose lhs is 'AA AND BB'. The implied condition is not, however, the presence of the concatenation:

AA + AND + BB

in the database. Instead, it is the simultaneous presence of 'AA' and 'BB' *anywhere* in the database. Again, the action implied by the rhs is not the literal replacement of items with the concatenation

(+ OLD + * +)

because * is a *variable* whose value is the first element in the database. If, at the time of performance, that element is 'AA', the item added will be

(+ OLD + AA +)

whilst if it is 'BB', it will be

(+ OLD + BB +)

In what follows, we will try to be explicit about the relationship between the productions themselves, which are essentially just pieces of text, and the conditions and actions which are derived from them by the interpreter, to which we now turn.

2.3 The interpreter

We can conveniently think of the interpreter as consisting of two main parts: the *interpretive* part, and the *control* part.

2.3.1 The interpretive part. We already alluded to the interpretive part of the interpreter in the last section: it is essentially that part of it which is responsible for defining *what* condition and *what* action are associated with a particular production.

A useful (though not entirely accurate) way of summarising this is to say that the interpretive part of the interpreter defines, for any single production p the two 'primitive' operations:

1) Test(p) – i.e. evaluate the condition of p.
2) Apply(p) – i.e. execute the action of p.

2.3.2 The control part. A PS computation or part thereof, must in some sense consist of a sequence of test and apply operations. Very roughly, we can regard the control part of the interpreter as that which determines the nature of such a sequence. At this point we need a term to denote the set of principles employed by the control part which cause it to behave the way it does. This we will call a *control strategy*. In short: the interpretive part of the interpreter determines the *how* of the primitive operations, whilst the control part determines their *when* and, in the case where the database consists of several items, their *where* i.e., the item, or items, to which they apply.

Realize that the state of the database at a given instant is entirely a function of the sequence of applications that have taken place up to that instant. If, therefore, two different control strategies cause different sequences of applications, there is no reason a priori to think that the terminal databases induced by each strategy will be identical. The consequence of this is that the computation effected by a PS is partly determined by the control strategy employed. We will be able to return to this issue in greater detail below, but before doing so, it would be well to make some concrete use of the concepts so far introduced. For we have now arrived at the stage of being able to construct a pure PS, and watch it in operation.

3. AN EXAMPLE OF A PURE PS

2. p1: AE   ⟹ AE1
   p2: AE   ⟹ AE2
   p3: AE1   ⟹ TERM
   p4: AE2   ⟹ (AE OP AE)
   p5: TERM ⟹ x
   p6: TERM ⟹ y
   p7: OP   ⟹ -
   p8: OP   ⟹ +

The productions in 2 are essentially a set of ordinary context free rewrite rules, which, within a generative linguistic framework, could be used to specify the well formed strings of a very simple language of arithmetic expressions of which the following are examples:

x; (x + y); (x + (y - x)); ((x + y) - (x - y))

and the following are counter-examples:

+; ( ); (x); (x +; x + y;

By specifying details for the appropriate kind of interpreter, we can build a production system which performs a large part of the task of recognising the well formed strings of this language. Recall from chapter 1 that a recogniser for a language L must, given any string S, either affirm, or deny, the membership of S in L.

3.1 Details of the interpreter

A) Interpretive Part: The rewrite interpretation of productions (see section 2.2) is employed, taking the *rhs* as condition and *lhs* as action.

B) Control Part: At each cycle, we determine the set of applicable productions, and then apply one.

Assuming the initial database: (x + (y - x)), we might expect the series of operations depicted in 3 to take place.

3.	database	applicable production set
	(x + (y - x)	{p5 p6 p7 p8}
	(TERM + (y - x)	{p3 p5 p6 p7 p8}
	(AE1 + (y - x))	{p1 p5 p6 p7 p8}
	(AE + (y - x))	{p5 p6 p7 p8}
	(AE + (y - TERM))	{p3 p6 p7 p8}
	(AE + (y - AE1))	{p1 p6 p7 p8}
	(AE + (y - AE))	{p6 p7 p8}
	(AE + (TERM - AE))	{p3 p7 p8}
	(AE + (AE1 - AE))	{p1 p7 p8}
	(AE + (AE - AE))	{p7 p8}
	(AE + (AE OP AE))	{p4 p8}
	(AE + AE2)	{p2 p8}
	(AE + AE)	{p8}
	(AE OP AE)	{p4}
	AE2	{p2}
	AE	

Since there are no more applicable productions the computation must stop. Note carefully that it contains the single item 'AE'. In grammmatical terms, each application can be regarded as a kind of 'direct derivation' (see chapter 1). Thus the database after an application can be said to be directly derived from the one immediately preceeding.

To say that two databases are related by a sequence of applications is then equivalent to saying that the string represented by the latter can be derived from the string represented by the former. Since the last database corresponds to the 'initial symbol' of the 'grammar', the run of this PS has proved that this latter can be derived from the string corresponding to the initial one.

Conversely, if the last database is anything but 'AE', the string is not in the language. This is illustrated in 4.

4. *database*   *applicable production set*

database	applicable production set
x + y	¦ p5 p6 p8 ¦
TERM + y	¦ p3 p6 p8 ¦
AE1 + y	¦ p1 p6 p8 ¦
AE + y	¦ p6 p8 ¦
AE + TERM	¦ p3 p8 ¦
AE + AE1	¦ p1 p8 ¦
AE + AE	¦ p8 ¦
AE OP AE	

3.2 Final databases and goal conditions

The simple interpreters described so far stop when there are no more applicable productions. We will call the database which results in such a case *final*. Suppose, however, that we wish to define the computation in terms of a *desired* state of the database. If, for example, we wanted our recogniser to return a definite yes or no, we would have to convey to the system that if it reached the state 'AE' it should say yes; otherwise, it should carry on with the computation. But of course, the system cannot continue if the database is final, in which case, it should return no.

To generalise a little, we can say that the stipulation of a desired state or goal condition defines the computation by providing two possible modes of termination: *success*, if a database fulfills the condition, or *failure* if it does not and is final.

In what follows, we will sometimes refer to a state fulfilling a goal condition as a *solution state*. But we must be careful to distinguish the solution state defined by a goal (i.e. the *intended* computation) from any state *actually* computed: for we might want to say that 'the solution state is never reached'.

4. APPLICABILITY OF SEVERAL PRODUCTIONS

The astute reader may have noticed that one detail of the interpretive part of the interpreter was skipped over with a deliberate amount of haste in the preceding section. We said that at each cycle, 'we determine the set of applicable productions, and then apply one'.

The process of selection from a set of applicable productions is usually referred to as *conflict resolution*. In this case, the criterion used was to pick the production with the lowest number. This amounts to an almost blind method for resolving conflicts, since there is no particular significance intended by the order in which they appear. There are, of course, many other ways of resolving conflict. One might, for example, wish to favour or disfavour productions which had been recently applied, or those which were special cases of others in the conflict set. A useful comparison of these and other strategies is discussed in McDermott and Forgy (1978). We will return to the topic below.

4.1 Irrevocable control strategies

The other characteristic of the control component illustrated in the last section is that it implements *irrevocable* control:

> In an irrevocable control regime, an applicable rule is selected and applied irrevocably without provision for reconsideration later. (Nilsson 1980: 21)

In general, irrevocable control strategies are easy to implement, since only one production application need be considered at a time. However, their use presupposes either that the order in which applications are applied is not crucial to the attainment of the solution state, or that the conflict resolution strategy is sufficiently intelligent to make the right choice.

4.1.1 Commutativity and non-determinism. Order of application is never crucial when the production set is commutative, i.e. when the database that results from applying all the applicable productions in some sequence is invariant with respect to the particular sequence chosen, as is the case for the system in the last section. For this reason, we could have had a much shorter 'derivation tree' by simply applying all the applicable productions in some arbitrary order at each cycle – e.g.

5. $(x + (y - x))$ $\xrightarrow{\hspace{2cm}}$ (TERM OP (TERM OP TERM))
   $\quad$ p5 p6 p7 p8

Because the PS is commutative, the final result after several such applications would not be affected.

Unfortunately, commutativity is a luxury that we cannot always take for granted. For the point is – and this is the essence of non-commutativity – that the application of a production *changes* the state of the database. If it happens to affect the very piece of data that is responsible for the applicability of some other production, then after application of the first, the second will no longer apply. Thus, the application of one excludes that of the other.

Thus, when several non-commutative productions apply to a given state, the system could proceed along different computation paths, each leading to a distinct result. There is therefore a space of (equally legitimate) computation paths, which can be pictured in the form of a tree (see 6), whose nodes represent states of the database, and whose arcs, the application of individual productions. We will subsequently refer to such a tree as a '*P-tree*', and the space it represents as the *solution space*.

6.

The combination of non-commutativity with an irrevocable control strategy implies that we pursue just one 'computation path' through the space of possibilities, so that the final state is entirely a function of the conflict resolution scheme – for once (and if) a final state is reached, the computation must halt.

This is satisfactory provided that the irrevocable choices are made upon evidence which is sufficient to guarantee that the correct path will always be followed. However, for many applications, there is insufficient information to make the appropriate choice. When this is the case, there is no alternative but to search the space of possible applications, and their consequences. Another way of saying this is that the computation is inherently *non-deterministic*, because if nodes in the tree represent 'states' of the PS computation, then a node with several branches indicates a *set* of subsequent states.

4.1.2 Solution Sets. A commutative production set implies that all solution paths are equivalent. Therefore the specification of a goal defines a single solution state. If the production set is non-commutative, the goal may define several solution states even if the goal condition is strong enough to identify a unique database configuration. For now, 'identical' databases may appear in different parts of the P-tree. The computation specified by the goal is therefore to be identified with a set of successful states, which we will subsequently refer to as the *solution set* of the computation. It is important to realise that the solution set is entirely determined by the interpreted production set, and the goal condition. It is therefore independent of any control notion.

4.2 Simulating non-deterministic computations

There are essentially two ways to perform a non-deterministic computation. If we have an arbitrarily large number of processors at our disposal, we could simply assign a processor to run each sub-PS, and perform the computation directly. However, if, as is usually the case, we have only one processor, then we are forced to *simulate* the computation deterministically. Although any such simulation must in some sense realise each path through the P-tree, we can broadly distinguish between control strategies which explicity construct and maintain the entire tree, or at least, several branches of it (parallel search), and those which realise at most one branch at a time (backtracking search).

4.2.1 Parallel search. The defining characteristic of parallel search is that the several states of the simulated computation corresponding to the individual application of the several productions are explicitly represented in the simulating computation. Intuitively, the states available correspond to a single level in the P-tree. We can achieve this by defining a new PS whose database always corresponds to the set of databases at that level.

Call the initial database of the simulated computation i, and let the set of databases reachable from a given state in the simulated computation be called the *continuation set* of that database. The initial database of the simulating computation is the set $\{i\}$. Execution of the simulating computation then proceeds by constructing the union of the continuation sets of each member of its database.

The advantage of parallel search is that 'parallel' states of the simulated computation are simultaneously available to the simulating computation, which is therefore in a position to manipulate them explicitly. By constructing the union, for example, multiple representations of the same state are eliminated, which, for a real machine, implies saving of the computational effort expended on generating their continuation sets.

On the other hand, parallel search is clearly going to require an amount of storage which is proportional to the number of states at a given level. This is combinatorially explosive, so that for anything other than trivial computations, maintenance of an entire level may not be computationally feasible.

4.2.2 Backtracking search. Parallel search effectively simulates a non-deterministic computation by representing the result of all possible choices simultaneously. Under the mode of simulation known as backtracking, the choice to follow a single path is made, but it is made in such a way that it can be undone if necessary. Nilsson (1980) calls this mode of control *tentative*:

> In a tentative control regime, an applicable rule is selected (either arbitrarily or with good reason), the rule is applied, but provision is made to return later to this point in the computation to apply some other rule. (Nilsson 1980: 21)

This amounts to depth first search of the P-tree, which can be accomplished by saving the state of the simulated computation (i.e., the database together with some indication of the choices left) each time a choice is made. This information is kept in a pushdown store or stack, which guarantees the orderly traversal of the P-tree one branch at a time.

The advantages and disadvantages of parallel search are reversed in the case of backtracking. Because only one branch of the tree is explicitly maintained, storage requirements are minimal. But then, each time a sub-branch 'disappears', so does all the information it contains – which could be of use in preventing the subsequent regeneration of an identical sub-branch.

Automatic backtracking simulation of non-deterministic computation is employed in programming languages such as PROLOG (Roussel 1975) and PLANNER (Hewitt 1971). A fuller discussion of the disadvantages of automatic backtracking, which led to the development of the language CONNIVER appears in Sussman and McDermott (1972).

5. TAXONOMY OF CONTROL

5.1 Controlled production systems

Every arc in the P-tree is associated with the name of the production which caused that particular transition. A single path through the graph thus corresponds to a word whose 'characters' are production names. The entire set of paths can therefore be regarded as a set of such words.

It is this observation which motivates Georgeff's (1982) conception of a *controlled* PS, which is essentially a PS augmented with a *control language* C. This comprises the 'control' words corresponding to possible execution paths through the P-tree. States of a controlled PS are pairs of the form '(w, d)', where d is an element of the database, and w the control word corresponding to the current history of the computation.

> Execution may terminate successfully if d satisfies the goal condition. Alternatively, execution may continue by considering all productions p such that wp is a prefix of some word in C. Let us call such productions *active*. The condition of each active production is evaluated, and all those applicable form the conflict set. If the conflict set is empty, execution terminates unsuccessfully. Otherwise, a production

p is (nondeterministically) selected from this set, and execution continued from a (not necessarily unique) state *(wp, d')*, where p applied to d yields d'. (After Georgeff (op cit))

The *computable* solution set of a particular problem is defined by an initial database, a goal condition, an interpreted production set, and a control language.

Within this model, we can elaborate on the rather low fidelity conception of control presented in section 2.3.2 For now, we can distinguish

A) the *generation* of a control language, and
B) its *execution*, which may involve conflict resolution.

These have rather different properties. The control language may be generated in many different ways, some of which will cause the solution set to be computed more efficiently than others. Below we examine two of these.

5.2 Order of expansion

Each branch point in the P-tree represents a situation where there are several applicable productions. If the solution resides in only one branch, it would clearly be desirable to search that branch before any of the others. There may of course be several paths to the solution. If the same solution resides in two or more branches, then the one which contains the shortest path to it is to be preferred. So in 7, an optimum strategy would first pursue the branch labelled 3.

7.
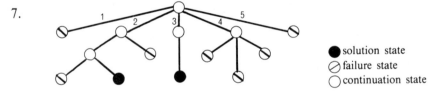

- ● solution state
- ⊘ failure state
- ○ continuation state

When the choice is made at random, we say that the search is *blind*. In practice, however, it may be possible to rank the branches in order of preference by using domain-specific knowledge. This sort of information is usually called *heuristic* to indicate the fact that it is not infallible.

5.3 Direction of evaluation

If a solution path exists, then there will always be an inverse solution path which starts at the solution and ends with the initial database. In cases where productions are reversible (such as the rewrite interpretation), and when the architecture of the system permits it, it is sometimes advantageous to arrange for the path to be discovered in reverse.

The reason that such a reverse solution might be preferable arises from the geometry of the P-tree. From top to bottom, there is a larger degree of branching, and therefore, a larger overhead in simulating the non-deterministic search than there would be in the opposite direction. In the limiting case of a truly tree shaped graph, the latter search is completely deterministic, permitting an irrevocable control strategy. In 8, for example, a non-deterministic strategy would be required to arrive at 'S' working *forwards* from state 'I'. On the other hand, by starting with 'S', the path to 'I' working *backwards* is without branches. This is exactly the shape of graph associated with the production set discussed in section 3. Hence the adequacy of the control strategy employed in the example PS.

8.

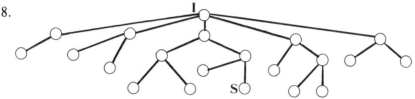

The technical term for PSs which discover solutions in reverse is 'goal directed'. We discuss the concept further in section 7.

Georgeff's claim is that whatever strategy is employed for generating a control language, it merely affects the efficiency of solution. It does not in itself change the nature of the computable solution set.

5.4 Conflict resolution

The other side of the control strategy coin is *execution* of the control language. A situation in which there are several applicable productions is inherently a situation of conflict. If a control strategy resolves that conflict by making a *selection* amongst the possibilities (as opposed to a mere *reordering*), then there is a risk of discarding some crucial branch, and changing the nature of the *computable* solution set. Suppose that for some interpreted production set, the P-tree were as illustrated in 9.

9.

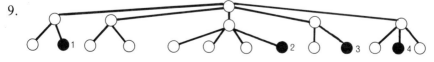

Let nodes 1, 2, 3 and 4 constitute the solution set associated with a given goal condition for this tree. Now suppose we employed a blind conflict resolution strategy which was such as to discard the branches marked 'x' and 'y', e.g. one which ignored every 4th possibility. Then the *computable* solution set associated with this control strategy would be 1 and 3. In the limiting case, the *intended* solution set might never be attained by the use of a conflict resolution strategy. But this could never happen with either of the 'optimisation' strategies mentioned above.

Within the controlled PS model, the distinction between the two types of control arises out of the architecture of the system.

6. PSs AND PROCEDURAL PROGRAMMING LANGUAGES

We said earlier that PSs constitute a scheme for describing computational processes. Despite the extreme generality of this statement, it raises the issue of comparison between PSs, and procedural programming languages (PPLs) such as Pascal or Algol – whose ostensive purpose is similar at an equivalent level of generality. To answer this question, we need some framework for making a comparison.

6.1 Procedures calls versus production invocations

Our point of comparison is the notion of a *basic procedure*. For those who are unfamiliar with this notion, it may be considered as an instruction which 'does something'. For example, an assigment statement:

10. X := Y

is a basic procedure which, when invoked, causes the variable X to take on the value of the variable Y. PPLs provide facilities for structuring basic procedures into complex ones. Thus, the ALGOL 'block':

11.   begin
            X :=Y;
            Z :=Y;
            Y :=X
            end

is a *complex* procedure which, when invoked, causes the sequential invocation of the three basic procedures in the order written. Other control constructs, such as conditional branching (*if* statements) and iteration (*while* and *for* loops) are also provided. The details need not concern us, however.

The other major kind of construct provided in PPLs is the possibility of giving names to complex procedures. Thus, we might call the above block 'P'. The power of this is not mere abbreviation. For once the name is defined, it can be used anywhere in a program, including the definition of other procedures. This permits the *hierarchical organisation* of procedures.

Define Q =
      if X > Y then P
        else X := X - Y

A call to *Q* now causes the invocations of several procedures. Note that the pattern of invocations mirrors the hierarchical and sequential organisation of the program. Note also that a newly defined procedure will *never* be called unless a call to it is anticipated by the programmer, and explicitly included in the program.

Let us now turn back to PSs and compare this notion of a procedure call with the invocation of a production. At a purely abstract level, there are many similarities. The invocation of a procedure changes the 'state' of the running program. A procedure call can be viewed as a mapping between states of the running program (McCarthy 1963) – just as a production invocation can be viewed as a mapping between states of the database. Thus PPLs and PSs can both be seen as ways of specifying computations consisting of procedure invocations. But there are important differences.

6.2 PPLs and determinism

A PPL program can be thought of as a text which describes a single complex procedure which is built using the structuring methods outlined above. Conceptually, the program is *run* by an interpreter, and takes the form of 'appropriate' invocations of sub-procedures as defined in the program. The crucial feature of PPLs is that at run time, the program effectively *tells the interpreter exactly which procedure to invoke next*, and there is never more than one. In other words, the interpreter *never* has to choose.

The interpreter of a PPL, then, is the slave of the program. But this means that the program is all-responsible. This contrasts sharply with the production set of a PS, which does not describe a sequence of production invocations. With a PS, it is the interpreter which decides on the basis of current evidence (i.e. the database) what sequence will be applied. Another way of saying this is that PPLs are restricted to the specification of deterministic algorithms, whilst PSs are not.

Here then, is the essential difference between specifying algorithms using PSs and PPLs. With a PPL, one is forced to do one thing at a time, and consequently, one has to be concerned with the order in which things are done. PPLs explicitly cater for this by providing control constructs for conditional, iterative, and recursive execution of procedures. In complete contrast, the procedures of a 'pure' production system – as specified by the production set – are not ordered. In principle, every one of them could be active simultaneously, and it is the result of their *collective* execution, as decided by the interpreter, and possibly in parallel, that constitutes the computation.

7. PSs, PARSING AND CONTROL

A useful way of regarding parsing for the purposes of discussing this issue is as a problem solving activity. In these terms, the problem statement is the input sentence, and the goal is the discovery of some description of the sentence which satisfies certain constraints. In order to arrive at the goal, the parser employs knowledge about language, which, although diverse, essentially takes the form of rules for the transformation of descriptions.

7.1 Ill-structured problems

The unfortunate truth about the problem of parsing natural language is that it is, for the most part, what Simon (1973) coined an 'ill-structured' problem. A problem, that is, whose solution involves the invocation of often diverse 'Knowledge Sources' (a term used by Hayes-Roth and Lesser (1977) which subsumes procedures, theorems, inference rules), but where it is difficult to specify when a particular invocation should take place in advance, and for the *general* case. Consider, for example, the choice of a method for determining the referent of a pronoun, or analysing a verb phrase. In each case, there will certainly be many alternative methods: finding the correct one, however, will almost certainly depend on the situation at hand.

The architecture of PSs is suited to the solution of ill-structured problems in so far as there is a clear and explicit separation between the knowledge available to the system (i.e. the production set), and the method for harnessing that knowledge in the solution of a particular problem (i.e. the control strategy). This is quite unlike the solutions to problems stated in PPLs, where there is no such explicit separation. There, the knowledge used is buried in the control structure implicit to the algorithmic description.

Although procedurally stated problem solutions are 'efficient', they run the risk of being unduly specific. Thus, a slight change in the problem specification may well require an entirely new procedure –

even though the general principles for solving the problem remain invariant. The reason is that the general principles are often of the form 'use knowledge K in situation S'. This kind of imperative is simply not available in PPLs. Another major disadvantage is that the addition of a new piece of knowledge (i.e. a new procedure) may disrupt the existing control flow. This makes the *incremental* construction of a problem solver harder in PPLs than in PSs, where addition of object level knowledge is essentially a question of augmenting the production set.

A case in point is the ATN (Woods 1970), which in its pure form, can be regarded as a PPL that has been deliberately downgraded for honourable reasons. Although a given grammar can cope with a fairly wide class of syntactic constructions, it is extremely difficult to modify it by simply adding to the networks already defined, for essentially the reasons just stated. Instead, the entire grammar has to be rewritten.

Another approach to widening the class of sentences acceptable to an existing ATN grammar is to relax the conditions on arcs (see Weischedel and Black 1980). So instead of failing when a state is blocked, one is left with a set of partial parses one of which has to be selected on the basis of the information present. It is hardly surprising that arbitrary heuristics have to be employed (longest input parsed), because the information just *isn't* present. If a test has failed, but is persuaded to succeed willy nilly, the subsequent state is totally undefined with respect to the original grammar. The problem with this approach is that it does not attack the crucial issue: the syntactic knowledge used by an ATN is not sufficiently distinguished from its use of that knowledge.

So, although some progress can and has been made by adopting procedural solutions, this generally involves abandoning the goal of incremental construction. In other words, it implies the choice of a limited domain before the parser is constructed. This is quite feasible when the characteristics of the language, and therefore the use of knowledge in parsing it, is well understood in advance, as is the case for programming languages. Natural languages present more of a problem because it is not clear *what* knowledge is required, never mind *how* it is used; and this is the case for even apparently simple domains. For this reason, we should only abandon the goal of incremental construction as a last resort.

If we view a parser as a problem solving system then, certain requirements are crucial. In particular:

A) The ability to represent *states* of the problem.
B) A formalism for the expression of linguistic knowledge which addresses and transforms states of the problem.

C) A mechanism for controlling the application of linguistic knowledge in a strategic way, which includes, for example, the possibility of expressing *goal states* and methods to achieve them.

Below we argue that pure PS architecture constitutes a suitable framework for (A) and (B), and this claim is substantiated with respect to the notions of a PS database (section 7.2) and a PS production set (section 7.3). However, with respect to (C), *pure* PS architecture seems to offer very little. In section 7.4, we discuss some of the control techniques that are clearly relevant, but note that they are all outside the domain of the pure PS.

7.2 The database

There is of course no restriction on the data structure used to implement a PS database, and therefore, no restriction on the kind of information representable within it. This has advantages and disadvantages. On the negative side, there nothing in the definition of a PS to stop the database being used as a general dumping ground for control information. But this tends to destroy the uniformity of the database, and therefore the transparency of the system as a whole.

On the other hand, the database can be crafted to suit the application, so that in parsing, it is possible to identify the database with the *state* of the parse. PS databases can, and have been used to fulfil requirement (A) above. Below we give some examples:

7.2.1 Databases for parsing. In the abstract, the state of a parse *with respect to some segment of the sentence* can be conceived as being information about 'objects', typically, either of a *classificatory* nature (e.g. that an object is an instance of a particular kind of syntactic category such as a word or verb phrase), else of a *relational* nature: that two objects are adjacent to each other, or that one object dominates another.

The relations of dominance (which subsumes category membership as a special case) and adjacency define *trees*, for which there are too many representations to mention here (but see Knuth 1971). Marcus (1980), for example, uses a linear buffer, which contains words, and a stack of nodes, each of which has a unique type, and a set of features. The use of lists and parenthesised strings is also feasible (see below), since trees can always be linearised.

7.2.2 Chart parsers. Systems which parse left-to-right and 'consume' input words implicitly treat a *unique* text segment that is always defined by the current word. Where this is not the case, information about the state of the parse must be relativised to the segment to which it applies.

The state of the parse is then defined by the totality of 'tree labellings' for each segment. An interesting class of data structures which explicitly caters for this situation is the *chart* (see chapter 5), which not only permits the explicit representation of adjacency between labellings, but also the relationship of *alternation* allows the ambiguous labelling of a given statement to be explicitly stated. Intuitively, the set of spanning paths through the chart (which is a directed graph) represents the current set of readings for the entire sentence. Chart data structures differ according to the structure of information on the arcs of the graph (e.g. lists (Pereira and Warren 1980); bracketed strings (Colmerauer 1970); graphs (Kaplan 1973)) and on the ways the geometry of the chart itself is implemented. Pereira and Warren's system, for example, constructs the graph out of PROLOG (Roussel 1975) clauses, which are a restricted form of assertion in predicate calculus.

7.3 The production set

The production set expresses the object-level knowledge used by a PS. As we mentioned in Section 1, the only restriction on the form of productions is that they have a lhs and a rhs. However, for productions to be *perspicuous*, the interpretation conferred upon them should not be overly complex. If the interpretation of productions is straightforward, the conditions under which a production is applied, and the effect of that application, are immediately apparent: this is why we deliberately employed the rewrite interpretation of productions in the above examples. Actually, the advantages of this particular interpretation are not purely pedagogical. For the addition of variables to the rewrite interpretation raises the expressive power of productions to a level where significant linguistic generalisations are stateable, although not at the expense of legibility. For such variables remain strictly *local* to the production in which they appear; their value cannot be changed by other productions.

The object level facts employed by a parser are facts about language. Although it is unfashionable these days to claim a distinguished status for facts of syntax, it seems unreasonable to deny that such facts are going to play some role in the construction of any parser. If we look to the linguists for a formalism in which to express these facts, we find that, since the advent of Chomsky, the notion of formal grammar has been almost universally adopted. There is more than a passing resemblance between a formal grammar, and the production set of a PS: it is not simply that each is expressed in the form of rules, but also that in neither is the exact usage of the facts preordained. These observations suggest that for at least one class of facts that are demonstrably useable for parsing, a PS is an appropriate kind of formal device for using them.

Of course, this is not to say that facts of syntax are sufficient for parsing Natural Language. But then, the notion of production is so general that it can certainly be used to represent other kinds of information. It is comparatively simple, for example, to augment the structure of the database so as to include semantic information in the structure being assembled, and to arrange for productions to manipulate it. From another, more general perspective, the database can simply be regarded as a collection of arbitrary 'true' assertions, and productions as rules that permit the inference of other true assertions. Now assertions can essentially be used to represent *any* facts at all. From this point of view, a parser is a special case of a generalised inference machine. Definite Clause Grammars, originally described by Colmerauer (1975) and subsequently developed by Pereira and Warren (1980), for example, seem to embody this philosophy exactly.

7.4 Control and pure PS architecture

In the above two sections, we argued that an appropriately designed PS database, combined with an appropriately designed set of productions, could in principle suffice to express the *object* level knowledge required for a Natural Language parser. However, as we have stressed throughout this section, a successful problem solver is not simply judged by his knowledge of the problem domain, but by his ability to use the right knowledge at the right time. The question, therefore, is whether the architecture of a PS permits the knowledge of language embedded in its production set to be effectively used to solve an arbitrary parsing problem. In answering this question, we are simply going to assume that the amount of linguistic knowledge used by any substantial parser will be large, and that this will be reflected in the number of productions expressing that knowledge.

A pure PS has but one producion set; we must therefore assume that this will be large. Statistically, the larger the production set, the larger the set of *applicable* productions for a given database state, and therefore, the less feasible computationally the search of the entire solution space. Now there *do* exist techniques for either avoiding the presence of large conflict sets, or for dealing with them if they are allowed to arise. The problem is that such techniques are simply not defined within the pure PS framework.

For example, one rather useful way of preventing explosion is to employ what Lenat and McDermott (1977) call 'multiple production memories' – in other words, to *partition* the production set so as to ensure that the number of productions under consideration at any moment is small. Partitioning is a powerful structuring device that is almost certainly *necessary* to the design of a flexible control strategy. But structuring devices alone will not solve the control problem. It is one thing to define a partition; but quite another to arange for it to be 'active' at the right time. Needles to say, most PS parsers (Marcus 1980, Colmerauer 1970) employ partitioning in one form or another – even if the usage of the partitions is non-optimal. The point is, partitioning of the production set is outside the scope of pure PS architecture. Within that architecture, the methods available   for controlling production invocation are limited to

A) the conflict resolution strategy
B) the conditions of productions

In organisational terms, it is important to realise the distinction between these two options. Within the pure PS philosophy, it is the PS designer who decides upon the conflict resolution strategy, but he cannot tell the user which productions to employ. By contrast, the user is entirely responsible for the conditions of productions, but cannot change the conflict resolution strategy supplied. This distinction is often lost on the fact that the designer and the user are one and the same person. But in the end, it has to be the user's view that counts.

7.4.1 Conflict resolution. It is always possible to ensure that a small number of productions will be applied by supplying a savage conflict resolution strategy. Although this manoeuvre takes responsibility out of the user's hands, the problem does not magically go away, since suitable criteria must now be given by the designer to define the strategy.

If conflict resolution is regarded as a last ditch alternative, which it often is, the strategy employed is typically based on simplistic criteria (e.g. first match or rule order), having nothing to do with the problem as such. For this reason, it is likely to make the wrong choice in the general case. It is the user who suffers, for he is then coerced into writing productions in an unnatural way (i.e. with knowledge of the conflict resolution strategy).

If this is to be avoided, conflict resolution has to be *reliable*. For this to be feasible, it is difficult to resist the conclusion that the strategy must have access to explicitly represented meta-level knowledge about the problem domain, a concept discussed in Hayes (1977), Davis and Buchanan (1977), Davis (1980a), and employed by Bundy et al. (1979) and in TEIRESIAS (Davis 1980b).

The use of meta-level knowledge in some form or other seems necessary. But its employment radically changes the nature of the PS *from the point of view of the user.* For the expression of meta-level knowledge, and therefore, the nature of the conflict resolution strategy,

is now in his hands. This is particularly apparent in the case of
TEIRESIAS, where a meta-level PS is used to resolve conflicts, and
thus control the 'object-level' PS. Indeed, it is possible to envisage a
hierarchy of PSs arranged in this way.

There is nothing wrong with the conception of the designer/user.
What is important is that the 'user-at-a-level' should be able to rely
upon the resolution strategy of the 'designer-at-level+1', and express
his knowledge without resorting to the usual hacks. But it should be
recognised that this organisation *is* quite foreign to the pure PS
philosophy.

7.4.2 Strengthening production conditions   The number of productions
applicable to an arbitrary state is inversely proportional to the average
strength of their condition parts. By making conditions more selective,
therefore, the user can impose a measure of control. However, to do
this effectively he must know exactly which conditions to strengthen,
and how to strengthen them. This is sometimes feasible if the production
set is small, and there is enough information in the database to permit
the right conditions to be expressed, as is the case with Parsifal (Marcus
1980), with its limited access buffer and stack.

Where the production set is large however, the user may not be in
a position to express the appropriate conditions either because the
structure of the database is insufficiently rich to support the necessary
information, or because the language for the expression of conditions
is too feeble to express what is in fact there. In Q-Systems (Colmerauer
1970), for example, the database is such that information pertaining
to the *geometrical* structure of a parse tree is represented in the same
way as information pertaining to the labels on the *nodes* of a parse
tree. This leads to a combination of the difficulties mentioned when
trying to express conditions which seem *linguistically* natural.

It is always possible deliberately to create 'distinguished' conditions
in the database which will cause unique productions to become
applicable. This approach was used by Moran (1973), who arranged
for production *sequencing* by getting the first member of the sequence
to deposit some special symbol in the database which is only recognised
by the second; the second doing the same for the third, and so on.
The problem with this is if these symbols are to do their job properly,
then provision must be made for productions which contain them to
run at a higher priority than the rest. As Georgeff observes, this is
not bad in itself, but it does change the nature of the system. It also
renders it less modular and in the case of OPS (Rychener 1977),
which generalises the same idea to other control constructs, spectacularly
opaque.

It is often said that sequential control notions are contrary to the
'spirit' of PSs. However, it might be suggested that this judgement

stems not from the nature of sequential control per se, but from the ad-hoc methods which have often been used to achieve it. Unfortunately, pure PS architecture leaves the user with little option but to destroy the integrity of the system.

A far cleaner way to specify sequential control is available in Georgeff's controlled PSs. For here, the user is in a position to define control words which cause pre-determined sequences of productions to be applied without cluttering up either the database or the production set. An additional payoff of this approach is that the use of *context-free* control languages permits something like the hierarchical control framework provided in PPLs. That is,

> We can interpret each non-terminal symbol appearing in the grammar as the name of a 'procedure' in the controlled PS. Now (top-down) left-right generation of control words produces possible execution sequences of the controlled PS, where each expansion of a non-terminal is interpreted as a call to the procedure having that name. (Georgeff 1982: 185-6)

Although sequential application is something of a special case, the ability to hierarchicalise the production set by defining 'procedures' in this way is another powerful structuring device because it enables knowledge to be packaged into more manageable chunks. But again, controlling a PS in the way suggested by Georgeff takes us out of the pure PS domain.

7.4.3 Goal directed invocation of productions. In a pure PS, the only 'handle' on knowledge represented by the production set is the condition part of each production. This implies that the invocation of productions is essentially directed by the contents of the database. However, as illustrated in Section 5.3, if the solution space (or some part of it) is tree-like, and the current database state is the root of the tree, it makes computational sense to work backwards from the goal towards the current state. For this to be possible, the computation must be goal-directed. That is, the productions whose actions are relevant to that goal must be retrieved, and their conditions set up as sub-goals.

Thus, another 'handle' must be provided for using it, including, for example, an operational definition of relevance.

An early problem solving system that used goal directed invocation was GPS (Newell, Shaw and Simon 1963). Given a goal G and a current state S, GPS calculated a description of the 'difference' between S and G. This difference was then used to index a precompiled table which linked differences with those productions whose application reduced that difference. The process was recursively applied to the subgoals generated by the conditions (note the plural) of each production selected. This technique, known as 'means-end analysis', was also used by the robot problem solver STRIPS (Fikes and Nilsson 1971). The technique has its limits, however, particularly when the order in which the subgoals are achieved is crucial. A great deal of research has been devoted to the construction of problem solvers that accept and achieve several goals simultaneously (Sacerdoti 1975, Sussman 1975, Waldinger 1977).

Goal-directed and data-directed invocation of productions can be regarded as two different ways of using the same piece of knowledge. But they are two of many. If a system is to achieve general problem solving ability, then it must be able to effectively employ a rich set of invocation criteria. The majority of existing problem solving systems do not allow the user to exercise his right to define the invocation criteria that he believes to be appropriate to a particular kind of solution. Typically, he has to make do with the few that are hard wired into the system interpreter. With all such systems, the limit is reached when the user knows *what* behaviour is required for the solution of a particular problem, but the system does not have the capacity to understand the description of that behaviour. The use of 'content directed invocation' (Davis 1977) is a notable attempt to break out of this scheme of things.

From the foregoing paragraph, the reader will no doubt infer that the architecture of a system admitting but one criterion of invocation is seriously lacking, because it offers the user precious little in the way of facilities for the description of general problem solving skills. The pure PS is just such an architecture.

8 CONCLUSION

In some ways, our final assessment of PSs bears a resemblance to what is said in chapter 4 regarding ATNs. That is, to make any criticism at all, we first have to pin down what seem to be the criterial features of the architecture. To do this, we may have to take as our example something which is more restricted than what is generally accepted to be an exemplar of that architecture. If this takes the form of a pure PS, then it has to be admitted that for an arbitrary programming task, and this, of course, includes parsing, almost any other programming formalism (with the possible exception of Turing Machines) is to be preferred.

Unlike ATNs, however, the exemplar we have chosen exhibits one principle which is profoundly important: the separation between system knowledge and system control. It is arguable that only by observing this principle will we ever make progress. For on current evidence, it is those that observe it who develop the programs which display some of the generality and robustness that we all require.

4

Parsing with Transition Networks

R. Johnson

1. INTRODUCTION

This chapter is about a class of representations for grammars (and parsers), known as *transition network grammars*, which for the last decade have enjoyed considerable success in computational linguistics.

Many variants on the same basic principle are now in existence, but it is generally acknowledged that the 'standard' form is the *augmented transition network* model of Woods (1970), usually abbreviated to *ATN*. Woods is generally credited as the inventor of ATNs, although the original 1970 article acknowledges earlier work on similar lines by Conway (1963), Thorne, Bratley and Dewar (1968) and Bobrow and Fraser (1969).

This chapter will concentrate mainly on the 'classical' ATN model of Woods, but with the aim of trying to characterise the 'spirit' of ATNs and related models, much as chapter 3 was concerned with the 'spirit' rather than the intricate details of Production Systems. We shall thus not be greatly concerned with specific details of representation, with particular applications, or with what have been called, in another context, 'mere notational variants'. Such information is easily available in the literature – cf. *inter alia*: the original 1970 article by Woods, Bates (1978) for a tutorial overview; Grimes (1975) on ATNs as a medium for linguistic descriptions; Kaplan (1972, 1975) and Stevens and Rumelhart (1975) on ATNs as models of human sentence processing; Waltz (1978), and Woods, Kaplan and Nash-Webber (1972), summarised in Woods (1977), on ATNs as front-end processors for data-base interrogation.

The chapter is divided into three parts: the first is an overview of the basic design philosophy of transition network models, as embodied in relatively simple objects called *recursive transition networks*; the second describes how the more complicated ATN can be constructed around the basic RTN nucleus; and the third examines briefly some claims which have been made in favour of ATNs as a basis for writing language analysers.

To explain some of the theoretical reasoning which underlies the transition network approach, it is useful to be able to appeal to a number of standard results on the equivalence between standard rewrite grammars and a class of abstract machines called *automata*. Relevant results are summarized very informally in the next section, but for a serious treatment the reader is referred to one of the standard sources – especially Chomsky (1963), Hopcroft and Ullman (1969). Readers already familiar with the basic results in formal language theory are advised to proceed directly to Section 2.

1.1 A note on grammars and automata

A set of rewrite rules, or *grammar*, can be thought of not only as an intensional definition of the sentences of a language, but also as the description of an abstract machine which is able to *accept* (or *generate*) just those strings which belong to the language. These machines are called (abstract) *automata*, and the complexity of their potential behaviour is directly determined by the internal complexity of the rules of the grammar to which they correspond.

All such machines may be characterised in terms of a set of states, an input device which can access one input symbol at a time, and a *control unit* which can examine and read input and cause the machine to shift from one state to another. In addition, such machines may have *memory*, which can be accessed by the control unit for storing and testing symbols. The computational power of the machine is determined essentially by the complexity of its memory and of the operations which can be performed on the memory.

The simplest of these automata are called *finite state machines* or *finite state automata* (FSAs), and the languages they can accept are called *regular languages*. Regular languages have all of the properties of context free languages except centre-embedding, and thus can always be recognized by an automaton with a finite number of states. Finite state machines have no internal memory, so that their behaviour must be determined entirely by the symbol currently being read and the current machine state.

To illustrate the behaviour of such a machine, consider the simple grammar

1. S → aB
    B → bB
    B → c

which generates the regular language ab*c.

The equivalent automaton may conventionally be represented by a *state diagram*

2.

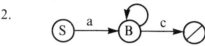

in which the nodes stand for *states* and the arcs for *transitions*. Labels on the arcs give enabling conditions on the input for a transition to take place. Nodes marked with a diagonal bar have a special status and are called *final states*. Note that the translation from rewrite rules to state diagrams is relatively straightforward for this particular automaton: non-terminal symbols go to states and terminal symbols to transitions.

The behaviour of the automaton can be described as follows: computation begins in a designated state called an *initial state* (here S); the first symbol in the input sequence is examined to see whether there is a possible transition which matches that symbol; if there is, the machine follows the transition to the next state and *consumes* the input symbol – i.e. shifts its attention to the next symbol in the sequence. This process continues until the machine *blocks* – i.e. until no more transitions are possible. If the machine blocks in a final state and all the input has been consumed, we say that the string has been *accepted* (or *recognized*).

Note that the same automaton can be made to generate strings just by changing the nature of the action on a transition from input to output.

If we add to a finite state automaton memory which is restricted to a last-in-first-out list (i.e. a push-down stack), plus some control conventions for manipulating it, then we convert the FSA to a *push down automaton* (*PDA*), which by virtue of its extra stack memory now has the ability to handle centre-embedding. PDAs are able to accept just the class of context-free languages.

By removing the restriction to stack organisation on the internal memory, applying only the constraint that the memory size be a linear function of the length of the input, we create a more powerful automaton known as a *linear bounded automaton* (*LBA*). If we wish, we can organise the internal memory so that part of the memory is organised as a stack and the rest as random access storage, thus preserving an obvious hierarchical relationship with the less powerful class of PDAs. LBAs are capable of recognizing a very general class of languages, defined by so-called length increasing grammars, which include the context-sensitive constituent structure grammars familiar in linguistics.

Finally, if we remove the last constraint on internal memory to allow it to be unbounded in size, we arrive at the most general class of automata known as *turing machines* (TMs). The corresponding grammars are *unrestricted rewrite systems*, in which rules are allowed to rewrite anything as anything. Turing machines are the abstract analogue of ordinary general purpose serial computers.

One of the primary issues in the theory of automata is the question of decidability, which can be informally stated as the problem of knowing *a priori* whether a given class of computations can be guaranteed to halt in finite time. In particular, the problem of recognition of a string which does not belong to the language corresponding to a particular automaton is not in general decidable for TMs. It is in principle decidable for all classes of less powerful automata.

2. RECURSIVE TRANSITION NETWORKS

An ATN is just an extended version of an ingenious CF recognition device called a *recursive transition network* (*RTN*). As well as being necessary for a proper understanding of ATNs, the RTN itself merits attention in its own right as an interesting departure from the ubiquitous rewrite rule representation for grammars. The rest of Section 2 of this chapter is devoted to a consideration of RTNs and their theoretical status vis-a-vis CF rewrite systems.

2.1 Rationale of RTNs

Consider the simple grammar

3. R1(a) : S   → NP (Aux) V (NP) PP*
    R1(b) : S   → Aux NP V (NP) PP*
    R2   : NP → (Det) (Quant) Adj* N* N PP*
    R3   : PP → Prep NP

which defines a context-free (CF) language over the alphabet {Aux, V, Det, Quant, Adj, N, Prep}.

Although the rules R1-R3 look somewhat more complicated than the 'standard' CF rewrite rules normally found in linguistics, the grammar is still CF in terms of its weak generative capacity. The extensions to the usual notation are parentheses, which enclose optional elements, and the asterisk, which indicates that the symbol to which it is superscripted may be iterated zero or more times in the expansion of the right hand side of the rule.

The right hand sides of these rules may also be regarded as defining expressions for regular languages, or regular expressions – respectively over the alphabets {NP, Aux, V, PP} for R1, {Det, Quant, Adj, N, PP} for R2, and {Prep, PP} for R3 – and can each therefore be represented in terms of an equivalent finite state automaton. For example, the state diagrams for the automata corresponding to the two parts of rule R1 are:

4. A1(a):

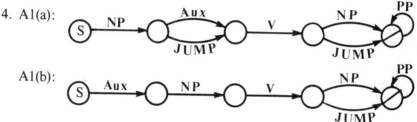

A1(b):

where the symbol *JUMP* is the normal convention in the ATN formalism for marking the unconditional transition which consumes no input.

We can observe immediately that the state transition representation allows us to merge the right hand sides of R1(a) and R1(b) into a single diagram, since the two rules are identical from the symbol V onwards. This gives a more compact characterisation of the information in the two rules than the rewrite formalism permits. Merging the two diagrams A1(a) and A1(b), we then have the following three state transition diagrams corresponding to the four rules R1-R3:

5. A1:

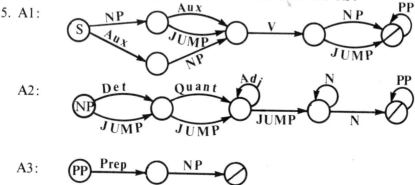

A2:

A3:

We now have a problem with the transitions *NP* in A1 and A3 and *PP* in A2. In order to justify the finite state representation we had to treat them as terminal symbols, whereas they are clearly non-terminal in the original grammar from which the state diagrams were derived. But if they are not terminal then how can they ever be recognised by the corresponding finite state automaton?

There is an obvious interpretation we can impose on these 'non-terminal' transitions, if we treat the three automata A1-A3 as a *system*. We no longer require A1 to try to recognise the symbol *NP* at all, but let it pass control temporarily to A2, delaying its decision on the transition until A2 returns the information whether or not an *NP* can be recognised at the current input position. Similarly, A2 has to pass responsibility for a decision on a transition on a *PP* to A3, which in turn recursively 'calls' A2 for recognition of an *NP*. It is clear that a simple FSA is no longer adequate to handle this kind of recursive process, because it has no way of remembering where it came from and how to get back there after an embedded computation. However, it turns out that if we add a pushdown stack, converting the system of FSAs into a PDA, the device now has sufficient resources to handle all the auxiliary operations of saving and retrieving states of computation that occur strictly on a last-in-first-out basis as control is suspended and restored.

This essentially procedural interpretation of symbols as labels for transitions is reflected in the standard ATN notation. When control is passed to an embedded process, the current machine state is *pushed* onto the stack, so that computation can be resumed from the same point when control is returned. In the ATN formalism, transfer of control to a state named, say, *NP* is invoked by a transition labelled *PUSH NP*. The corresponding convention for final states is to add a dummy arc labelled *POP*, reflecting the fact that when a process terminates the original machine state is restored from the stack. (A useful side effect of the use of dummy *POP* arcs on final states is that it allows exit from a process to be ordered with respect to other possible options at that state.)

We still have to account for the status of the other transitions like Aux, V, Det, ... , which themselves are unlikely to be genuine input symbols unless our intention is to parse a string of grammatical category names. We have not yet specified how transition network grammars handle dictionaries.

One possibility is to suppose that the dictionary can be expressed as a collection of rewrite rules of the type:

6.   R4(a) : Det ⟶ 'a'
     R4(b) : Det ⟶ 'the'
     R4(c) : Det ⟶ 'some'

and so on. We can then use the same techniques as before to restate the rewrite rules in state transition form like

7. A4: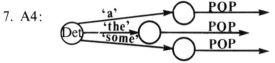

and plug the result into a grammar network like A1-A3 (see 5).

Alternatively, as usually happens in standard ATN practice, we can define a set of functions which can be invoked as transitions, and which consult a pre-defined dictionary. The format of the dictionary then becomes more a function of the language in which the transition network grammar is embedded than of the grammar itself. The most widely used of these dictionary lookup functions, usually called *CAT*, tests a predefined CATegory name against the dictionary entry for the current input word.

We are now in a position to represent the network grammar A1-A3 in a form more closely resembling the standard notation for RTNs, with transitions distinguished between lexical category tests (CAT) and calls to sub-processes (PUSH), and with final states labelled by dummy POP arcs. Here it is:

8. A1':

A2':

A3':

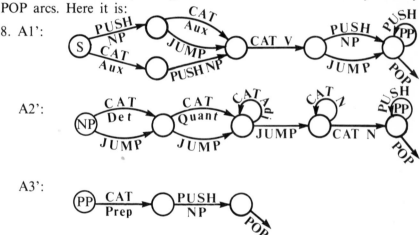

2.2 Procedural nature of RTNs

The method of representation described in the last section is at an abstract level equivalent to a system of CF rewrite rules, in the sense that any CF rewrite rule grammar can be translated into an equivalent RTN. There is, however, a very important feature of the RTN representation which is not present in rewrite rule systems, namely the notion of *process*. If we want to use a grammar to construct a recognition procedure for a language, then the rewrite rules specify *what* is to be done; the automaton which underlies the RTN also describes *how* to do it.

Compare, for example, a production system for CF recognition based on rewrite rules, and an RTN implemented as a recogniser for the same language. When we design the production system, we are free to design into the interpreter decisions on questions like what rule to apply next, what piece of data to consider next, and how to perform the 'rewrite' operation on the data base. In the RTN version, notice how much of the responsibility for the same control decisions is a priori removed from the designer of the interpreter because they are already implicit in the semantics of the grammar representation. The RTN formalism, in fact, especially when it is translated into some linear representation for computer input, exhibits many of the characteristics of conventional procedural programming languages – conditional and unconditional *goto* (state transitions), statement labels (state names), and procedure calls (PUSH and POP).

The one important feature of procedural control which is not implicit in the notation is the behaviour of the interpreter when it arrives at a state from which more than one transition may be taken. (The 'normal' mode is to take transitions in order, starting at the first, and to proceed top-down and depth-first by pursuing each path as far as it will go and accepting the first path which arrives at a final state with empty input and empty stack).

There is an important contrast here with the production system approach, in which the rewrite form of the rules does not in itself presuppose any particular process. The very act of constructing an RTN network requires that the writer think in terms of a top-down, left-right recognition process in order to be able to follow his own rules.

This implicitly procedural orientation becomes explicit when we come to add the extensions which transform recursive transition networks into augmented transition networks.

3. AUGMENTED TRANSITION NETWORKS

An RTN as described so far is just a way of describing a strategy for CF recognition. We now look at the basic augmentations which are required to convert a simple RTN into an *augmented* transition network.

3.1 'Standard' ATNs

An RTN as it stands is not a very useful parsing device. It can only recognize CF languages, and anyway provides no means of producing structured output which we expect a parser to produce.

It is, however, well known that for a fairly large subclass of rewrite rule systems, known as constituent structure grammars (Chomsky & Miller 1963: 292-296), it is possible to construct a parse-tree as output from a recognition procedure, simply by reinterpreting the rewrite symbol as a hierarchical dominance operator. Thus, if a rule

9. A → X Y Z

has been applied during the course of a successful recognition of a string, the subtree

10.

can be assigned automatically as the part of the parse-tree dominating that substring which is generable from the sequence of non-terminals X,Y,Z. It is relatively simple to arrange for any CF recognizer to construct such a tree as it tries to recognize some string, and to output that tree at the end of the process, if the string has been accepted.

In the case of the RTN, though, if we want to use it to do even context-sensitive parsing, we have to think a little harder. There is no direct way to translate either of the standard forms

11. X A Y → X BC Y

or

12. A → BC / X - Y

of a context-sensitive phrase structure rule into the transition network representation, since the formalism gives no immediate means of testing more than one symbol at a time. The inherent top-down, left-right serial technique of description (not even application) inherited by the model from the crude architecture of a finite state recogniser makes even thinking about this kind of rule awkward in a transition network framework. (It is interesting to note that there seems to be no great conceptual difficulty about handling this kind of contextual dependency with very straightforward bottom-up application of rewrite rules.)

Top-down, left-right treatment of context sensitivity requires essentially the ability to postpone decisions until we have had a chance to see what is coming up later. In terms of the mechanistic orientation of transition networks, this means assigning extra memory in which details of previous transitions can be stored and retrieved to supplement conditions on some later transition. In ATN nomenclature, we add to each level of the network a set of *registers*, along with some pre-defined functions for manipulating them. (The most important operations provided on registers in standard ATNs are an assignment function SETR, and a function GETR which returns the current value of a register.)

Use of registers makes transitions much more complicated, because they now not only have to carry tests on the category of the constituent being sought; they also must hold register assignments as well as arbitrary register tests which can now be used, in conjunction with category tests, to determine whether or not to take the transition.

Although we can make an RTN recognize context sensitive languages (at least) by adding registers and associated operations, we lose the useful property, which was true for CF languages, of being able to construct a parse tree automatically from the trace of the traversal through the grammar. However, ATNs also provide a structure-building function *BUILDQ*, which allows construction of any list structure whatever out of literals and register contents, and these arbitrary lists are normally interpreted as trees. By astute use of *BUILDQ*, it is possible to build and save in the registers almost any kind of tree structure simultaneously with the process of CF recognition.

All we need to make something of these structures is a way of outputting them. ATNs provide output by allowing POP arcs to return a value back to the calling process, where the   value returned is accessed conventionally via a special register called the * register. The output from the entire network which actually appears as the result of a parse is the value returned by a top-level POP.

With the addition of registers, output, and the ability to control transitions by tests on the registers as well as on the input, the basic recursive transition network becomes an augmented transition network. In this form, the ATN already has the capability of a general purpose device for transducing strings of words into trees.

There is not, unfortunately, any real standard definition or implementation of an ATN. The basic design features of transition network grammars derive from a graphical representation of abstract automata. Since these grammars are normally intended to be run on a computer, there comes a point where the graphical notation has to be translated into some appropriate linearisation. Choice of that linearisation depends in large measure on the decision of the implementer and the characteristics of the host language, although certain naming conventions for standard features are normally – not always – adhered to.

In addition to the standard features, moreover, an ATN designer, or even user, is in theory free to define any arbitrary function he wishes and use it as a condition or action on a state transition. In most ATN implementations, freedom to define new and arbitrary functions is limited only by the user's reluctance to tamper with the basic ATN control mechanism and the accessibility of the host language within which the ATN is embedded.

This unlimited freedom to add to and modify the basic operations of the system makes it somewhat difficult to characterise precisely what an ATN is. Consider, for example, a conventional ATN implementation, in which the ATN notation is embedded in LISP. The dictionary access functions, like *CAT*, have not been implemented. On the other hand, the ATN is embedded in LISP, so that any arbitrary LISP function may be called from any transition, including functions which can directly read, build and test structures of arbitrary complexity. Is this still an ATN, or is it just a way of partially ordering the collection of LISP programs on the 'transitions', or is that what an ATN is anyway?

4. CLAIMS ABOUT ATNs

Since its introduction, the ATN model has become established as one of the standard tools of computational linguistics. Many and varied arguments have been extended in support of its use. The next few paragraphs consider just some of the claims and counterclaims which have been made.

4.1 Efficiency

The 'normal' implementation of an ATN parser uses a top-down, depth-first traversal, following strictly the order of arcs in the basic transition network. A breadth-first traversal which explores all paths from a given state 'in parallel' is also quite common. There is no reason in principle why any kind of parsing strategy should not be feasible – although perhaps less natural.

If necessary, to simplify implementation of other strategies, the interpreter may even make a first pass through the ATN itself to try to decompose the underlying RTN into its component CF rules, *provided* the system is then able to keep track of register operations in the right place at the right time. It is not clear that this is in general possible without severely constraining the use of the registers.

A very common criticism of ATNs running in the normal depth-first mode is their dependence on blind backtracking when trying to recover from an incorrect analysis path. For example consider a fairly standard syntactically oriented ATN confronted with the English sentence

13. [$_S$ [$_{NP}$ The mnemonic labels [$_{PP}$ in the program]]] [$_V$ enhance] [$_{NP}$ readability]]

Up to the word *program*, in a left-right parse, there is an alternative bracketing

14. [$_S$ [$_{NP}$ The mnemonic] [$_V$ labels] [$_{PP}$ in the program] ...]

which is only rejected on finding the verb *enhance*. If, going depth-first the ATN happens to start off down the wrong analysis path, it will then have to back up from *enhance* all the way to the beginning of the sentence and start the parse again, including a second traversal of the PP *in the program*, although this constituent will already have been successfully computed once by the first (failed) analysis.

Various schemes have been proposed to make this kind of backtracking more efficient, including, notably, a suggestion of Woods (1973) to incorporate a special data structure called a *well formed symbol table* (*WFST*). Each time a constituent is successfully recognised – even during traversal of an unsuccessful path – information is stored about it in the WFST. Then, whenever the system tries to PUSH for a constituent, it first checks the WFST to see if a constituent satisfying the right conditions has already been found at the corresponding point in the input. This method involves a trade-off of computation time against storage space and retrieval time for all possible partial constituents which may be unacceptable in some environments.

An interesting alternative idea for avoiding backtracking in inherently combinatorial situations, to be described in chapter 5, is to use a rather more complicated, problem-oriented data structure called a *chart*, perhaps in conjunction with an ATN-like strategy.

4.2 Efficiency of representation

A related issue is that of the efficiency, not of execution but of the representation itself. RTNs, it is claimed, provide, in the network notation, a more compact form of expression than the equivalent CF rewrite rules. An important side-effect of this facility for compaction is that it can permit some degree of hand-optimisation of the run-time process, through combining together of common partial paths to reduce search time. This is a valid claim in itself, although there may be a trade-off between compactness and descriptive clarity which needs to be evaluated carefully in deciding how desirable this facility is for a given application.

4.3 Perspicuity

Woods (1970) remarks of Transformational Grammars:

It is not possible in this [the TG] model to look at a single rule and be immediately aware of its consequences for the types of construction that are possible. The effect of a given rule is intimately bound up with its interrelation to other rules, and in fragments of transformational grammars for real languages it may require an extremely complex analysis to determine the effect and purpose of any given rule. The augmented transition network provides the power of a transformational grammar but maintains much of the perspicuousness of the context-free grammar model.

Now RTN representations do seem to have a certain appeal, they are very easy to draft out, and they allow a number of different but related bits of linguistic knowledge to be captured simultaneously. I know a number of linguists who prefer to sketch out their (CF) grammar rules in RTN form as an aid to thinking about potential grammar organisation, even when they have no intention of using an ATN or RTN parser for the real thing.

On the other hand, it seems likely that CF grammars are easy to understand precisely because they describe objects which themselves have a relatively simple structure. I suspect that even the most enthusiastic ATN user, when presented with a complex ATN with all the trappings of register tests and assignments, complicated BUILDQs, and anything else we care to define, would find it difficult not to agree with the rather mischievous paraphrase of Woods:

> It is not possible in this [the ATN] model to look at a single transition and be immediately aware of its consequences for the types of construction that are possible. The effect of a given transition is intimately bound up with its interrelation to other transitions, and in fragments of ATN grammars for real languages it may require an extremely complex analysis to determine the effect and purpose of any given transition.

Or is perspicuity perhaps in the eye of the beholder?

5. CONCLUSION

Because of the enormous amount of flexibility in the definition of what you can do to an RTN to make it into an ATN, the precise characterisation of what an ATN really is is rather an elusive notion. Nonetheless, some distinctive characteristics do emerge which seem to be invariant. The basic notion at the heart of it all is the RTN graph, which starts out life as an alternative notation for collections of CF rules and finishes up as a kind of scheduling device for organising sequences of conditional structure-building actions, centred around the recognition of (possibly embedded) distributional categories.

Apart from the issue of the sufficiency of context free phrase structure grammars to describe observable language use, which is likely to come up again many times in this book, it seems to me that the determining factor in accepting or not accepting ATNs is going to be one's position on the procedural-declarative issue (Winograd 1975a).

Like any procedural model, an ATN gives extensive possibilities for optimisation and tight control over details of parsing strategy. The price to be paid in return is a danger that as the system increases in size, its logic becomes obscure, modification progressively more risky, and debugging more and more problematic.

If you want to write a small system, syntactically oriented, that goes fast, then an ATN may do the job. If the system has to be large, modular, easily extensible, and processing time is not absolutely critical, then it may be a good idea to look elsewhere.

5

Charts:
a Data Structure
for Parsing

G.B. Varile

1. INTRODUCTION

This chapter is intended as an elementary introduction to a data structure known as a *chart*. It draws on the classical work on charts by Kay (1976) and Kaplan (1970), to whom the merit for the ideas goes, the mistakes being the author's responsibility.

The present chapter has a somewhat special status in this volume, in that it is mainly concerned with a *data structure for parsing* and other linguistic data processing, while the other chapters are mainly devoted to the *parsing process*. It is important to keep in mind that there is a strong interaction between a data structure and a process which works on it, but having said that, this interaction will largely be ignored for the purpose of this introduction, although in Section 5 an example of a special parsing algorithm working on charts will be shown. Readers especially interested in the interactions are referred to Colmerauer (1970) and Kay (1980).

The basic problem of natural language processing is to compute the correct relationships between the different parts and subparts of a text (depending on the language, this may apply down to the level of morphemes). Given the state of the art, this presupposes the *possibility* of being able to compute, if necessary, all possible (legal) relationships between parts of a text. In other words, in order to obtain the desired result (which in some cases will be non-unique due either to true ambiguity, lack of contextual knowledge, or lack of linguistic knowledge) it is often necessary to compute a large number of possible partial results, and to represent them. Charts were invented to accomodate this need.

2. WHAT TO REPRESENT WHEN PROCESSING LANGUAGE

When processing natural language, one must deal with, and be able to represent strings, (of characters), like:

1. flies

ordered sequences of such strings, like:

2. Mahomet goes to the mountain.

(which is not the same as 'The mountain goes to Mahomet'), and relations between strings and sequences of strings, as in:

3.

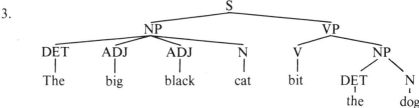

Assume we process the string in 3 with a data driven algorithm, obtaining at some stage the partial results:

4.

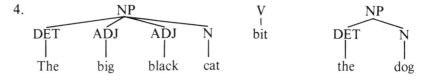

This is usually called a string of trees, and we must be able to represent it too. But that is still not enough. Due to the inherent ambiguity of language, it is often necessary to compute several or all legal subparts of a sentence (so called well-formed substrings) in order to obtain the desired result. If we had to process:

5. I saw the village dead.

we would like to obtain both 6 and 7.

6.

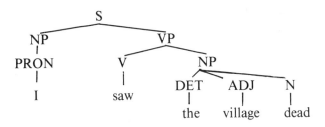

7.

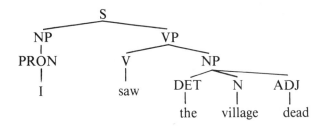

In processing 5, we may obtain the following intermediate results:

8.

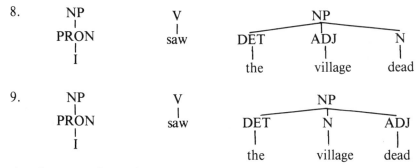

9.

that is, two strings of trees (8 and 9).

In general, we must be able to operate with a list of strings of trees having common subparts (since not everything is always ambiguous). We call such a list of strings of trees a family of strings of trees. We therefore need to represent strings (of characters), linear order (of strings and trees), hierarchical dominance (in a tree) and alternatives (in a string of trees). Charts allow us to represent all this, and do so in an economical and perspicuous way.

3. CHARTS

A chart is a graph, that is a set of nodes and a set of arcs linking them. The arcs are ordered and oriented, and there is a unique first and last node. No loops may occur in a chart and each of its arcs bears some (possibly complex) information called a *labelling* which is not the same thing as a *label*; a label is part of the complex labelling.

As an example, the following is a chart representing the ordered sequence of words of 5:

10.

I assume for the moment that the labelling of each arc consists of just a tree (in the example all trees have just a root). Later on we will see that the labelling can be arbitrarily complex.

Let us now assume that we had to process 10 using the set of production rules given below, which are only intended to aid explanation and are, of course, unrealistic.

11. I   = = > PRON(I)
    saw   = = > V(saw)
    the   = = > DET(the)
    village = = > N(village)
    dead   = = > N(dead)
    dead   = = > ADJ(dead)
    PRON(?X)   NP(PRON(?X)
    N(?X) + N(?Y)   = = >ADJ(?X) + N(?Y)
    DET(?X) + N(?Y) + ADJ(?Z)= = >NP(DET(?X) N(?Y) ADJ(?Z))
    DET(?X) + ADJ(?Y) + N(?Z)= = >NP(DET(?X) ADJ(?Y) N(?Z))
    V(?X) + NP(?Y)   = = >VP (V(?X) NP (?Y))
    NP(?X) + VP(?Y)   = = >S(NP(?X) VP(?Y))

where the conventions are:

A) trees are represented as lists plus a root, with the usual interpretation
B) '+' is the string (of trees) concatenation symbol (i.e. expresses a partial path through the chart)
C) '➤' is the rewrite symbol to which the interpreting algorithm gives meaning.
D) symbols prefixed with '?' stand for arbitrary trees or lists of trees

There is no distinction made between dictionary rules and other grammar rules

Now assume the following rather simplistic interpreting algorithm for 11: whenever a partial path in the chart (data base) matches the lhs of a rule of 11, build a new path spanning the matching path, according to the specification(s) of the rhs of the matching rule. Repeat this until no more rules apply, taking care not to apply the same rule twice to the same data.

Conceptually all rules which are potentially applicable to a certain data base are applied simultaneously. The simultaneous application of all potentially applicable rules to a data base constitutes one iteration of the interpretation of the grammar.

What we have described is very close to a classical production system, whose interpreter applies the rules 11 to a data base which is a chart (10 in our example), producing successively 12 and 13.

12.

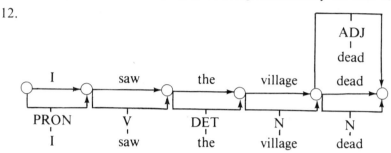

If we look at 13 we see that there are two spanning arcs whose root of the labelling is S in the resulting chart. One notices immediately that both of the trees labelling the arc have the same structure:

14.

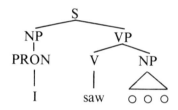

differing only in the internal structure of the right NP. Now, one of the claims about charts which we hinted at earlier was their economy, in space *and* in computation. But to obtain 13 we have computed *VP* and *S* twice, and have also represented it twice. Another claim for charts was perspicuity. But 14 seems intuitively a more natural, and therefore perspicuous structure for 5 than we have obtained in 13. How could we obviate these inconveniences and profit fully from the advantages of a chart?

If we look at 5 we see that what we need is to represent alternatives inside the structural description of a sentence. We know that trees do not allow us to represent alternatives in a straightforward way, but charts do. Since charts also allow us to represent linear order (or precedence) and hierachical dominance, why not represent trees themselves as charts?

13.

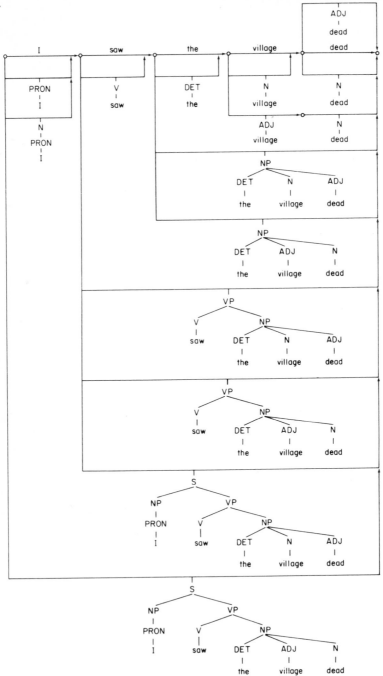

4. TREES AS CHARTS

There are two types of relations in a tree, hierachical dominance and linear order (precedence). The first relation is explicitly indicated by the branches of a tree, while the second is implicitly indicated by reference to the parent node. If in:

15.

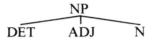

we make precedence explicit and dominance implicit we obtain something like

16.

The bottom line looks like a chart, the only difference being that the information is contained in the nodes, while in a chart all information is carried by the arcs. We can now easily transform 16 into :

17.

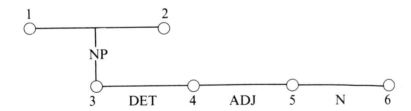

which is a chart.
Note that in 17 the chart 18

18.

19.

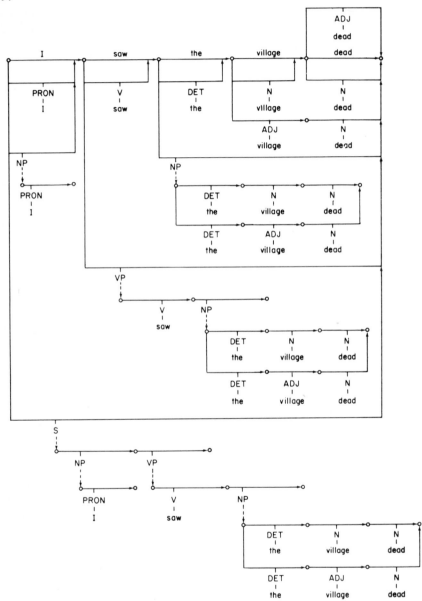

is part of the labelling of the chart with a single arc from node 1 to node 2. One has to be careful to distinguish between solid arrows which are arcs of a chart, and dotted arrows which are pointers, part of the labelling of an arc.

If we now modify the interpreting algorithm in order to make sure that two arcs spanning the same space and having the same root are present only once in the data base, in processing 10 with the modified algorithm, we would obtain 19.

5. MORE ON CHARTS

Following the discusion of Section 3 we can define charts to be loop-free chain graphs with unique entry and exit nodes, whose arcs are ordered and oriented and have a unique (possibly complex) labelling. There are other possible definitions. I would like to give here the classical one by Kaplan (see Kaplan 1971).

First, let us call the arcs of a chart *edges* and its nodes *vertices*, in order to avoid confusion with linguistic trees. We also use the term 'indicator', following Kaplan, to refer to what we have called the 'labelling' on an edge.

Now, since from any vertex more than one edge can originate, a vertex defines a set of edges or *edgeset*:

20.

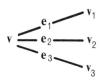

The interpretation of the edges emanating from one vertex is that they are mutually exclusive alternatives. The subset of edges from a given edge to the end of the edgeset to which that edge belongs is called a *tail* (since edges are ordered, this makes sense). For example (e_1, e_2, e_3), (e_2, e_3), (e_3), and 0 (the empty set) are all tails.

Now one can define a chart to be a set of edges and edgesets (the vertices). The structure of a chart is fully defined by four functions:

21. EDGESET   (vertex)   = edgeset-of-vertex
    FIRSTEDGE   (tail)   = first-edge-in-tail
    EDGEALT   (tail)   = rest-of-tail
    GETI   (edge indicator) = value-of-indicator

EDGESET, given the name of a vertex, returns the corresponding edgeset. That is, for each vertex we can know the list of all edges originating in that vertex. FIRSTEDGE and EDGEALT return for each tail (e.g. an edgeset) the first edge in the tail and the rest of the tail respectively. (Those familiar with LISP can think of FIRSTEDGE as corresponding to CAR and EDGEALT to CDR.)   These two functions define the order amongst the edges in an edgeset.

So far we have seen functions which define the geometry of a chart. The fourth function, GETI, gives access to the information carried by an edge, i.e. it defines the internal structure of an edge. An edge can be seen as a set of properties each one consisting of a pair (attribute.value). Kaplan calls such attributes indicators (GETI stands for GET Indicator). Apart from LABEL an edge has at least an indicator for its left DAUGHTER (i.e. the leftmost vertex it dominates) and for its right SISTER vertex. An edge may, and usually will, have other indicators carrying information relevant for natural language processing (for example case relationships between the edge and other parts of the text).

An example will illustrate the meaning of these four functions. Let us consider the chart:

22.

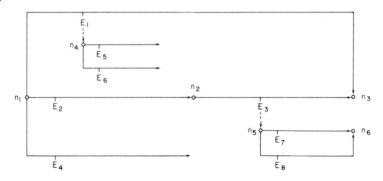

then:

   FIRSTEDGE (EDGESET (n1))

returns a pointer to the edge labelled E1, i.e.

   GETI (FIRSTEDGE (EDGESET (n1)) LABEL) = E1

Furthermore:

   GETI (FIRSTEDGE (EDGESET (n1)) DAUGHTER) = n4

Also:

   FIRSTEDGE (EDGEALT (EDGESET (n1))

returns a pointer to the edge labelled E2, and:

   GETI (FIRSTEDGE (EDGEALT (EDGESET (GETI FIRST-EDGE (EDGESET (n2)) DAUGHTER)))) LABEL) = E8

A program processing linguistic data in the form of a chart always works on one edge at a time. This edge is called the focus. To define the focus it is useful to have stored the following information:

23. EDGE: the current edge
    EDGES: the tail of which EDGE is the first edge
    VERTEX: the edgeset to which EDGE and EDGES belong
    CHART: the current sub-chart

A program working on one edge at a time implies that the program works on different edges at different moments. How are the above variables reset? In two ways. Either the focus shifts to a successor edgeset or else to the next alternative in its own edgeset. In the first case, it shifts either to the right sister edgeset or to a daughter edgeset. This can be achieved in the following way:

24. VERTEX becomes GETI (EDGE SISTER) or GETI (EDGE DAUGHTER)
     EDGES   becomes EDGESET (VERTEX)
     EDGE   becomes FIRSTEDGE (EDGES)

In the second case the shift of focus is achieved in the following way:

25. EDGES   becomes EDGEALT (EDGES)
    EDGE   becomes FIRSTEDGE (EDGES).

6. Q-SYSTEMS

A Q-system is a set of rules to transform a chart-like graph into another chart-like graph. It can be seen as a production system whose data base is an acyclic oriented graph with unique entry and exit nodes, whose arcs each bear a tree.

Q-systems were designed in the late sixties by A. Colmerauer (see Colmerauer 1970), and have been used in the machine translation system TAUM-Meteo. Q-systems are general string of trees to string of trees transducers operating on an acyclic chain-graph whose arcs bear trees (Colmerauer calls such graphs graphs of strings). A path in such a graph represents therefore a string of trees, and the whole graph a family of strings of trees. The rules of a Q-system are of the form

26. lhs == rhs/condition

meaning the lhs rewrites (==) as the rhs, provided the condition is true (for the lhs). lhs and rhs are specifications of a partial path through the graph (i.e. they are descriptions of strings of trees) and are of the form:

27. $tree_1 + ... + tree_n$

In the description of such a path in the graph, one is allowed to use variables (called parameters by Colmerauer). Variables match a class of structures instead of just one. In order to restrict such classes there are conditions which are general boolean expressions augmented by two operators which express inclusion and disjunction of trees and list of trees.

The interpreter which applies the rules of a Q-system to the data base (i.e. the graph) is described in Colmerauer (1970) in the following terms:

A) first phase:　creation of new arcs –

for each path of the graph (i.e. string of trees) for which there is a rule with matching lhs, create a new path spanning the matching one according to the description given by the rhs of the rule, taking care not to apply the same rule twice on the same path. This phase terminates when no rules are left which can be applied.

B) second phase:　deletion of arcs –

first delete all arcs belonging to a path which has participated in a successful match, then delete all arcs which are not part of a path from the entry to the exit node.

Let us see how one could analyse:

28. The black cat bit the dog

with the following Q-system:

29.

```
a. the      = = DET (the).
b. black    = = ADJ (black).
c. cat      = = N (cat).
d. bit      = = V (bit).
e. bit      = = N (bit).
f. dog      = = N (dog).
g. DET (X*) + ADJ (Y*) + N (Z*) = = NP (DET (X*), ADJ (Y*), N (Z*)).
h. DET (X*) + N (Y*)      = = NP (DET (X*), N (Y*)).
i. V (X*) + NP (Y*)       = = VP (V (X*), NP (Y*)).
j. NP (X*) + VP (Y*)      = = S (NP (X*), VP (Y*)).
k. NP (X*) + N (Y*)       = = NP (*X, N (Y*)).
```

where:

1) 'X*', 'Y*', 'Z*' are variables for (lists of) trees,
2) '(　)' indicate dominance,
3) ',' separate trees in a list.

29g could also be written as:

30. A (X*) + B(Y*) + C (Z*) == NP (A (X*), B (Y*), C (Z*)) /
A = DET -ET- B = ADJ -ET- C = N.
(-ET- is the Q-system 'and'), the reverse slash separating rhs and conditions.

The chart constructed by the first phase of the interpreter will be as in:

31.

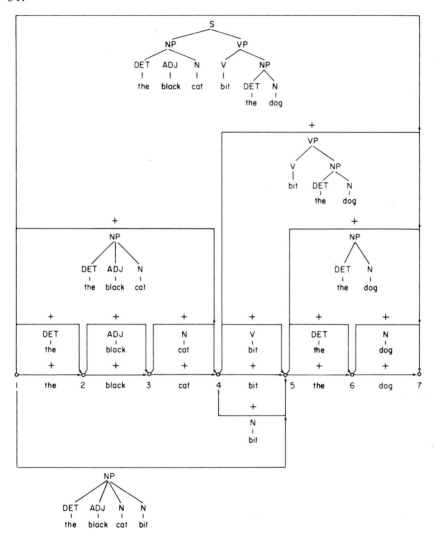

(Note that arcs which participated in a succesful mach are marked with a '+').

Now marked arcs are deleted, leaving the only two unmarked arcs which are 1-7 and 1-5. The latter is deleted because it is not part of a path between the entry and the exit node (everything between 5 and 7 has been deleted). So we are left with the result:

32.

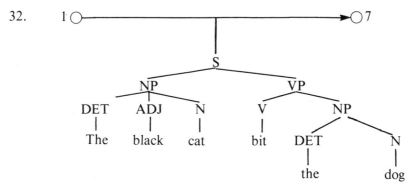

7. CONCLUSIONS

I hope that it has been shown that charts are a very powerful data structure for parsing.

First they provide a very general framework for representing input, output and intermediate results of all sorts of linguistic data processing.

The second advantage of charts is economy. Economy of space in that common subparts of families of strings of trees are represented only once. And economy of computation because rules which involve common parts of families of strings of trees need not be applied as many times as there are members in the family. And also because on back up after failure, well-formed substrings need not be recomputed (as for example in ATNs).

Their third advantage is perspicuity and flexibility of representation. It is important to be able to represent linguistic structures in the way that seems most natural and to do that you need a very flexible data model.

Last, but not least, charts enable good software design. Since very complex programs, like those which manipulate linguistic data, are very difficult to write and debug, it is good programming practice to break them up into manageable modules. This is possible only if one knows at every moment on what data each module will be working. In other words one must be able for each module to specify exactly what its input and output are. Once the communication between modules has been clearly defined, relative program independence becomes an achievable goal. (This is even more important if one considers co-routines as a way of processing language. In this case one must be able to ensure that every module be capable of working on data only partially processed by a co-module.) Charts are well suited for exactly defining in general ways data to be processed, therefore meeting the above needs, without prejudging the type of approach to linguistic data processing: procedural (e.g. ATNs) or of more declarative nature (e.g. production systems). Charts have been used with both.

Section II

Developments in Syntactic Parsing
Introduction

The linguistic theory assumed in Section 1 was the Standard Theory of Transformational grammar. Work in recent years has led to considerable extension and revision of the theory Although the prime motivation for revision has been purely linguistic – the desire to develop a more satisfactory theory – nonetheless many of the extensions and revisions proposed have a direct influence on the construction of practical parsers.

The first chapter of this Section describes one such parser, and discusses the linguistic theory underlying it. The central theme is the question of determinism: the attempt to construct parsers which do not need to carry around multiple alternatives but which can be relied upon to make the right choice when a choice presents itself. Obviously, if it can be shown that a deterministic parser can adequately cover all the phenomena of natural language, ipso facto the nature of the parser changes, since the problem of remembering and dealing with multiple alternatives automatically disappears. The parser described in chapter 6 makes considerable use of trace theory, which is discussed in more detail in chapter 9. This chapter then serves as an introduction to the ideas of chapters 7 and 9, as well as standing in its own right.

Chapter 7 takes the parser described in chapter 6 and describes a development from it to deal with 'semi-grammatical' input. One constant difficulty in giving an abstract account of natural language via a grammar is that the grammar itself necessarily defines the language it is intended to describe. If the users of natural language always observed the rules of the parser's grammar, this would not matter. But, in practise, of course, they do not. (Whether this is because the grammar itself is wrong or incomplete, or because the language user makes mistakes is irrelevant to this discussion). For the construction of a practical parser this raises a problem: either the parser must give up, or it must assume that the input text is reasonable and find some way to carry on. The self-repairing parser described in chapter 7 takes this latter option, dealing with input not foreseen by its own rules.

(Special thanks should go to Eugene Charniak for allowing us to include this chapter, which was not one of the original Lugano papers.)

The final two papers of this Section pick up specific issues within linguistic theory of relevance to parsing. Chapter 8 is concerned with the power of a grammar needed to describe natural language. A transfomational grammar is known to be over-powered for the treatment of natural language. On the other hand, one of the prime reasons behind the introduction of transformational grammar was the claim that grammars of lesser power were not adequate for the description of language. This claim has recently been challenged. Chapter 8 therefore discusses the counter-claim that context-free grammars may, after all, be powerful enough. Should this prove to be true, the nature of the parser needed changes completely. The grammar rules are theoretically much simpler, just because they take no account of the surrounding context. Consequently, the interpreter needed to apply the rules also becomes much simpler to construct, and faster and more economical to run.

Trace theory, described in chapter 9, changes both the nature of the linguistic representation aimed at by the parser, and, in consequence, the kind of tools needed to arrive at it. The number and complexity of the transformations required to construct a representation including trace is greatly reduced, if not entirely eliminated. In consequence, a parser based on trace theory can be much simpler than one based on the standard theory.

6

Deterministic Parsing

G.R. Sampson

This chapter is devoted to the theory of deterministic parsing advanced by Mitchell Marcus, on which the standard reference is Marcus (1980). All otherwise-unspecified page references will be to this book. Milne (1980b) discusses an extension of the theory; other secondary literature will be referred to as the chapter proceeds.

One reason for regarding Marcus' theory as important is that it can be seen as essentially the first serious attempt to make good an I.O.U. which has been issued by theoretical linguists repeatedly for more than a decade. One of the central claims made by Noam Chomsky and his many followers is that there exist certain non-trivial, surprising properties which appear to be common to the syntactic structures of all human languages, and that these 'syntactic universals' reflect characteristics of our mental language-processing machinery. (Chomsky goes on to argue that the characteristics which give rise to the syntactic universals must be innate rather than developed by learning, but for our purposes this is really a side issue.) What Chomsky himself has never done is to make proposals about just what sort of processing machinery would give rise to the syntactic properties he discusses: Chomsky and some of his associates have specified the syntactic universals quite explicitly and precisely, but they have inferred from these only that there exist *some* fixed processing-mechanisms, 'they know not what'. I am not making this point in a critical spirit; it is not clear that Chomsky has been under any obligation to expand his theory in this particular direction. But obviously one hopes that the theory *can* be filled out in this way, and that is what Marcus claims to have done. He has produced a model of a parsing system which has features that are attractive *a priori* for a model that is claimed to correspond to psychological reality, and which at the same time turns out to require the languages on which it operates to obey many of the universal constraints which are central in Chomsky's theorising.

The key feature of Marcus' system is that it is deterministic. Unlike, for instance, the Augmented Transition Networks ('ATNs') used by Woods (1970, 1977), Marcus' system never changes its mind about a partial analysis already carried out, it does not constantly backtrack from what turn out to be blind alleys or clone itself into several systems operating in parallel when it reaches a point where different moves are equally legal. *Exactly* what it means to call the model 'deterministic' is a difficult question (to which I shall return shortly), and it is also controversial whether Marcus' system is as wholly distinct from ATNs as Marcus claims; but, if we can take the notion of 'determinism' intuitively for the moment, we can (I think) agree that it is attractive to suggest that a model of human parsing should have this property. When we listen to speech or read prose we do not feel that we are constantly trying one wrong analysis after another; normally we seem to go straight to the right analysis. (There are certain 'trick' sentences where we *do* find ourselves misanalysing and having to go back and correct our original parsing, and these 'garden path' sentences will play a key role in Marcus' theorising; but the odd feeling that these sentences give us just serves to demonstrate that with the great majority of sentences we do not seem to do anything of the kind.)

It is important at the outset to point out that the goal of Marcus' theory is rather different from the goal of many Artificial Intelligence language-processing systems, such as Woods' LUNAR. LUNAR is an outstandingly successful example of a model that is meant to serve a practical purpose in an artificial system – a question-answering system, in that particular case. Marcus' system is a 'linguist's parser' rather than an AI man's parser, in the sense that it is designed to try to answer a theoretical question about how human beings process language rather than to provide a practical tool to allow machines to process language. Woods' ATNs are designed to have Turing-machine power, unless constraints are placed on the range of acceptable augmentations. Marcus' system, on the other hand is deliberately designed as austerely as possible; Marcus tries to give the system the minimum flexibility compatible with actually being able to handle the things that do crop up in real languages. That means that one probably would not want to use Marcus' theory to design an artificial parsing system that was going to be used for some practical purpose, such as answering questions or translating; or at least one would not want to use Marcus' theory for that until it has been tested over a long period, because at this early stage there is far too high a likelihood that some piece of data from some language will crop up which turns out to force a modification of the theory – that is the price one pays for designing a model which incorporates a strong, falsifiable theory of how human language-processing works. This does not mean that Marcus' theory is just paper speculation which has not been implemented; in fact he *has* implemented quite a complex grammar of English. But obviously there is plenty of English syntax which Marcus has not yet got round to handling, and he has not examined other languages at all. If in due course it turns out that Marcus' model, or some variant of it, *is* adequate to handle all the problems that natural language pose, then probably it *would* be a very good system to incorporate into a practical artificial language-processing system, because its theoretical austerity would make it a very efficient, cheap parser. But at present someone whose aims are practical would undoubtedly do better to use a relatively inefficient but flexible system like ATNs, which cannot be stymied by some awkward bit of grammar that is lurking just round the corner. Marcus' aims are theoretical, not practical.

In what follows, we shall begin by seeing how Marcus' system works, and then go on to look at psychological evidence which suggests that people work that way too; in the last part of the chapter we shall examine how the system may be used to predict Chomskyan universal syntactic constraints.

First: what exactly does Marcus mean by saying that other parsers are 'non-deterministic'? As he points out, it cannot mean that the mechanisms that implement them are endowed with free will – any artificial machine that implements a parsing program, or any other program, is physically quite deterministic. Nevertheless, such systems commonly *simulate* non-mechanical systems that face choices between sets of more than one alternative move, each of which is equally legitimate. The simulation works either by parallel processing – faced with a choice the machine splits itself into two or more machines, each of which carries on with one of the possibilities to see where it leads – or by backtracking – alternative choices are tried in series rather than in parallel, with a tally being kept of choices that did not work. Compare the problem of finding the way through a maze. One way to do it, if your biological technology were up to it, would be to pause each time you got to a fork, split into as many clones as there were paths, equip each clone with a walkie-talkie, and proceed on the understanding that whichever clone reaches the exit will broadcast an instruction for all the other clones to commit suicide. The other way is to make a chalk mark whenever you walk down one side of a fork and always walk down the leftmost unchalked path. Either method seems rather wasteful; but this sort of wastefulness will happen a lot in parsing with an ATN, for instance. Suppose the sentence to be parsed begins with an adverbial clause such as *Although it goes against the grain*, ... You begin any parse by pushing for an S; the initial node will have masses of arcs sprouting out of it corresponding to the different ways one can start a sentence:

1.
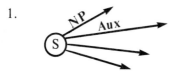

First you try pushing for an NP (and the act of pushing for an NP will probably imply setting up a bit of tentative structure involving an NP node attached to the root S – in ATNs as opposed to RTNs it is not inevitable that the output structure is a map of the sequence of successful pushes, but in this case it probably will be). The initial node of the NP network in turn will have a bunch of arcs sprouting out of it:

2.

so you will go through them in turn – is *although* a Det? No; is it a Proper Name? No; and having run through all these possibilities you have to conclude that the first element of the sentence is not an NP at all, so you go back to the S network (discarding the bit of tentative structure built when you pushed for an NP) and try for an Aux instead. Is *although* an Aux? No; so you doggedly grind on through all the possibilities until you happen to hit the arc which pushes for an adverbial clause.

There are ways of reducing the amount of wasted effort here; in particular it is standard to arrange the arcs leaving a given node in order of relative frequency of the corresponding construction, so the likely possibilities are always tried first. But this will still leave most sentences involving a fair amount of wasted effort. Furthermore, sometimes quite a lot of structure will have been built up only to be eventually thrown away. Consider the sentences:

3. Is the liquid spreading across the floor?
4. Is the liquid spreading across the floor blood?

The phrase *spreading across the floor* is the complement of the verb *is* in 3 and a modifier of the noun *liquid* in 4; so, at the point when the ATN moves on from *floor* to examine the next element of the text (question-mark in one case – we assume the parser is working on *written* input – and *blood* in the other), in one or the other case (depending on which order the relevant arcs were arranged in) it will discover that its tentative analysis of that whole phrase was wrong. This could have involved an enormous quantity of testing wrong arcs and triumphantly finding successful ones, all of which might have to be discarded. (Admittedly, Marcus does seem to take insufficient account of the way that Woods' ATNs are capable of revising their analysis of a constituent in the light of subsequent input without always having to go back to square one (Woods 1970: 603); but it is probably fair to say that quite a lot of this backtracking does have to occur even when that particular aspect of Woods' system is fully exploited.)

So far I have been describing the operation of the ATN parser on the assumption that it is solving the maze by the chalk method – which is wasteful of time. On a computer system it would be equally easy to arrange for the maze to be solved by the cloning method, which would be efficient in time but wasteful in terms of amount of machinery used. Both of these come down to wasting money, in practice. Marcus wants to arrange for the maze to be solved in a different way: he wants to send the person in with instructions that will tell him, whenever he hits a fork, *which* path is the right one – so that he never needs to turn round at a dead end *or* clone himself, but just walks through as fast as possible and straight out the other side.

If we go back to sentences 3 and 4 it is obvious that *no* set of rules about how the English language works, no matter how complete, can tell a mechanical system how to take the word *spreading* if it operates purely left-to-right and cannot look ahead to see what follows *floor* – or at least any rules one did give would necessarily be wrong either for 3 or for 4. So Marcus' system depends crucially on incorporating what he calls 'lookahead'. But if you just say that a parser can look ahead as much as it wants, then it seems that it might be vacuous also to say that it is deterministic – what is the difference between getting to a choice-point, looking ahead to see which of the choices allowed by the grammar is realized, and choosing one's forward path accordingly, or on the other hand moving along a path until it turns out to be a blind alley and retreating to try another path? These seem to be just two ways of thinking about the same sort of procedure. Therefore a key component of Marcus' system is that it has very *limited* lookahead. To go on with the metaphor: when the man walking through the maze hits a fork, he does not clone himself; but he is equipped with a sort of flexible periscope, let us say, of a fixed and limited length, which he can use to peer a certain way down the various paths before he takes one. The rules he is given do not always tell him which path to take just on the basis of what he can see unaided when he hits a fork; but what he can see at the fork itself and the information provided by the periscope, taken together, will always be enough to choose the right path.

One of the ways in which Marcus explains the difference is that ATN parsing is purely 'top-down' or 'hypothesis-driven', whereas his system is to some extent 'bottom-up' or 'data-driven'.

It is worth stressing, I think, that the claim that Marcus' system is 'strictly deterministic' may not be as meaningful and true as Marcus says it is. If 'looking ahead' and 'backtracking' are just two metaphors for the same thing (and obviously neither of them are anything more than metaphors – those computers do not really have little homunculi inside them peering round corners or turning on their heel) then it may be that all Marcus can claim is that his system is *relatively* deterministic because his lookahead is *limited* – it may be that determinism is a more/less rather than yes/no predicate, or at least that the only languages which could be parsed by completely deterministic parsers were ones whose grammars permitted no local structural ambiguity so that cases like 3 and 4 simply never arose. Marcus argues (p. 24) that this is not so and that there is a sense in which his system really is completely deterministic, but I am not fully convinced; perhaps that is my fault, though cf. the discussion of Swartout's critique, below. But in any case, even if the system is only relatively deterministic it is clearly much *more* deterministic than other parsers, and interesting on that account alone.

Incidentally, before proceeding I should briefly discuss the obvious question of what a 'deterministic' parser does when faced with a sentence which is globally ambiguous, such as:

5. The old men and women are muttering.

– where no amount of lookahead tells us whether to take *old* as an immediate constituent of *men* or of *men and women*. Marcus' parser, in such a case, cannot produce two alternative outputs (or it would be obviously non-deterministic); but he says it can be arranged to produce one of the alternative structures supplemented with a flag indicating that the sentence is ambiguous – so that some wider system in which his deterministic parser is embedded might step in to work out the alternative structure if it had a reason to do so. This is perhaps not unrealistic, psychologically – when we encounter an ambiguous sentence, it seems to me that typically we notice just one of its senses rather than being aware of both at once with equal vividness. But Marcus does not pursue this point and I shall not do so either.

Now to the workings of Marcus' system. The system analyses a sentence by building and modifying two data-structures: an *active node stack*, and a *buffer*. The active node stack is a stack of nodes for which daughters are being sought; the buffer is a sequence (n.b. not a last-in-first-out stack) of nodes seeking attachments to mothers.

CURRENT NODE

rule packets which become active when their nodes become current

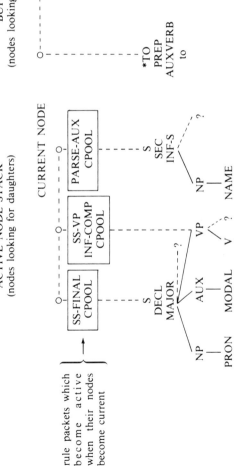

... been waiting for hours.

items in buffer may be single words or complex constituents but there may never be more than three in all.

Two specimen rule-packets:

PARSE-AUX: If 1st (item in buffer) is [VERB] then create an AUX node (i.e. insert such a node at right-hand end of active stack, where it automatically becomes the current node). label it with the person, number and tense features of 1st, and activate the rulepacket BUILD-AUX.
If 1st is [*TO, AUXVERB] and 2nd is [TNSLESS], then create an AUX node with the feature [INF]. attach 1st to this node as TO, and activate BUIL-AUX.
If 1st is [AUX] then attach it to current node as AUX, activate PARSE-VP, deactivate PARSE-AUX.

BUILD-AUX: If 1st and 2nd have features [*HAVE] [EN]. then attach 1st to current node as PERF and label that node [PERF].
If 1st and 2nd have features [*BE] [ING], then attach 1st to current node as PROG and label that node [PROG].
If 1st and 2nd have features [*BE] [EN]. then attach 1st to current node as PASSIVE and label that node [PASSIVE].
If etc...
Otherwise, shift the current node into the buffer. ('Otherwise' is an informal way of saying that this rule is ordered after the others in the packet; Marcus provides a formalism permitting any amount of mutual ordering as desired.)

I use a diagrammatic notation of my own to represent states of the parser; 6 shows an example. In this diagram, the ordering of nodes in the active node stack is represented by left-to-right ordering of the various vertical dotted lines on the left of the diagram; the oldest node is to the left, the newest or 'current' node is to the right and this is always the one being worked on. (The geometry of linguistic phrase-marker trees makes it much more convenient to diagram the active node stack left-to-right, rather than bottom-to-top as is conventional for push-down stacks.)

The grammar of the language is represented by a set of rules, which are arranged in 'packets' (with names such as SS-FINAL, CPOOL); each node in the active stack is associated at any given time with a set of rule-packets, and the significance of this is that when a node becomes the current node (perhaps because the node to the right of it has given all its daughters and hence popped off the stack), the rules in the packets associated with the new current node will determine what the system does next.

(Incidentally, Marcus regards the distinction between active node stack and buffer as the most original aspect of his theory. Without contradicting this, it is perhaps fair to detect a family resemblance with Lyn Frazier and Janet Fodor's 'Sausage Machine' (Frazier and Fodor 1978, cf. Wanner 1980, Fodor and Frazier 1980).)

Elements in the buffer are constituents, which may be individual words or higher-level nodes with various daughters, granddaughters, etc. dangling from them. But at any given time there can be no more than three elements in the buffer (and these are referred to, left to right, as '1st', '2nd', '3rd'). The buffer represents the limited lookahead: the system may inspect the three following constituents but no more. [1]

How do things get into the buffer? Individual words enter at the right when an active rule asks about the features of currently-empty buffer-slots; thus if the buffer contained just an NP constituent and an active rule asked whether the pattern [NP] [VERB] occurred in the first two buffer-slots, the first word of unconsumed text would be read in as 2nd element with all its possible features as supplied by the dictionary. For instance, if the word were *had*, this would be inserted along with the features *HAVE (meaning that it is an inflected form of the root *have*), VERB, PAST, EN (the latter two features meaning that *had* could be *either* the past-tense *or* the past participle of *have*) and other features. In this case the pattern of the active rule would match and the rule would execute; but even if the word entering from the unconsumed text turned out not to match the pattern being looked for, once it has left the input text for the buffer it has to stay in the buffer until attached to a node in the active stack; it cannot be put back in the input string.

Non-leaf constituents (nodes with offspring) enter the buffer at the left, when the system decides that the current node in the active stack has had all its leaves attached but cannot yet itself be attached to a mother. In this situation it is moved from rightmost position in the active stack to leftmost position in the buffer, and the node which had been immediately to the left in the active stack becomes the current node. The fact that nodes are regularly 'dropped into the buffer' in this way means that the rules cannot afford to be too incautious about looking ahead (i.e. bringing words from text into the buffer): it might be that there would be room for the next word of text in the 3rd buffer-slot at a given time, but if immediately thereafter the current node were to be dropped into the buffer there would be an overflow – which means failure to parse. When the current node is dropped into the buffer as '1st', the previous '1st' automatically becomes '2nd' and '2nd' becomes '3rd' – the buffer-positions are like beads on a string rather than fixed pigeon-holes. (When the current node has been supplied with all its daughters *and is already attached to a mother* it is simply popped without being moved into the buffer – in my diagrammatic notation this corresponds to rubbing out the vertical dotted line above it.)

In diagram 6 the system is partway through parsing the sentence *We can expect John to have been waiting for hours.* (Various features have been omitted from nodes in the active stack which have already been parsed and will not be considered further.) The question-marks attached to the active nodes indicate that the system has not yet decided whether these nodes are to receive one or more further daughters – that is what it means to be a node on the active stack. (In fact all the active nodes in this case are destined to be given further daughters; the root S will be given the full stop as its rightmost daughter.) Daughters are always added to the right of all their older sisters. The two specimen rule-packets shown contain the rules used in the next few moves by the system (although to finish parsing the entire sentence several more packets are needed).

From the state portrayed in 6, the system will proceed as follows. (The reader may wish to use pencil and paper to simulate the actions of the system.) The active rule-packets (those associated with the current node) are PARSE-AUX and CPOOL – it happens that the rules in CPOOL are never actually needed in the moves that follow and so they are omitted, but those in PARSE-AUX are shown. The second rule in PARSE-AUX is applicable (the items in the buffer have the listed features), so a new node is added to the right-hand end of the active stack labelled TO and dominating the set of features in 1st position in the buffer); and 'BUILD-AUX' is written on the oblong label associated with the new current node.

At this point PARSE-AUX is no longer active, since the node with which it is associated is no longer current. Control passes to BUILD-

AUX. The first rule in BUILD-AUX asks about the elements in the first two buffer positions, but only one is currently filled; so the word *been* is read in from the unconsumed text with all its features (*BE, VERB, EN). Then the first BUILD-AUX rule applies, and adds a second branch below the AUX node, transferring to it the material in the buffer associated with *have*. BUILD-AUX is still active, so its second rule causes *waiting* to be read into the buffer (which has the feature ING, meaning that it is a present participle), and a third branch is added to the AUX node.

After this has been done, none of the 'If ...' clauses in the BUILD-AUX rules apply to the resulting state (and no CPOOL rule applies), so the 'Otherwise' rule in BUILD-AUX is executed: the AUX node with its various daughters becomes the 1st element in the buffer, and the S node which was current in the state shown in 6 is again current. Therefore PARSE-AUX is active, and the third of its rules applies: we have just dropped an AUX node into 1st position. Accordingly that node (with its daughters) is retrieved from the buffer and attached as right sister of the NP dominating *John*; and, in the oblong box associated with the S node, the item 'PARSE-AUX' is deleted and replaced by 'PARSE-VP'.

Since this node is still current, control now lies with the rule-packets PARSE-VP and CPOOL; neither of these packets are displayed in the diagram, so my exposition of the working of the system must stop here. I hope I have said enough to clarify its operation. When the whole sentence is successfully parsed, the root S as current and only node in the stack will be popped off the stack, with the buffer empty.

The above sample of the working of Marcus' system is by no means fully representative of the kind of things it does. In particular, the rules used in this sample depended for their applicability wholly on the properties of the buffer-contents; in general it is possible for rules to be dependent also on certain properties of the stack. We shall look at this later.

At this point we have seen enough of Marcus' system, though, to introduce into the discussion an extremely interesting critique of it by William Swartout (1978). Swartout sets out to make clearer how Marcus' system works by showing how it would look translated into ATN notation; according to Swartout such a translation is entirely possible. States of the network, in ATN terms, correspond in Marcus' system to sets of rule-packets active at a given time; and a distinctive feature of Marcus' system turns out to be that, whereas an ATN state normally represents one particular 'hypothesis' about the nature of the structure being parsed, in Marcus' system a state will commonly represent a disjunctive hypothesis (the structure is *either* X *or* Y ...). Swartout suggests that it is a strength of Marcus' system that (although in general austere) it can easily incorporate such disjunctive hypotheses.

On the other hand, Swartout also casts doubt on Marcus' claim that this system should be regarded as strictly deterministic. We have seen that Marcus insists that the 'lookahead' facility provided by the buffer does not amount to non-determinism – for Marcus, the crucial point is that his system 'neither discards nor ignores any of the structure that it creates' (p. 24). The term 'structure' is most naturally understood as applying to the nodes, node-labels, and connecting branches found in active stack and buffer, and in this sense Marcus' claim is quite correct: any such structure, once created, is never altered and always appears in the output. However, if the equivalent in Marcus' system of ATN network-states are active rule-packets, it becomes relevant to notice that these are frequently de-activated or ignored while active; this does not 'feel' like 'discarding structure', but possibly that may say more about how we tend to perceive Marcus' model than about the intrinsic properties of the model itself.

At this point, let us take up the question of psychological reality. So far we have spoken as if Marcus' system will unerringly be able to find the right parsing for any English sentence. Even equipped with a periscope, the maze-walker in our metaphor might not always be able to avoid mistakes, if the design of the maze were such that even finite lookahead did not provide enough information to distinguish the correct from the incorrect paths unambiguously. But the suggestion has been that English, and other human languages, are the sort of mazes in which limited lookahead *will* suffice.

But Marcus in fact says that this is not quite true, though it is *almost* true. There are certain kinds of sentence on which we, as human readers, can detect ourselves going wrong; and one of the virtues of his system is that these coincide with the sentences on which the system goes wrong. The cases in question are so-called 'garden paths', such as:

7. The grocer always orders a hundred pound bags of sugar.
8. I told the boy the dog bit Sue would help him.
9. The horse raced past the barn fell. [2]

Although a human reader can understand each of these, typically our comprehension of them is not the smooth, unconscious process which it is for most sentences; rather, there comes a point in the middle of the above sentences where we consciously catch ourselves having made false assumptions which have to be given up in the light of what follows. Marcus suggests that this experience may be interpreted as corresponding to an automatic parser getting stuck and invoking a more sophisticated component of our intelligence to step in and untangle the analysis; since his deterministic system is intended as a model of the lowest-level, automatic component of our total human ability to make sense of sentences, it should break down on sentences which cause humans to 'garden-path'. (Breaking down could correspond to failure of all active rules to be applicable, or to overflow of the buffer.)

Rather than examine the detailed operations of Marcus' parser and grammar rules with respect to sentences 7-9, let us note that the implication of the limited buffer is that breakdown should be inevitable whenever a sequence of three constituents all have alternative analyses which can be resolved only in the light of a fourth constituent: the fourth constituent can be brought into the buffer and inspected only after at least one of the ambiguous constituents has been attached to the active node stack, which means that a decision has been made about its analysis. In a deterministic parser any such decision is irrevocable, so whenever it turns out to be the wrong decision the system will break down. For cases 7 and 8 this is clearly so: in 7 *a* might need to be attached to a quantifier node (*a hundred*) or to an NP node (*a hundred-pound bag*), the attachment of *hundred* is similarly ambiguous, *pound* might be the latter part of *hundred-pound* as a complex modifier or might be a simple adjective, and all of these have to wait for the plurality of *bags* in order to be resolved; likewise in 8 the roles of *the dog*, *bit*, and *Sue* all separately depend on the fact that a verb rather than full stop follows.

I must admit that it is not clear to me why the famous 'garden path' sentence 9 is similarly problematic, since it would appear that only two constituents, *raced* and *past the barn*, have to wait for their resolution by the word *fell* (and indeed the attachment of the prepositional phrase seems unambiguous independently of the analysis of *raced*). Marcus claims this sentence as another verification of his theory and it is undoubtedly my fault that I do not understand why. (It is clear that Marcus' system *equipped with the particular grammar rules Marcus gives* will break down on 9; what I do not understand is why the grammar rules cannot be modified, preserving the general nature of the system and in particular the limitation of three buffer elements, so as to parse 9 correctly.) Milne (1980a) argues with respect to other examples that 'garden pathing' does not always conform to Marcus' predictions and is influenced by semantic considerations.

Leaving aside the question whether there are exceptions to Marcus' claims, I should stress that Marcus' discussion of garden paths depends on empirical research on various subjects' reactions to different sentences – perhaps unusually for an artificial-intelligence specialist (or even a linguist!) he does *not* merely rely on his personal intuitions about the status of sentences and arrange for his system to reflect these. One of his points concerns the sentence:

10. Have the packages delivered tomorrow.

(n.b. English readers should avoid being distracted by the fact that *Have N Verbed* is an unusual construction in England; in America, where Marcus did his work, it is a much more usual form of imperative.) Marcus finds it counter-intuitive that such a short sentence as this should be a garden path, but he finds that half his subjects do in fact 'garden-path' on it, taking it for a question until they hit *tomorrow* or perhaps the full stop – this despite the semantic clues (a package can easily be delivered but can scarcely deliver). It is therefore particularly satisfying that the theory predicts that 10 should be a garden path: *have, the packages*, and *delivered* are all of ambiguous ancestry until the lack of noun following *delivered* shows that that word must be being used passively.

There remain, of course, the half of Marcus' subjects who did not garden-path on 10; and in general he found that sentences which caused some subjects to garden-path usually did not cause everyone to do so. I should have thought there were several adequate let-outs for Marcus from this *prima facie* awkward fact. If a sentence is locally ambiguous then a proportion of subjects might opt for what turns out to be the correct analysis by chance; and, even if all English-speakers use the same rules, and ought therefore all to garden-path on the same sentences, it could easily be that some of us are less conscious of this momentary interior hitch than others are. Marcus chooses a different and more interesting explanation: he suggests that the size of the buffer may not be constant across all individuals, but rather that some people may learn to expand their buffer to four or even five places. (I think this suggestion would imply that the individuals in question would also complicate their grammar rules, though Marcus does not say this, because unless I am mistaken a set of rules designed for a three-place buffer would be unable to take advantage of the more sophisticated processing capacity offered by a four-or-five-place buffer.) This is a very un-Chomskyan proposal – it is always treated as axiomatic by Chomsky that our general language-processing machinery, as opposed to the particular rules of individual languages, is invariant across the species and that individuals are not 'better' or 'worse' than one another as speaker/hearers however different their general cognitive abilities might be. But Marcus' suggestion is perhaps not to be scorned merely for that reason. Certainly it does not reduce his general theory to vacuity, as some readers may perhaps suspect; the theory still predicts that, the *more* constituents remain separately ambiguous-as-to-ancestry at a time, the *fewer* people will comprehend without garden-pathing (and, since someone with a four-place buffer should presumably be able to use it wherever it is advantageous, the theory also predicts constancies across given individuals' reactions to diverse sentences – but Marcus does not appear to have researched on this).

Finally, as Marcus points out, sentences which are garden paths in writing usually are not in speech, where intonation is available to resolve ambiguities. Marcus argues – I believe rightly – that this is a point in his favour. Humans are so organized that automatic parsing virtually always works deterministically on 'natural', i.e. spoken, language. Written language is a relatively artificial system which provides only part of the data needed by our parsing device, and therefore the latter sometimes breaks down; the accuracy of Marcus' model is shown by the fact that its performance degrades in the same way as the human's performance in response to similarly-inadequate input.

I turn now to an explanation of how, according to Marcus, this theory succeeds in predicting some of the universal characteristics of language discussed by Chomsky, and thus redeems the I.O.U. issued by Chomsky when the latter says that these universals reflect processing machinery.

Before I can give this explanation, though, I must say something about the nature of the output of Marcus' parsing system. Up to now I have been silent on this issue, and from my silence the reader will perhaps have inferred the default implication that the system outputs Chomskyan 'deep structures' or logical forms of the sentences input to it. In many respects this is just what the system does. Thus, it re-orders the elements of an interrogative sentence such as *Has John VERBed ...?* to give a structure in standard declarative order prefixed by an interrogative marker: *Q John PERFECT VERB ...*; or, faced with an imperative sentence, it supplies the subject *you*. Marcus claims, in fact, that his system can carry out these operations in a particularly elegant fashion. But there is one important respect in which the results of the parsing differ from philosophers' 'logical forms', or from 'deep structures' as envisaged by 'classical' transformational grammar (where 'classical' refers to anything between about 1965 and 1975). Where 'classical' transformational theory treated a noun-phrase as having been shifted from one place to another in a sentence, the output of Marcus' parser leaves the NP where it is in the input, but includes a so-called 'trace' or dummy NP, supplied with a pointer to the surface NP, such that the position of the trace shows where that NP logically belongs.

Let me stress that these 'traces' are not used merely to simplify the task facing Marcus' parser. They may incidentally do that; I have not looked into the question whether it would be possible to use Marcus' mechanisms to parse sentences into deep structures of the 'classical' type. But the use of traces rather than shifting NPs has been standard in linguistic theory for several years now, and was introduced for purely theoretical reasons having nothing to do with parsing algorithms. (On trace theory, see Lightfoot (1980), or chapter 9 of this volume). Thus Marcus is simply arranging for his system to output the structures which his linguistic colleagues nowadays would want a parser to output.

Some examples are given in diagrams 11 to 13 (I do not guarantee that every detail of the structures shown here is as Marcus envisages, but the details relevant to this discussion are correct.) 'Traces' are shown as NP nodes dominating just the letter *t*, with a dotted line leading to the surface manifestation of the NP. (In the implementation each node of a tree is numbered, and the pointers are realized by including the number of the pointed-at node in a designated slot in the representation of a trace node – but this is an engineering issue, it has no conceptual relevance.)

11.

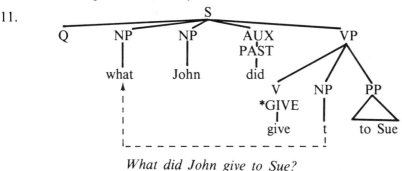

What did John give to Sue?

12.

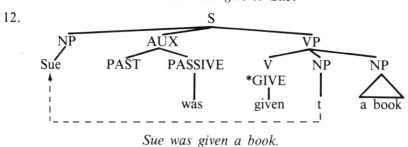

Sue was given a book.

13.

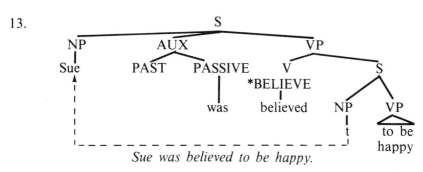

Sue was believed to be happy.

Note that strictly the nodes at which traces point are the nodes labelled 'NP'; in my diagrams I draw the arrowheads pointing to the material underneath the NP nodes simply because the diagrams are easier to draw that way. In a diagram incorporating traces, what are relevant to the *sense* or *logical form* of the respective sentences are exclusively the positions at the *beginning* of the dotted lines; the items at the *end* of the arrows are relevant only for the surface *pronunciation* of the sentences. You may ask: in that case, where are the logical subjects of the passive sentence in 12 and 13? In classical transformational theory such sentences would be derived from underlying *Someone gave/believed ...*, with passivisation to *Sue was given/believed ... by someone* and subsequent deletion of the *by*-phrase by an optional rule. But in modern transformational theory it seems that passive sentences are regarded as having no logical subject at all – so it is quite appropriate that the only 'subject' in 12 and 13 is an item at the head of a trace-pointer and thus logically non-existent. And one must concede that in some ways this seems more satisfying than positing a deleted *someone*: after all, the sentence in 12 may mean the same as *Someone gave Sue a book*, but it would be rather risky to equate 12 and 13 with *Someone believed Sue to be happy* – in many contexts the sentence would be better translated by *Everyone* (or, *Most people*) *believed Sue to be happy*. Classical transformational theory forced you to specify some particular NP as the one which occurred underlyingly in an agentless passive; the modern theory leaves this question open, which seems more realistic.

Another point which needs a word of explanation in connection with interpreting the diagrams is that, where a leaf-node is labelled with an inflected form such as *given*, or *was*, or *believed*, what is relevant to the sense of the structure is the root form which is included as a feature of the node immediately above – in the case of *given*, the form *GIVE, in the case of *was* in 12 the morpheme PASSIVE. The inflected words in the input sentence are all displayed in the output structure, to show which word corresponds to which bit of meaning, but what counts for defining the meaning is the material dominating the words in small letters. Strictly I ought to have shown the word *Sue* as dominated by a node labelled *SUE, and so forth – but that would have been unduly pedantic, so I have shown the roots in capital letters only when they are realised by words carrying special inflections.

In the light of these explanations, it should be clear in what sense the tree-structures in 11 to 13 represent the meanings of the ordinary-English sentences written to the left of them.

Now let me show how one of these trace nodes is created by the parser. Diagram 14 displays the state of the parser in the middle of analysing sentence 12; *was given* has been analysed as including the morpheme PASSIVE by the rule-packet BUILD-AUX discussed, and the system is currently looking for daughters for the VP node initiated by *given*.

14.

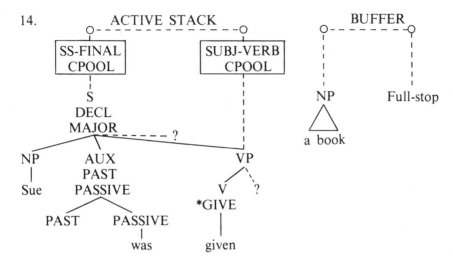

The relevant rule-packet at this point is SUBJ-VERB. (CPOOL is also active but as it happens it is inapplicable, so let us ignore it.) SUBJ-VERB includes the following rules among others (I omit irrelevant details):

If the AUX of the 'closest S' [see below] has the feature PASSIVE, and the closest S lacks the feature NP-PREPOSED, then:

1) give the closest S node the feature NP-PREPOSED [one of the things that this feature achieves is to prevent the rule applying over and over again – it has another motivation which we shall ignore here];
2) create an NP node labelled TRACE [this automatically becomes the current node, of course];
3) set the pointer of the current node to the NP immediately dominated by the closest S; and
4) drop the current node into the buffer.

Otherwise, [...] if the closest S has the feature MAJOR then activate SS-VP [...] and deactivate SUBJ-VERB.

These rules introduce a key property of Marcus' system which I have not discussed so far: the active node stack, though in most respects a push-down store, has the feature that *two* rather than one of its elements are accessible at any given time – the node at the 'top' (in my diagrams, at the right), but also the nearest node in the stack to that 'current' node which is labelled 'S'. Thus a grammatical rule may depend for its applicability on the contents of any or all of the three buffered nodes and either or both of these two nodes in the active stack. For a node to be 'accessible' means that the system can look at it and at everything hanging from the bottom of it; but there is no mechanism for looking *upwards*, thus in diagram 14 it is not possible for a rule to ask whether the current node, which is the VP, is dominated by a DECL S node. Allowing grammar rules freely to ask questions about the material above a given node would add a major increment of flexibility to the system; in harmony with his general aim of producing a system that is as austere as is compatible with doing its job, Marcus includes the 'closest S' facility as the smallest possible increase in power (by comparison with allowing the machine to look at just the current node and what is below it) that enables it to carry out various operations that are necessary for parsing natural language.

(For the benefit of linguists who may wonder why exactly *this* is Marcus' preferred way of incorporating a limited amount of looking upwards in trees, it should be pointed out that the computer-formalism in which trees are represented makes it technically enormously more difficult to find the mother of a given node than its daughters, so any system which avoids having to do the former is going to look like a relatively weak system to a computer specialist. Whether this is *only* a fact about artificial computer technology or something more I am not sure.)

The idea that the parser can look leftwards in the stack but only to what is currently the nearest S node is connected with the principle of transformational grammar called 'cyclical application of rules' (see e.g. Chomsky (1966: 63)), i.e. that the ordered sequence of transformational rules applies separately to each clause in a structure containing nested subordinate clauses. There is a complication here: in very recent (since 1976) writings Chomsky has argued that transformations cycle on NP as well as S nodes, and because of this when Marcus introduces the notion that two nodes in the active stack are accessible he says that the one of these which is not the current node will be the closest cyclical node, S *or NP*. However, later in the book (p. 162), he points out that treating NP nodes as cyclical creates a problem with respect to the universal phenomenon I shall be discussing below. Marcus does not mention the fact that until very recently no-one ever suggested that NP nodes *were* cyclical; but since that is the case, I shall assume that 'classical' transformational theory is correct so that only the closest *S* node can be accessed and Marcus' problem disappears. (It may be that this decision would create problems for *other* issues that Marcus discusses – I have not gone into this.)

When SUBJ-VERB is applied to the structures shown in figure 14, then, the result will be:

15.

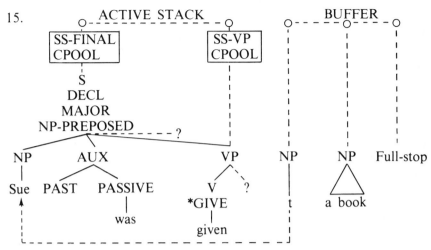

The active rule-packet is now SS-VP, and this will take the NPs from the buffer and attach them successively as daughters of the current VP node. The reason why the trace node was first dropped into the buffer by SUBJ-VERB and then retrieved by SS-VP (rather than being attached to the VP node immediately by SUBJ-VERB) is that, in a sentence such as *John was believed to be happy*, a trace node will also be created following *believed* but in this case it will *not* be attached as direct object of that verb (rather it is subject of *to be happy*) – therefore it is arranged that the system reserves a decision on the syntactic role of a trace immediately following a passive construction until it has invoked a rule-packet (SS-VP) which is sensitive to the difference between verbs like *give* that take only NP objects and verbs like *believe* which can also take clause objects.

The fact that SS-VP takes NPs from the buffer and attaches them as objects of a verb has nothing to do with the fact that the sentence in question is in the passive, of course – SS-VP would do the same in parsing the sentence *John gave Sue a book*, and the rule-packet is quite indifferent to the fact of whether an NP it manipulates is a trace or an ordinary NP, and whether it entered the buffer from the input string or from the active stack. Marcus points out that, although we commonly think of the relationship between passive and active sentences in English as quite a complex one, the only differences in the operation of his parser with respect to the two sentence-types are that BUILD-AUX detects passive morphology in passive sentences (just as it detects other features of auxiliaries), and that SUBJ-VERB inserts a trace in the buffer (and the feature NP-PREPOSED in the clause node) – in this way the desired output structure follows automatically from the operation of other rules that are needed anyway for active sentences.

So much for 'trace theory' and the way it is incorporated into Marcus' system. Now let us turn to the question of linguistic universals.

Chomsky and his followers have proposed quite a wide range of syntactic and other properties as apparently universal features of all human languages, which do not have to be learned by children from experience with their elders' language but are in some sense 'known' at birth as part of our innate endowment. For references to the various publications in which such proposals have been put forward, see e.g. Sampson (1980 : ch. IX). Much of modern linguistics consists of testing such proposals against the data of various languages and modifying or extending them accordingly. Marcus takes several of the universal properties which are central in Chomsky's philosophical arguments for innatism and shows how a parsing system such as he has described requires any language to which it is adapted to possess these properties.

I shall illustrate this aspect of Marcus' theory by considering just one of the universals he deals with, the 'Complex NP Constraint' originally proposed by J.R. Ross.

In terms of classical (i.e. pre-trace) transformational grammar, the Complex NP Constraint is a constraint on how transformations are allowed to move constituents around. Ross phrases it as follows: 'No element in an S dominated by an NP with a lexical head noun may be moved out of that NP'. Any transformation which would otherwise be applicable to a given phrase-marker will be blocked from applying if its action would violate that constraint. Thus, consider:

16a. Mary read a statement which was about that man.
 b.*The man who(m) Mary read a statement which was about is ill.
 c.*Who(m) did Mary read a statement which was about?

The NP *a statement which was about that man* has a lexical head (*statement*) followed by an S (the relative clause); therefore if *that man* in 16a is replaced by a relative or interrogative pronoun, which must obligatorily be moved to the front of a superordinate clause by the *Wh*-Fronting transformation, a bad sentence results. Note that if the relative clause in 16a is reduced to a non-S modifying phrase as in 17a no comparable ungrammaticality occurs:

17a. Mary read a statement about that man.
 b. The man who(m) Mary read a statement about is ill.
 c. Who(m) did Mary read a statement about?

Likewise, compare the badness of 18b and c, in which a *wh*-word has been extracted from a clause in apposition to a noun (*the report*), with the goodness of 19b and c where the clause alone constitutes the object of the higher verb:

18a. Mary believed the report that Otto had taken the plans.

b.*The plans which Mary believed the report that Otto had taken are secret.

c.*Which plans did Mary believe the report that Otto had taken?

19a. Mary believed that Otto had taken the plans.

b. The plans which Mary believed that Otto had taken are secret.

c. Which plans did Mary believe that Otto had taken?

(Incidentally, some people who are not familiar with data like these tend to react by suggesting that it is not necessary to posit some subtle syntactic constraint to explain them – the starred sentences are 'bad' for semantic or pragmatic reasons: 'No-one would ever want to say anything like that so of course it sounds odd'. One obvious retort to this is: '*Why* wouldn't people ever want to say e.g. 16c if they might quite easily want to say 17c' – the two seem to mean exactly the same, and normally there is only a trivial difference of style between a relative clause beginning *which is* and a modifying phrase from which these words have been elided. The other point is that there exist languages in which the equivalent of *wh*-words are not fronted but left in their logical position – in which one says things like *You are reading what?* rather than *What are you reading?* – and in such languages the translations of sentences which in *English* violate the Complex NP Constraint sound perfectly natural and usable, as Ross's theory predicts; this seems to establish that what is wrong with the starred sentences in 16 and 18 is purely a *syntactic* matter rather than a matter of the sentences saying things which it is not useful to say.)

Marcus' first point about Ross's principle is that Ross has stated it in a form which is stronger than is justified by any data he has given. According to Marcus the evidence justifies only the following weaker principle, and it is this that he demonstrates to follow from the nature of his parser:

No *NP* in an S that is dominated by an NP with a lexical head noun may be moved out of that NP by *whatever rules form questions and relative clauses.*

Furthermore, since within trace theory question-forming and relative-clause-forming rules no longer move NPs at all, what Marcus will show is that his parser does not permit traces to be created and correctly linked to antecedent NPs by rules for parsing questions and relative clauses, if the traces occur in Ss within 'complex NPs'. If human beings cannot parse a given sort of structure correctly, it would presumably follow automatically that human speakers would not produce such structures – this is not a logical truism, but it is surely a fairly straightforward practical implication.

Marcus divides the task of showing that his system predicts the limitation quoted in the last paragraph into two parts; he shows first that it is true with respect to the parsing of complex NPs containing relative clauses (e.g. 16) and secondly that it is true with respect to the parsing of complex NPs containing complements in apposition (e.g. 18).

If 16b and c could be parsed the output would have to look broadly as follows (in the case of 16b structure 20 will itself be embedded in a superordinate clause):

20.

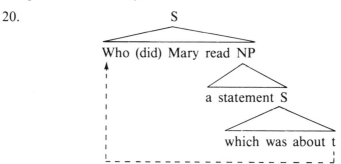

Marcus deals with this rather quickly: he says that the trace could not be linked as shown, because at the time it is created the 'closest S' will be the lower S so that the system would have no access to the constituent *who*. It seems to me that this is a bit cavalier; Marcus really ought to show that there is no way of writing rules in such a fashion that the trace can be created and linked *before* the lower S is created. But although Marcus gives no proof that this is impossible (perhaps because an earlier discussion of another constraint has adequately established the point - see pp. 142-143 of Marcus' book), it is easy to agree that it would be difficult, given that all elements of the relative clause preceding the trace (which must include at least subject and verb) would have to be held in a limited buffer. And it is clearly true that with 17b and c the difficulty evaporates; the analysis of these sentences will contain no S node subordinate to the *read* clause, so the S dominating *read* will be the 'closest S' when the trace is created and hence it can easily be linked to the *who* dangling from that S.

Marcus discusses the problem of 18 in more detail. Again, if 18b and c were parsable their structure would have to be broadly as follows:

21.

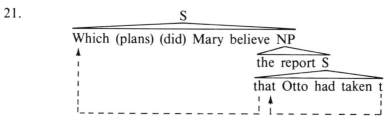

By the time the trace following *taken* is created, the S dominating that clause will already be on the stack and hence will be the 'closest S' (at least, if we accept the argument for structure 12 we must accept the parallel argument here); therefore the only possibility of linking the trace with *which (plans)* will be to do so by a two-stage process, in which first the word *that* (or perhaps another trace associated with it) is linked to the antecedent while the top S is still the closest S, and then the trace at the end of the sentence is linked to the source of the first linkage. There are some complications about just what the analysis of the intermediate element in this linkage should be and whether it is the first element of the subordinate S or the last element of the NP which is outside the S, but we may neglect these since they scarcely affect the present argument. Notice that it is normal enough for traces to be linked to their surface manifestations by double links; for instance that will happen in the parsing of *John was believed to have been shot*, which will be broadly as in 22 (In such double linkages only the *ultimate* source – in this case the trace following *shot* – is relevant to the logical form of the sentence, each of the positions at the arrowhead end of a link has to do exclusively with grammatical realisation.)

22.

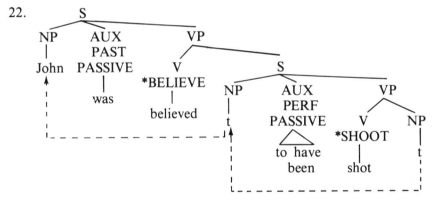

The question is whether it will be possible to create the double linkage in 21. On the face of it this does look as if it should be possible. The difficulty comes, Marcus says, from the fact that *the report that ...* might turn out to introduce a relative clause rather than an appositional one (that is, when it hits the word *that* the machine does not know that it is not in the middle of reading a sentence such as:

23. Which plans did Mary believe the report that Otto published to discuss?

But if it *does* turn out that 23 is the sentence being input, then it will turn out to have been an error to have linked *that* with *which plans*. Sentence 23 has to parse into the following structure:

24.

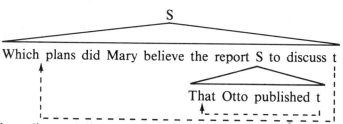

The 'long-distance' link in 24 poses no special problem, since, well before the sentence-final trace is created, the relative clause *that Otto wrote* has been completed and popped from the stack, so that the main S is again the 'closest S'. But in a deterministic system it is not possible to create a link from *that* to *which plans* in 18c 'on spec', being prepared to destroy it if the sentence turns out to have the structure of 23, since it is of the essence of determinism that any aspect of structure, once created, is preserved and not destroyed. Therefore structures 21 and 24 may not co-exist in a language; Q.E.D.

19b and c on the other hand pose no problem because there is no possibility of interpreting *that* as introducing a relative clause – any relative clause must have an antecedent. So it is safe to write rules linking *that*, when encountered, to *which*, knowing that *that* in turn will be linked to a trace to be created when a 'gap' in the logical structure is encountered.

However a point not mentioned by Marcus is that on this theory the badness of 18b and c is crucially dependent on the fact that the word which introduces a complement clause in English is homophonous with one of the relative pronouns. That is to say: suppose that instead of saying *Mary believes that John is a buffoon*, we said in English something like *Mary believes bonk John is a buffoon*, with some word *bonk* quite different from the relative pronoun you get in *Mary found the book that she wanted*. Then Marcus should presumably predict that it *would* be all right to say sentences such as:

25. Which plans did Mary believe the report bonk Otto had taken?

– when you get *bonk* it is quite safe to create a link to *which plans*, because *bonk* cannot be interpreted as beginning a relative clause as in 23. This means that if there is a language with two words like *bonk* and *that* it should violate Ross's Complex NP Constraint.

It happens that a number of European languages resemble English in having complementisers which are homophonous with relative pronouns – French uses *que* in both roles, German *dass* is homophonous with *das*. Slavonic languages, however, do not use homophones for these functions. Czech, for instance, uses *že* for *that* in the 'bonk' sense, and this word is not homophonous with or even similar to any of the Czech relative pronouns. Czech versions of examples 19c and 18c/25 would be respectively:

26. Jaké plány věřila Marie, že Otto ukradl?
27. Jaké plány věřila Marie zprávě, že Otto ukradl?

Unfortunately, according to the intuitions of my colleague Igor Hajek (whom I thank for his help), while 26 is 'a little archaic or contrived, but quite acceptable', 27 is 'utterly and completely impossible'. In other words, Czech obeys the Complex NP Constraint with respect to these examples despite the fact that, in parsing 27, it would be quite safe to create a trace bound to *jaké plány* in the complementizer slot without reading past *že*. This surely implies that Marcus' explanation for the fact that *English* obeys the constraint cannot be correct?

Perhaps Marcus may be able to answer this rather specific criticism in a way which preserves the cogency of his explanation for the Complex NP Constraint. There is a more general problem, however, about Marcus' approach to the Chomskyan linguistic universals.

Suppose for the moment that the Complex NP Constraint is indeed obeyed in just the cases where Marcus' parsing theory predicts that it should be obeyed. The complex NP Constraint is only one of the Chomskyan universals; and Marcus claims that a number of others also (the 'Subjacency Constraint', the 'Tensed S Constraint', the 'Specified Subject Constraint') all turn out to follow from the basic principle that the parser is (in some sense) deterministic. Since the notion that humans parse deterministically is attractive *a priori*, Marcus appears to have achieved a significant measure of scientific explanation, in the sense that he has shown how several rather disparate and surprising-looking facts (the Complex NP and other constraints) are consequences of a single relatively unsurprising fact (deterministic parsing).

But it is not clear that this is indeed a fair assessment of what Marcus has done. First, Marcus' is not the only attempt to explain the Complex NP and various other constraints in terms of unified and relatively clearly-motivated principles, though the previous attempt (Cattell 1976) is perhaps not specially cogent and has not been generally accepted. Secondly, at least in the case of the Complex NP Constraint, and I think also in the case of the other constraints discussed by Marcus, it is not really true that he deduces the observable facts from the postulate of deterministic parsing alone; rather, he deduces them from the conjunction of that postulate with the postulate about accessibility of the 'closest S node' as well as the current node in the stack. And while the determinism principle is the sort of postulate that one might well want to adopt *a priori*, the 'closest S' principle looks much more *a posteriori*. That is, there is a hint of possible circularity here – maybe the decision about how the active stack can be accessed was influenced by the need to reflect the observed constraints, in which case the 'explanation' of the constraints is purely *ad hoc* and unpersuasive.

Even if this suspicion has some foundation, Marcus might respond by saying that to derive a *number* of assorted universal constraints from a *single* principle of stack-accessibility (plus the principle of determinism) would be an achievement that cannot be dismissed as *ad hoc*; but unfortunately it is not clear that he can claim to have done this, since (a point that was alluded to above) Marcus hedges somewhat on whether the node other than the current one which is accessible in the stack is the nearest *S* node always, or the nearest *NP-or-S* node – on p. 163 he adopts a solution of making the accessibility principle differ in different circumstances, which goes perilously far in the direction of arranging a separate accessibility principle for each of the universals to be 'explained'.

On the other hand, at Lugano Eric Wehrli of M.I.T. argued that Marcus' problem may stem from his having worked with an out-of-date formulation of the Complex NP Constraint, and that the formulation now believed to be accurate might be compatible with a less *ad hoc* version of Marcus' parsing system. I have not followed this up.

In any case, I believe it would be a mistake to cavil too much at the apparent adhockeries in Marcus' work. What he has tried to do is something that linguists ought to have attempted years ago. There is every reason to continue working on Marcus' system, in the hope that it may be developed and improved into a fully satisfactory theory.

NOTES

1. Marcus (ch. 8) has to complicate his buffer mechanism considerably in order to handle the internal structure of NPs. In this introductory exposition of Marcus' theory I shall ignore these complications. It is fair to say, however, that this aspect of the system reduces the persuasiveness of Marcus' suggestion that this theory achieves the goal of predicting a rich and diverse set of data on the basis of an austere set of axioms.

2. 9 is a 'classical' example of garden paths, introduced by Thomas Bever (1971).

7

A Parser with Something for Everyone

E. Charniak

1. INTRODUCTION

Syntactic parsing in Artificial Intelligence (AI) has always had its share of controversies. Many in AI have seen in this work 'much wasted effort' (Riesbeck 1975a) because things would be much more efficient if parsing were more closely integrated with semantics. More generally, some have felt that 'the heavily hierarchical syntax analyses of yesteryear may not be necessary' (Wilks 1975c). At the same time, syntactic parsers have been attacked by those in linguistics as 'devoid of any principles which could serve as even a basis for a serious scientific theory of human linguistic behaviour' (Dresher and Hornstein 1976). And, while psychologists have been kinder, they must surely have their own quibbles; any psychologist must be uncomfortable with theories which, if taken literally, would predict that people cannot understand ungrammatical sentences – a prediction which is false.

In this paper we will propose a parser, named 'Paragram', which goes some way to answering this criticism. In particular:

A) The parser is 'semi-grammatical' in the sense that it takes a standard 'correct' grammar of English and applies it so long as it can, but will accept sentences which do not fit the grammar, while noting in which ways the sentences are deviant.

B) The rules of the parser are intended to capture the relevant generalisations about language in much the same way as a good transformational grammar. Paragram's rules are nearly in one-to-one correspondence with those proposed in some versions of transformational grammar. [1] Despite the fact that augmented transition network (ATN) parsers are based upon transformational grammar, when examined closely typical ATN grammars (Woods 1973) seem to be far from the above ideal.

C) The parser is reasonably efficient, and would be very efficient if implemented on a machine with limited parallelism, so that the rules of the grammar all test the input in parallel (but only one is actually applied).

The next section will concentrate on the problem of ungrammatical input. There we note that Paragram is based upon Marcus' parser 'Parsifal' (Marcus 1980), and motivate this choice by showing how a semi-grammatical parser could not be based on the obvious alternative, the ATN. We will then describe Parsifal in some detail, and follow by describing the major differences which allow Paragram to handle ungrammatical input. Section 3 will start with a description of some of the failures of ATN parsing to live up to its transformational origins, and show how Parsifal, while better in some ways, has many problems of its own. We will then show how Paragram does better than either of the two in 'capturing the relevant generalizations'. Efficiency considerations will be covered briefly in section 4.

2. HANDLING UNGRAMMATICAL SENTENCES

2.1. The problem

That people are quite capable of understanding ungrammatical sentences has led to doubts about the plausibility of models that depend heavily on the grammaticality of the input. Few people have trouble understanding a sentence like:

1.*The boys is dying. [2]

In response, those who have favoured the use of syntactic parsers have pointed out that while our understanding of the above sentence is not affected by the lack of subject verb agreement, in some cases the expectation that they will agree is crucial. So, a parser that did not check for agreement would not distinguish:

2a. The fish is dying.
 b. The fish are dying.

What is needed is a 'semi-grammatical' parser that would enforce the rules of grammar when possible, but admit defeat gracefully when not. Note however that it will not do simply to build non-grammaticality into the grammar. While it would be perfectly possible to write a grammar of English which would accept ungrammatical sentences this approach is incompatible with the goal of having a one-to-one correspondence with plausible rules of transformational grammar. Furthermore, if taken literally such a grammar would not explain why people recognize that some of the constructs the parser accepts are grammatical while others are not.

2.2 Why we need a deterministic parser

As we noted above, Paragram is a modification of Parsifal. We will explain Parsifal shortly, but first let us explain why we chose it as a starting point. Probably the best known parser in AI today is Woods' ATN parser (Woods 1973). However it would not be possible to base a Paragram type parser upon the ATN parsing model. To see why this is so, we need only consider that when Paragram finds an ungrammatical situation, it must simply recognize it as such, and continue as best it can. ATNs simply do not work this way. When an ATN finds an ungrammatical situation it takes it as evidence that it made an incorrect decision earlier in the sentence, and hence backs up to find the correct path. So, consider:

3. Jack sold the ball.
4. Jack sold Sue the ball.

Suppose that an ATN parser initially decides to parse 'Sue' in 4 as a direct object, just like 'the ball' in 3. When it gets to the second noun phrase in 4, 'the ball', it has no way to handle it, and hence it backs up and tries making 'Sue' into a dative which has been moved before the direct object. But suppose we had the ungrammatical sentence,

5.*Jack sold Sue give.

Here the ATN would back up as well, but to no avail, since there is no way to get a grammatical sentence out of this. In this particular case we have not lost too much, since the sentence has little meaning (certainly Paragram does not get anything out of it), but it would be nice if the parser could at least tell us what is wrong with the sentence. But again, an ATN cannot do this. An error at any point need not imply that the sentence is ungrammatical there. Furthermore, an ATN would behave the same way on a less badly mutilated sentence such as:[3]

6.*Jack sold Sue ball.

Hence we need a parser in which the failure of rules at a given point may be presumed to be due to the sentence being ungrammatical at that point. This is exactly what Parsifal can do. Since Parsifal is deterministic (i.e., it does not back up) it may assume that it has parsed everything correctly up to the point where it runs into trouble. Thus the problem must be right there, and hence, in theory at any rate, it could simply make a guess at what was intended and continue on.

2.3 Parsifal

Parsifal has two basic data structures, a stack and a buffer. The stack contains the sentence constituents on which it is still working. If a constituent is complete, then it must reside in one of two places: first, it may simply hang off some larger constituent. So at the end of a sentence there is only one item on the stack, the topmost *s* node, and everything else hangs off it. Second, Parsifal may have a complete constituent, but not know yet where it should go. Such constituents are put in the *buffer* which is a storage area of limited size.[4] An obvious example would be an individual word (which is clearly complete). A less obvious example would be a noun phrase which, while complete, might be attached at any one of several places in the tree.

Rules in Parsifal are of the typical situation/action type. To decide if it is applicable, a rule will most often look to see what is in the buffer, although, with some limitations, rules may also look at the stack. Two positions in the stack are special, the bottom of the stack, which is named *c*, and the lowest sentence node in the stack, which is named *s*. To take a simple example, in Parsifal the rule for recognizing passive constructions is this:

(rule passive-aux
[= be] [= en] → Attach 1st to c as passive)
The rule is named passive-aux. It looks at the first two buffers and puts the 'be' on the bottom-most node of the stack (which will be an 'aux').

The two square-bracket groupings indicate what the rule requires in the first and second buffer. In particular, the '=' indicates that what appears in the corresponding buffer must have the feature specified, such as being a form of the verb 'be'. These individual 'atomic tests' make up the rule test which determines whether the rule is applicable. Everything following the '→' is the action portion of the rule. These actions are specified in a language called 'Pidgin', which is quite restricted but formulated to look like English.

Suppose we were applying this rule in the course of processing the sentence

7. Jack was taken to the house.

At the point where *passive-aux* is applicable, the state of the parser would be as follows:

8.

Here the *np* 'Jack' has been made a constituent of the top level sentence, but it is hanging off to the side to indicate that it is no longer on the stack, since it is a completed constituent. In the course of testing, Parsifal will see that 'was' is a form of the verb 'to be', while 'taken' is an 'en' form of the verb 'to take' and thus the buffers match the rule test. At this point the action would be executed, which is to put the 'was' on the *aux* which is currently the node Parsifal is working on. This will have the side effect of removing the 'was' from the buffer, at which point the words further along in the sentence will move in to replace those which have been removed from the buffer. Thus after the rule has applied we will have the following configuration:

9.

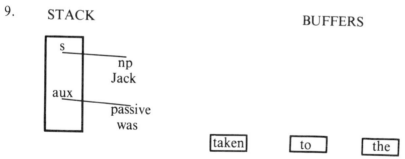

However, not all rules of the grammar will actually be tested at any given point. Indeed most of the rules would be completely irrelevant; while parsing the auxiliaries of a verb we would hardly expect to find direct objects. To prevent Parsifal from even looking, each of its rules is found in one or more 'packets' and only the rules which are in 'active' packets will be tried. The active packets are those which are attached to the bottom node of the stack, c. Should this node be removed, the packets on the next higher node will be active. The idea is that if Parsifal is working on a noun phrase, then noun phrase rules will be active. Once Parsifal is done with it, it will be removed from the stack, and the rules on the next higher uncompleted constituent, say a verb phrase, will become active once more. Which packets are attached to a given node is explicitly controlled by the grammar rules themselves, using commands to *activate* or *deactivate* certain packets. Thus the rule we just looked at, *passive-aux*, should have indicated in which packets it is to be found.

(rule passive-aux in build-aux
[= be] [= en] → Attach 1st to c as passive.)
This rule is found in the build-aux packet.

Furthermore, it is possible that of the rules that are in currently active packets, more than one might apply. To handle this situation, Parsifal rules also have 'priorities'. Rules are tried in order of their priorities, with lower numbers going first. A rule without an explicit priority, such as *passive-aux*, is given a default priority of 10. Typically, one gives more specific rules higher priority, and less specific ones low priority. For example, the rule which says, in effect, that if you cannot parse any more auxiliary verbs, then assume you are done with the aux, is this:

(rule aux-complete priority: 15 in build-aux
[t] → Drop c into the buffer.)

Note that this rule does not test the buffer at all (the test 't' is always true). Hence it will always be applicable; but since we do not want it applying in place of more specific rules like *passive-aux*, we give it a priority of 15 (remember: the higher the number the lower the priority) so that rules with the default priority of 10 will be tried first.

Finally, one last complication: many rules in Parsifal assume that noun phrases have already been put together, and dropped back into the buffer. For example *aux-inversion* effectively inverts the subject and *auxverb* in a sentence like:

10. Did the boy eat the frog?

to produce a sentence in the normal order, such as:

11. The boy did eat the frog.

The rule works by picking up the *np* after the *auxverb* and   attaching it as the subject of the *s*.

(rule aux-inversion in parse-subj
[= auxverb] [= np] → Attach 2nd to c as np. Deactivate parse-subj. Activate parse-aux.)

This rule assumes that the subject of the sentence, 'the boy', has been parsed as a noun phrase, and dropped into the buffer *before* Parsifal figured out what to do with the initial *auxverb* 'did'. This is accomplished in Parsifal by 'attention-shifting rules'. An attention-shifting rule is one which automatically goes into action (if its packet is active) as soon as it matches any part of the buffer. Furthermore these rules are applied before normal rules at each step of the parse. They are called 'attention shifting' because, should they match a part of the buffer which starts at a location other than the first location of the current buffer, then Parsifal's 'attention' shifts to the part of the buffer starting where the match was made, and, until the grammar shifts attention back, this becomes the effective start of the buffer. (The command restoring the previous start of the buffer is *restore buffer.*) In the case at hand, the rule for starting a noun phrase is an attention-shifting rule, and Parsifal is not told to restore the buffer until it has parsed the noun phrase and dropped it into the buffer. Thus, when *aux-inversion* is ready to be tried, the buffer will have the initial 'Did', followed by the *np* that was created by the attention shifting rule.

2.4 Parsing ungrammatical sentences

Naturally, Parsifal as currently constructed will only parse grammatical sentences. Should it be given an ungrammatical sentence, it will eventually come to a point where no rule applies, and it will simply give up.

Paragram differs from Parsifal in numerous ways, but allowing for ungrammatical input requires only a comparatively minor modification. Active Paragram rules, rather than being tested sequentially in order of priority, are to be thought of as being tested in parallel. Naturally, on current computers, they are really being tried sequentially, but it is useful to think of them all testing the input at the same time. Furthermore, unlike Parsifal, the result of a test in Paragram is not a yes/no decision. Rather it is a numerical 'goodness rating' which, the higher the number, the better the fit between the rule and the buffer/stack. Paragram then takes the rule with the highest number and runs it, allowing it to change the stack and buffers. It then repeats the process.

The goodness rating of a rule is the sum of the values returned by the rule's atomic tests. Each atomic test will add to the score if it succeeds, and subtract if not.

Atomic test	Add if succeed	Subtract if fail
category (e.g. np)	4	15
specific word (e.g. 'to')	6	15
semantics okay	0	8
other (e.g. agreement)	2	15

No great significance should be attached to the actual numbers. The basic idea is that the more tests succeeding, the higher the score, and failure is punished severely. Note in particular that this scheme means that we no longer need priority ratings to ensure that more specific rules apply before less specific ones. Simply because it has more atomic tests, a more specific rule can get a higher goodness of fit rating, and thus will be chosen if applicable.

Now the crucial point in all of this is that for an ungrammatical sentence, the various ratings that we will get at the point of ungrammaticality will all be quite low, since none of the rules of grammar will exactly match the input. *Nevertheless, one rule must still have the highest score, and hence will apply, even though it does not really approve of the sentence as given.*[6] So, for example,

1.*The boys is dying.

will be given a low rating when Paragram starts to parse the auxiliary 'is', at which point the best rule will be:

(rule subject-verb-agreement in parse-aux
[= verb] [test: The np of s agrees with 1st] ⟶ Create an aux. Activate build-aux.)

(This rule is not yet a Paragram rule. See the Appendix for the real version.) When applied to the above ungrammatical sentence this rule will have a goodness-of-fit rating of -11 since there is a match with *verb*, (implying a value of +4) but the subject/verb agreement fails (causing Paragram to subtract 15). Nevertheless, this is the best value at that point, so the rule is used anyway, and Paragram starts parsing the auxiliary verb, as intuitively it should. Note however that with sentences like

2a. The fish is dying.
 b. The fish are dying.

the above rule will succeed in each case, and in the process specify that the word 'fish' is to be understood as singular and plural respectively. Some other ungrammatical sentences handled by Paragram are:

13a. *Bill sold Sue book.
 b. *Jack wants go to the store.

There are however, many ungrammatical, yet understandable, constructs which Paragram cannot currently handle, a subject we will return to at the end of the paper.

Nevertheless, Paragram is 'semi-grammatical' in the sense we defined earlier, and its ability to parse ungrammatical sentences is not an ad hoc addition to the grammar, but rather stems naturally from the nature of its parsing mechanism. Furthermore, Paragram can tell the user where the sentence is ungrammatical, since it is only with ungrammatical sentences that the values of the scores go below zero. It is also possible that Paragram can tell 'why' the sentence is ungrammatical, if one makes the reasonable assumption that the sentence is ungrammatical 'because' the rule which succeeded, but with a low score, should have been matched exactly.

3. PARSING THE RELEVANT GENERALISATIONS

The second goal set out for Paragram is that it capture appropriate generalisations about language in much the same way as a good transformational grammar. This has proved an elusive goal in parsing programs. The most well known of AI parsers, Woods' ATN parser, has been based upon transformational grammar, and Bresnan (1978) points out that one could use the ATN framework to provide the link needed between her 'realistic' grammar of English and an actual performance model of parsing. Nevertheless, while ATNs are inspired by transformational grammar, the single extended ATN grammar I have seen often required several special-case rules to handle what is a single rule in transformational grammar. While we will not pursue this point in any detail, let us take a single example, taken from the ATN grammar for English given in Woods (1973).[7]

The rule of *there-insertion* in transformational grammar relates sentences like these:

14a. Some flowers were in the vase.
  b. There were some flowers in the vase.

15a. Policemen were hit by the bricks.
  b. There were policemen hit by the bricks.

The statement of the rule is something like this:

np(-def) *exist-verb* ... → There *exist-verb* np ...

This rule handles all cases of unstressed 'there' (as opposed to the 'there' in 'There is Jack'). However, Woods' ATN has four separate rules for *there-insertion* for handling each of the following cases:

16a. There were barnacles on the ship.
  b. Were there barnacles on the ship?
  c. The ship on which there were barnacles sank.
  d. The ship there were barnacles on sank.[8]

Having four rules, where one would do, is hardly capturing the relevant generalization, and there are other examples where this came from. So, despite the inspiration of transformational grammar, this ATN grammar has not done as well as one would like in the elegance of the rules it embodies.[9]

Now in many respects, Parsifal does better. The rule for *there-insertion* in Parsifal goes as follows:

```
(rule there in build-aux
[ = *be ] [ = np ] [ test: The pronoun of the np of s is 'there ] → Attach 2nd to
current s as np.)
```

This rule will work for all four of the ATN's special cases.

But this is not to say that all of Parsifal's rules are this elegant. Unfortunately, this is not the case. *Indeed, of the 57 or so rules which I have looked at in depth from the detailed grammar at the end of Marcus' book (Marcus 1980), only twenty or so correspond to transformational rules.* Of the rest, they may be categorized into three groups, depending on the particular deficiencies which required them to appear in the grammar.

Phrase Structure Rules. The majority of the 37 other rules, 21 in all, are there because Parsifal must have explicit rules in its grammar for the placement of phrase structure constituents. Thus, a rule like:

$$s \rightarrow np \ vp$$

is implemented by four separate rules in the grammar: one for creating an *s* when needed, one for attaching the *np* at the right spot, another for the *vp*, and finally one which says to stop parsing the *s*. Not only would it would be preferable to have a single rule, but the packet mechanism in Parsifal is really a phrase structure mechanism in disguise; thus these twenty one rules are redundant, at least in principle.

Wh-movement. Next, ten of the remaining rules are involved in the implementation of the *wh-movement* rule, as used in:

17. Who did Jack give the ball to?

Naturally we would rather have just a single rule, but deciding on the location of the 'gap' which *wh-movement* leaves behind is not easy. Marcus explicitly claims (Marcus 1980: 99) that for a deterministic parser it will not be possible to reduce *wh-movement* to a single rule, as in transformational grammar.

Miscellaneous problems. Finally, six of the rules are needed because of various peculiarities of the grammar and the parser. For these there is no single reason why it was not possible to capture the generalization.

We shall look at all three classes, although for the third we will simply take one particularly interesting example. This example will be concerned with the rule of *raising*.

3.1 Phrase structure rules and the control of the parser

While Parsifal does not use phrase structure rules, or anything else which corresponds to the base component of transformational grammar, Marcus does point out that the way in which packets are shuffled in and out is quite reminiscent of the use of base rules.[10] So he points out the following correspondences:

Constituent:	s	→	np	aux	vp	$(pp)^*$
Packet:	cpool		parse-subj	parse-aux	parse-vp	ss-final

If this can be done consistently, it would have the advantage of reducing the complexity of individual rules by eliminating the explicit activation and deactivation of packets, hence making the rules closer to their transformational equivalents.

However, as we noted above, there is another reason for introducing explicit phrase structure rules to eliminate the need for regular rules to do what, in a transformational grammar, would be done by the base component. In particular, for each base rule of the form:

A → B C

Parsifal needs, in effect, the following rules:

A) Creation rule: Create a constituent of type A.
B) Finishing rule: Decide to stop parsing an A.
C) Attachment rule: Pick up each right hand side constituent (B C) and attach it to A.

For example, the following are rules which actually occur in Parsifal's grammar, but which are really base rules in that they follow the above patterns.

(rule startaux in parseaux
[= verb] → Create a new aux node.)
A rule of the first type: creates a new aux node.

(rule auxcomplete priority: 15 in build-aux
[t] → Drop c into the buffer.)
A rule of the second type: finishes parsing an aux.

(rule future in parse-aux
[= aux] → Attach 1st to c as aux.)
A rule of the third type: attaches an aux to an s.

To eliminate most of these separate rules, as well as the need for explicit activation and deactivation of packets, we have added the following base rules to Paragram.

s-maj	→	s finalpunc
s	→	np aux vp

$$pp \;\rightarrow\; prep\ np$$

$$np \;\rightarrow\; \begin{Bmatrix} s \\ pronoun \\ proper\text{-}noun \\ (det)\ noun\ (s) \end{Bmatrix}$$

$$vp \;\rightarrow\; \begin{Bmatrix} v0 \\ v1\ np \\ v2\ np\ np \end{Bmatrix}$$

$$aux \;\rightarrow\; \begin{Bmatrix} (be^*\ ing) \\ (be^*\ en) \\ (have^*\ en) \\ (modal\ tnsless) \\ (will^*\ tnsless) \\ (do^*\ tnsless) \end{Bmatrix}^*$$

These base rules, in effect, automatically create rules of the second and third types mentioned above. That is, we need not explicitly include in our grammar any rules for finishing parsing a constituent, and only an occasional rightward-movement rule like *there-deletion* need explicitly attach a constituent to a higher one. [11]

Unfortunately, it has not proved possible, yet, to automatically create rules for the creation of new nodes. In both Parsifal's and Paragram's grammars such rules tend to be highly variable, and currently there does not seem to be any way to predict their form simply by looking at the base rules. We have seen one such rule above, for aux nodes. Contrast it with the following, for s nodes.

(rule that-s-start priority: 5 in cpool
[= *that] [= np] [= verb] → Label a new s node sec, comp-s, that-s. Attach 1st to c as comp. Attach 2nd to c as np.)

While by paying careful attention to such rules we have been able to reduce their variability somewhat, they have still resisted complete uniformity, and so we have had to explicitly state them in the grammar shown in the Appendix. Of course, we have reduced the number of such non-transformational rules from 21 to 9. Excepting the base rules, these are the sole examples of non-transformational rules in Paragram's grammar.

3.2 Wh-movement and semantics

Wh-movement is a rule of transformational grammar which accounts for the syntax of wh-questions and relative clauses by assuming that the *wh* (e.g. 'who', 'which', 'that') is moved from its 'logical' location in the sentence to the front of the sentence, leaving a 'gap' where the *wh* used to be. So, for example:

18a. Jack wanted to hit Bill in the stomach.
  b. Jack wanted to hit who in the stomach?
  c. Who did Jack want to hit in the stomach?

In this last sentence, the 'who' is moved to the front of the sentence, leaving a gap between 'hit' and 'in' where normally we would expect the direct object of 'hit'. (The reader might notice that we also had to add the auxiliary verb 'did' and place it before the subject 'Jack', rather than after. These changes need not concern us here.) All AI parsers use some analogue of this rule, but naturally they are presented with the much more difficult problem of trying to figure out where the gap occurs, so that they can then decide on the logical position of the *wh*.

Probably the best current analysis of *wh-movement* is to be found in grammars for ATN parsers. The reason is that ATN parsers can, by using backup, simply try assuming that the *wh* was moved from *every* place that would accept an *np*.[12] To see how this would work, consider the following example:

19. Where did Jack phone from?

As the ATN is parsing this sentence, once it has parsed 'phone' it must be prepared for a direct object, so that it could handle

20. Where did Jack phone you from?

In 33 the parser will not find any direct object, and since this is one place from which the *wh* might have removed, the parser could, at this point, start working on the assumption that the *wh* was indeed moved from there, as in the sentence

21. Who did Jack phone from Montana?

In 19 the parser will not find any direct object, and since this is one place from which the *wh* might have removed, the parser could, at this point, start working on the assumption that the *wh* was indeed moved from there, as in the sentence `
prepositional phrase.

But the relevant feature of ATN parsers here is backtracking, and we have already noted that it is not compatible with our desire for a semi-grammatical parser. Furthermore, Parsifal does not do so well. To see what does happen in Parsifal, let us return to 19. The relevant rule, which would apply after Parsifal has parsed 'phone', is this:

(rule wh-pp-build in cpool
[= prep] [* is not np] [*there is a wh which has not been placed*] →
Use the wh-word as the noun phrase in the prepositional phrase.)[13]

So in 19 the rule will see the 'from' followed by the final punctuation '?' in the buffer. Since the second is not a noun phrase, we use the *wh* as the noun phrase of the prepositional phrase.

Yet other rules for the placement of gaps depend on the semantic acceptability of the various possibilities. These rules, however, tend to be quite complex, and we will forego an example.

While this approach works, it is rather ad hoc. For one thing, Parsifal has two sets of verb-phrase rules. There is a normal set, which handles most verb phrases, but as soon as we must worry about gaps, we have a completely different set, of which the above rule is but a single example. Because we must worry about gaps, this second set continually checks the semantics to ensure that it has not gone astray. In fact, there are cases where it is only semantics that can tell the parser what to do. For example:

22a. What did Bob give the girl?
  b. Who did Bob give the book?[14]

The net result is that our single rule of wh-movement has become nine separate rules, requiring about three pages to state.

Paragram does without all of this by making two changes in the parsing mechanism. First, to avoid needing two sets of verb-phrase rules (with and without an unused *wh*), Paragram *always* checks to see if a constituent is semantically reasonable before it will add it to the syntactic tree. Thus, for 19 Paragram would initially try 'where' as the direct object, but since 'phone' normally requires a person as direct object, this would be rejected.[15] Note that the user need not explicitly specify that a call to semantics is required here. Indeed, if one looks at the sample grammar in the appendix, there are only two such calls, and they are probably due to a separate problem in the grammar. Rather, Paragram automatically adds such calls to the testing section of any rule which adds a constituent to the tree. Naturally, for many cases these tests are pretty much pro forma. For example, it is hard to imagine a case where semantics could object to the addition of a progressive tense to the *aux* of the verb, especially given that it does not even know what the main verb is at the time it is adding the progressive. Nevertheless, the call is made.

The second change is the way in which the parser decides to postulate that a *wh* might have been moved from a particular location. In Parsifal, this is done by explicit rules like the one given above. In Paragram, by contrast, there is the convention that *any* rule may, if it would help it fit the buffer better, 'hallucinate' a constituent. So, for example, when we talked about ungrammatical sentences, we gave the following as an example which Paragram can handle:

23.*Jack wants go to the store.

This is handled by the appropriate rule hallucinating a 'to' immediately before the 'go'. Naturally, there is a severe penalty in the goodness of fit rating, since Paragram should not hallucinate unless it has to, but it is an option if all else fails.

This same mechanism is used to insert *np*s except that if there is an unused *wh* the cost is much less. (We still want some penalty, since if there is something in the sentence which can fit, then it should be used in preference to sticking the *wh* in at that point.)

This scheme does have some problems, but we shall postpone their discussion until section 4.

3.3 Miscellaneous cases

Of the rules which do not correspond to transformational rules, six were cases where for one reason or another it was not possible to capture a transformational rule in a single parsing rule, but rather two or more were required. These cases do not fall into a fixed mould, and hence there is no single one which can serve as truly representative. Nevertheless, one in particular is quite interesting because it relates to an issue which has been much discussed in linguistic circles, that of *raising*.

Raising is the rule which is primarily responsible for the differences between these sentences:

24a. Jack believes that Fred is ill.
  b. Jack believes Fred to be ill.

This rule postulates that in 24b 'Fred' has been 'raised' so that it is no longer the subject of the embedded sentence 'Fred is ill', but rather is the direct object of 'believes'. There are various arguments which can be proposed to support this analysis, the most obvious being the difference in the sentences:

25a. Jack believes that he is ill.
  b. Jack believes him to be ill.

Note that when in the subject position 'he' appears in nominative case, while, in the raised example, the 'him' is in objective case. This is consistent with the belief that 'him' is no longer the subject of the embedded sentence, but rather the object of the main clause.

For reasons which need not concern us here, the rule of *raising* has been quite controversial within transformational linguistics, and Marcus (1978) has taken some pains to show that his analysis is not 'true' raising. To see what he means, consider this rule of his:

```
(rule inf-s-start1  priority: 5  in inf-comp
[ = np ] [ = *to, auxverb ] [ = tnsless ] →
Label a new s node sec, comp-s, inf-s. Attach 1st to c as np. Activate cpool, parse-aux.)
```

This works on sentences like:

26. Jack believes Bill to be ill.

After Parsifal has parsed 'believes' its buffer will have an *np* followed by the word 'to' followed by a *tnsless verb*. Hence the conditions for *inf-s-start1* to apply are satisfied. The actions taken by this rule are *a)* to create a new s node (which will serve as the embedded sentence), *b)* attach the given np as the subject of the embedded clause, and *c)* activate various packets.

Now, since we are going from surface to deep structure, the rule we are interested in would be one which *lowered* a noun phrase from the higher *s* to the lower one. Now in some sense the *np* from the buffer has been 'lowered' into the lower *s*, since that is where it ends up. Nevertheless, Marcus can claim that his is not, strictly speaking, a *raising* (or *lowering*) analysis because the *np* which has the subject of the embedded *s* was never the direct object of the higher verb. Rather, Parsifal assigned it as the subject before ever having given it a role in the higher *s*.

It turns out, however, that this analysis creates problems. In particular, consider the following sentences:

27a. I helped him to do it.
  b. I helped him do it.
  c. I helped do it.

Example 27a clearly matches the raising rule, and hence presents no problem. However, 27b does not match. The solution would seem to be to allow some verbs, like 'help' to insert a 'to' before the verb in the sentential complement. This would transform the second sentence into the first, which we already know how to handle. Marcus' rule for this is this:

```
(rule insert-to in to-less-inf-comp
[ = np ] [ = tnsless ] → Insert the word 'to' into the buffer before 2nd.)
```

However, this rule will not work for 27c since it has no *np* following the verb. To handle this case Marcus needs the rule

```
(rule insert-to-1 in to-less-inf-comp
I've clearly missed a generalisation somewhere.
[ = tnsless ] → Insert the word 'to' into the buffer before 1st.)
```

The comment in the above is Marcus' own. It shows that he is clearly aware that the two rules are only doing the work of one.

There is, however, a rather easy solution to this problem. All we need do is to make Marcus' 'pseudo-raising' rule into a real raising rule. That is, if our parser first makes the raised constituent into the direct object of the verb, and only then lowers it, the three rules *inf-s-start1*, *insert-to*, and *insert-to-1*, can be reduced to two:

(rule lowering in inf-comp
[= *to] [= tnsless] [test: c has an np.]   → Detach the np of c before 1st.
Label a new s node sec comp-s inf-s. Attach 1st to c as np. Activate cpool, parse aux.)
This puts the np into 1st and moves everything else over one.

(rule insert-to in to-less-inf-comp
[= tnsless] → Insert the word 'to' in the buffer before 1st.)

With our new version, our parser will take the sentence 27b and first parse the 'him' using the normal rule for picking up direct objects. Only then will it start on the sentential object, and since the direct object is out of the way, the rule *insert-to* need not distinguish between the cases with the direct object and those without. [16]

Marcus cannot have a true *raising* rule since he has tried to reduce the power of the grammar by imposing a constraint on the destruction of constituents. (This also enforces his claim to a deterministic parser, since it means he cannot simulate non-determinism by creating constituents and then destroying them.) While any reduction in the power of the grammar is a good idea on general principles, in this case it forces Parsifal to miss a generalization. For this and other reasons, we have not chosen to retain this constraint in Paragram, and to use a true *raising* analysis.

4. IMPLEMENTATION AND EFFICIENCY

4.1 The current implementation

The parser described here has been implemented, and has worked on all but three of the examples used to demonstrate Parsifal. [17] Parsing these sentences took an average of 0.3 seconds per word (including final punctuation). [18] The version of the parser which produced this figure was written in Brown's version Franz Lisp (Foderaro and Hirst 1980), compiled, and run on a VAX 11/780.

4.2 True parallelism

While this time is within respectable limits, it is, in some respects, misleading. Paragram was conceived of as testing all rules in parallel on the buffer in order to decide which has the best fit. Thus, another way to consider the efficiency of the program is to ask how long it would have taken if we really had the hardware to do this parallel computation. This would be significantly different, since 87 percent of the time taken in the above run was spent testing rules.

To take parallelism into account we also kept track of the time for each testing cycle, and how many rules were tried on that cycle. We then divided the total time by the number of rules. Taking this reduced figure as the time for the test cycle, the total time per word would now be 0.04 seconds per word.[19] Of course, in one sense this is optimistic, since the real time would be the time for the longest of the tests, but on the other hand it is pessimistic since in reality many of the atomic tests within a rule test could themselves be done in parallel, further reducing the time. Since we are not really concerned with the exact figure, we have decided to assume that these two influences cancel each other out.

We are assuming, of course, that Paragram's rules could actually be implemented in a parallel fashion. For the most part they are quite simple so no explicit analysis of this claim is called for. There is, however, one exception. As we have already noted, Paragram does a semantic feasibility check each time it attaches a node to the tree. The test run mentioned above used a very stupid program, one which was just short of a case-by-case analysis of the sentences at hand. In general, however, this call to semantics will have to be quite complex. For example, in an early sentence we claimed that a location could not serve as the direct object of 'phone', and hence in

19. Where did Jack phone from?

we would not be inclined to use 'where' as the direct object. This is not, however, strictly true. In the proper circumstances we could a) use a location to refer to a person or conceptual person (such as a corporation), or b) actually want to talk about calling a location rather than a person.

28a. Fred, you phone Chicago. (Instructions to call a regional office.)
  b. You can phone Chicago for 3 minutes for $995. (In a promotion for calling long distance.)

If semantics is to accept these, it must recognize the context, and from all indications such tests promise to be neither simple nor fast. Furthermore, it seems plausible that such sophisticated tests cannot be performed in parallel. There is no evidence for this, but it is usually assumed that the more complicated the reasoning, the less likely it is to be done in parallel; we are simply using a particular application of this general assumption.

To overcome this problem, Paragram does the simple syntactic tests first, and makes an initial ranking of the rules based solely upon the results of these tests. It then goes through and looks at each of the top-ranked rules and only uses semantics on those which might conceivably be first were the semantics found to be okay. Thus semantics can be done serially, and used relatively sparingly.

4.3 Improvements in serial time

Nevertheless, it seems unlikely that we will see a truly parallel version of Paragram any time soon, so we might ask if it is possible to improve its serial time. It would seem that for grammatical and semantically reasonable sentences, at least, there are several improvements which could be made. One comparatively simple idea is to associate a maximum rating value with each rule. This would roughly correspond to Parsifal's priorities. In Paragram we could compute this value for each rule, and test the rules in order of decreasing values. This is what Parsifal does, and by so doing it tries on the average only half of the rules. We could expect the same sort of savings, provided that the sentence is grammatical and hence some rule will achieve its maximum value. Assuming, as is likely, that the rules tried before have low scores because some atomic test failed, we could then immediately decide that the rule which succeeded with maximum value would be the overall winner, and hence there would be no need to go on to test the rest of the rules. This, however, has not been implemented.

More complicated schemes could be considered as well. For example, there exist ATN 'compilers' which turn ATN grammars into Lisp programs. One could imagine something similar for Paragram programs. Our current workaday parser here at Brown does this for Parsifal (Tom Grossi, personal communication). Doing the same for Paragram however would be trickier.

5. PROBLEMS

Naturally, there are problems. We will concentrate on three classes.

A) *Wh-questions* which Parsifal can handle but Paragram cannot.
B) Ungrammatical sentences which we cannot parse.
C) Excess complexity of the grammar and parser.

5.1 Wh-question problems

We have simplified Marcus' handling of wh-questions by refusing to use special rules designed only to place the *wh* in the correct spot. Instead, we depend on the grammar to recognize when an insertion of a *wh* would help, and constantly use semantics to ensure that the grammar is doing reasonable things. There are, however, problems here.

One class of sentences which Parsifal can handle but Paragram cannot is illustrated by the following:

29. Who did you want to give a book to Sue?

Many people report that they have trouble parsing this sentence. The problem for Paragram (and, perhaps, people) is that after the 'want' Paragram must decide who is the subject of the embedded *s* 'to give a book to Sue'. In a sentence like

30. Jack wants to hit Bill.

the logical subject is 'Jack' and the transformational analysis would be based upon the rule of *equi-np-deletion*, in which the subject of the lower *s* may be deleted when it is identical to the subject of the higher one. This is the analysis which Paragram assumes for 29 as well. The alternative, assuming that the subject of the lower *s* is the 'who', is less favored on the general grounds that Paragram does not assume that the question word goes into a particular gap unless the alternatives are ungrammatical or semantically deviant.

That Paragram cannot handle this does not bother me overly much, given that many people have trouble with this sentence as well. Secondly, Parsifal can handle this only by creating a dummy subject, and deciding what the subject really is when it reaches the end of the sentence. If it were necessary, Paragram could do the same, but my personal belief is that we really need a theory of error handling which could account for the parsing of 'slightly' garden path sentences.

Another sentence is more troublesome:

31. Jack sold Bill to Sue.

Here, when Paragram gets to 'Bill' it rejects the analysis of 'Bill' as the direct object of 'give', on semantical grounds – one normally does not sell people. On the other hand, 'Bill' would make a perfectly good indirect object, and this is what Paragram chooses, only it then runs into trouble with 'to Sue' since that is the real indirect object.

The solution here would be to make the rule for dative movement choosier about what can qualify, by requiring that there be two noun phrases in a row. That is, the buffer test should be:

(rule dative-movement
[= np] [= np] ➡ ...)

However, for reasons which are extremely complicated, this type of rule interacts in a rather nasty way with Paragram's handling of *wh-*

movement. Thus, interestingly enough, the real culprit seems to be *wh-movement*, and not anything particular to the immediate sentence. But any discussion must await some deeper understanding on my part of the issues involved.

5.2 Ungrammatical sentences

The following is a relatively 'obvious' ungrammatical sentence, and one might well expect Paragram to parse it in a 'reasonable' fashion.

32.*The boy did hitting Jack.

It is not clear if we should interpret this as progressive or not, but either that or past tense would be reasonable.

What Paragram actually does is give up trying to parse the *aux* altogether, and never recognize the 'did' as part of the *aux*. Then it interprets the *did* as the main verb of the sentence, leaving the 'hitting' as a rather acute embarrassment, and leading to a nonsensical parse which you would rather not know about.

Actually, an early version of Paragram successfully handled this sentence, but with the implementation of automatic generation of base rules, Paragram lost this ability. In the new version, Paragram gives up parsing the *aux* when there is nothing more to do which could lead to a score greater than zero (the rather arbitrary line between grammaticality and ungrammaticality). The older version, however, was more selective. Basically it had some idea of what sorts of things the *aux* rules were responsible for. In particular it had the rule that you could not stop parsing an *aux* if you had two verbs in a row. This is the case in the above sentence, and hence Paragram was forced to keep trying to parse *did* as an *aux* and so we got a reasonable parsing.

The new version forgoes this capability in order to have automatic generation of 'finish constituent' rules based on the phrase structure rules. This would have been of greater concern, except that the rule for stopping parsing an *aux* was getting out of hand anyway. In particular, the rule, 'there must not be two verbs in a row' does not work for the example:

33. The jar seems broken.

The standard analysis of this sentence has 'seems' as the main verb, with 'broken' seen as an adjective or possibly passive verb in a complement clause. If this analysis is retained, the aforementioned rule for finishing *aux*es has to be modified. At any rate it was beginning to seem somewhat ad hoc, so it seemed reasonable to get rid of the rule, and the ungrammatical sentence it would account for. Nevertheless, such examples deserve more study.

Paragram also cannot handle sentences with extra elements that should be ignored in order to get a reasonable reading. For example:

34. Jack is is here.

Scrambling also is beyond our capabilities:

35. Book did Jack Sue give.

At the moment I do not see how to write a parser that would see these as abnormal, yet understandable, variations on 'correct' sentences of English.

5.3 Constraints on the grammar

The reader is again encouraged to look through the appendix containing Paragram's rules, since we also point out there many of the detailed problems with the grammar as it currently exists.

Some of these we have already noted above – the fact that we must have explicit rules for starting new base rule constituents, such as a new *s* node. Others we have not covered at all. For example, the parser, if taken literally, would seem to imply that the particular form of *subject-verb* agreement found in English is a linguistic universal, since there is a test for it built into the parser, just as there are tests for, say, detecting that a constituent is a certain part of speech.

Also bothersome are the cases where we have pretty much built some feature into the parser (so that individual grammars need not concern themselves with the issue), yet there still remains a single rule or two which requires special treatment. For example, with the exception of two rules, no rule of the grammar explicitly requests help from semantics. One of the exceptions is *dative-movement*, which asks semantics for its ruling on the suitability of an *np* as the indirect object of a sentence. It must do this because Paragram currently only calls semantics automatically when a new constituent is added to the tree. *Dative-movement* does not do this, but rather inserts a 'to' into the buffer to allow the np to be picked up like a regular indirect object. Alternative analyses of *dative-movement* might make this special case unnecessary. Furthermore, through a long causal chain, this fix would also remove the call to semantics from the other rule, a rule for creating prepositional phrases.

6. CONCLUSION

Even if you should be sympathetically inclined to the model presented here, we have given no reason to take it seriously as a model of human cognition. The most one could claim is that it is as plausible as the obvious competitor, ATN grammars. Let us for the moment, however, suppose that our model has some psychological validity – then what?

There are two important questions which a psychological theory of syntactic parsing must answer. First and foremost, how does syntax fit into the overall parsing process? The traditional answer within Linguistics is to assume that syntax is the initial mechanism which takes the word string and produces as its output some 'deeper' representation that has properties that make it useful for the further processing to be done at the semantic level.

At one time this was the standard view, but it has been steadily accumulating critics. As we have noted, given this model it is not easy to understand why people have little or no trouble with ungrammatical sentences. Furthermore, there have been some psychological results which have led to some doubts about the reality of such syntactic processing – for example, the results of Slobin (1966) which show that so-called 'non-reversible' passive sentences take no longer than active ones.

But the question one must ask is, if not the 'standard' model, what then?[20] The two alternatives which have been 'in the air' are to do without a separate syntactic component (Riesbeck and Shank 1976, Wilks 1975c) or else to use some form of 'blackboard' model (Erman et al. 1980) in which both syntax and semantics work on the same input independently of each other.[21] However, both of these have their problems as well. As we noted earlier, many sentences are only completely understandable if one uses reasonably sophisticated syntactic rules, such as agreement. At an even more basic level, neither of the alternatives can explain the simple fact that people do have grammaticality intuitions. This is hard to explain if they are not doing syntactic processing. If they are doing syntactic processing, then either it must come before semantics or not. The latter seems unlikely. After all, one of the things syntax does is to put the input into a representation which is closer to the 'meaning' than the raw surface structure. To assume that semantics comes first, or is even concurrent, is to assume that semantics ignores the useful work which syntax has performed. One is then left with the same question, why have syntax at all?

Our answer to this problem is to return to the 'standard' model, and assume that there *is* a syntactic parsing phase, and it comes first, with the proviso that it is continually sending off constituents as they are attached for a decision on their plausibility. As for the problems with this model, that of ungrammatical input we have already covered. Concerning the psychological problems, it is my basic assumption that syntax is extremely rapid, and the time it takes has been swamped by other things. This is why I have stressed the efficiency of the parsing process described in this paper.

Such a model is not the traditional 'autonomy of syntax' model, since it has semantics sandwiched in along with the syntactic processing. Nevertheless, insofar as it claims that the syntactic processing of a constituent is separate and prior to its semantic processing, the model presented here is closer to that of traditional linguistics than many of its competitors.

Once we have decided to adopt a model in which syntactic analysis is done, and as a separate process (albeit one which is in constant communication with semantics), we must then answer the second major question: what is the relation of the syntactic parsing process to standard 'competence' models of syntax?

Again, at one time it was assumed that the relationship was reasonably direct. At an extreme it was proposed that people use a transformational grammar and start generating sentences until they find one with the same surface structure as the one they wish to parse. However, the computational problems with such a model are so severe that I can safely move on to less radical (conservative?) possibilities, and assume that we have some process which uses analogues of transformational rules, but which in some way has been optimized for the parsing process. Paragram is such a model.

Again, the arguments against such a model have been primarily on efficiency grounds (from people in AI) and psychological reality (from Psycholinguists). But a really efficient parsing process would, I believe, answer these objections. Thus, a psychologically real Paragram would argue that people do indeed have a competence grammar in their heads.

In coming to these conclusions I am reminded of a character in a story by Jorge Luis Borges who sets himself the task of repeating the creative act of writing Don Quixote. As Borges points out, this second version, written several hundred years after the first, differs in meaning from the original because of the cultural differences surrounding the two acts of creation. I feel somewhat akin to this character, since my conclusions would have been standard fifteen years ago. Only the circumstances have changed.

7. APPENDIX

This appendix gives the current rules for Paragram. The rules here are expressed in a slight extension of Pidgin, Parsifal's language for expressing grammatical rules. However, Pidgin has not actually been implemented for Paragram, and hence these rules are a translation of the actual rules into Pidgin. The translation is straightforward, and hence it is unlikely that the rules as expressed here differ from the actual rules used. Sections of italicized English are comments.

7.1 The base component

These rules are slightly more complicated than those in the body of the paper. In particular, a constituent may be indicated either by an atom, or an atom plus property (e.g., '(be*en)' indicates a form of 'to be' but also with the property 'en'). The property '+neutral' is basically a hack. It is there to make agreement rules mandatory, since only they add this property to a word. Some other way of enforcing the application of required rules should be found. '[ ]' indicates optional constituents. To avoid ambiguity, constituents inside brackets must be in parentheses, even if no extra property (e.g., 'en') is given. [xor...] indicates mutually exclusive options. [...]* indicates that it may appear zero or more times.

```
[base-rule  s-maj    →    s finalpunc ]
[base-rule  s        →    np aux vp ]
[base-rule  pp       →    prep np ]
[base-rule  np       →    s ]
[base-rule  np       →    [ (det) ] (noun +neutral) [ (s) ]]
[base-rule  np       →    pronoun ]
[base-rule  np       →    proper-noun ]
[base-rule  vp       →    (v0 +neutral) ]
[base-rule  vp       →    (v1 +neutral) np ]
[base-rule  vp       →    (v2 +neutral) np np ]

[base-rule  aux      →    [ [ xor(be*ing)
                              (be*en)
                              (have*en)
                              (modal tnsless)
                              (will*tnsless)
                              (do*tnsless) ] ] * ]
```

7.2 Creation rules

All packet names are generated by the base rules. A packet named x-pool is active whenever we are parsing an x. A packet named x → is parsed after we have created an x, but before we have parsed any sub constituents. Similarly, a packet named x → y + z is active while parsing an x, but after we have already attached a y and a z.

```
[rule: create-s in s-maj→
  [ = np ] → Create an s. ]

[rule: create-pp in (s-pool vp-pool)
  [ = prep ] [ test: 1st semantically goes with c as prep. ] → Create a pp. ]
```

[rule: attach-pp in (s-pool vp-pool)
  [= pp] ➤ Attach 1st to c as pp.]

Attach-pp *is a problem. It is the only explicit constituent-attachment rule, excepting rightward movement rules (which are a separate case). It is needed because we did not put* [pp]* *into our* s *base rule, so we need a rule to pick up* pps. *We did not do this with the base rule because we cannot restrict* pps *to the end of* vps. *This in turn, is the result of the fact that we handle dative movement by creating the 'to dative' phrase in place, directly after the verb, and before the direct object. That dative rule has to go.*

[asrule: create-np in (s-maj-pool s-pool vp-pool aux-pool pp-pool np ➤ det + noun)
  [= np-start] ➤ Create an np.]

This is currently the only attention shifting rule. An np-start   *is anything which might begin a* np; *nouns and dots are obvious candidates.*

[rule: create-vp in s ➤ np + aux
  [= v] ➤ Create a vp.]

[rule: create-aux in s ➤ np
  [= v = +neutral] ➤ Create an aux.]

[rule: s-comp-start in (vp ➤ v1   vp ➤ v2 + np)
  [= np] [=* to] [= tnsless] ➤
Neutralize 3rd.
Delete 2nd from buffer.
Create an np.
Create an s.]

Neutralize *says to make the verb not accountable to normal subject/verb agreement. This corresponds to the rule that verbs take the infinitive form when the subject of the sentence has been removed.*

[rule: that-start in (vp ➤ v1   vp ➤ vp2 + np)
  [=* that] [= np] [= v not = tnsless] ➤
Create an np. Create an s. Delete 1st from buffer.]

[rule: wh-relative-clause in np ➤ det + noun
  [= wh] ➤
Bind 1st to c.
Categorize 1st as np.
Hold 1st specially.
Create an s.]

The first action 'binds' the wh *to the* np, *roughly in the same sense as in trace theory. We certainly do not want to use the old idea of 'copying' the constituent. The* categorize *action is somewhat ad hoc. We want to make the* wh *look like an* np *so that it may be substituted into places which take* nps. *Note that we cannot handle non-np* wh-movement. *The hold action puts the* wh *into a special stack which enables us to determine easily if there is an unused* wh *or not.*

7.3 s-maj→ and s-maj-pool

Rules in these two packets are active at the start of sentences. In particular, they handle the obvious problem of distinguishing between imperative, declarative, wh-question, and yes/no-question sentences.

> [rule: you-insertion in s-maj →
> [= tnsless] [test: c is not a question.] →
> Label c imperative. Insert 'you into buffer.]

The second test above is to prevent 'Who do you like?' from being made into an imperative after we have already parsed the 'who'.

> [rule: aux-inversion in s-maj →
> [= auxverb] [= np] →
> Label c question. Invert 1st and 2nd.]

Aux-inversion *and* wh-movement *assume that if an* s-maj *is labeled* 'question', *then it is a yes/no-question unless marked wh-question.*

> [rule: wh-movement in s-maj →
> [= wh] [= v] →
> Label c whquestion.
> Categorize 1st as np.
> Hold 1st specially.]

> [rule: time-np-to-pp in s-pool
> [= np] [test: (= The pronoun of 1st is time.] →
> Insert 'during into buffer.]

This handles cases like 'Jack sold the book yesterday', by making the time modification into a pp.

7.4 s → np and aux→

Rules in s→np *and* aux→ *do subject/verb agreement and then parse all auxiliary verbs. They also reposition the subject* np *if they find a passive construction.*

> [rule: subj-verb-agreement in s → np
> [= v not= +neutral] [test: 1st agrees with the np of c.] →
> Neutralize 1st.]

Note that at the moment agreement is a primitive, in that rules for determining it are built right into the parser. This obviously needs revision.

```
[rule: affix-hopping in aux ➤
 [ = auxverb = +neutral ] [ = v not= +neutral ] ➤
 Label 1st with the affix of 2nd.
 Neutralize 2nd. ]
```

The standard rule of affix-hopping: takes 'is sitting' and transforms it into 'is+ing sit' where by neutralizing it, 2nd looses its tense.

```
[rule: passive in aux ➤
 [ = be* = en ] [ test: s has an np. ] ➤
 Detach the np of s after 2nd. ]
```

*'Jack was+en take to the store' will now be untransformed into q '*was+en take Jack to the store'. Note that this rule cannot handle passive 'by' phrases. However, since we would need a separate rule for deleting them, having a separate rule for attaching one is okay.*

```
[rule: there-deletion in aux ➤
 [ = be* ] [ = np ] [ test: The pronoun of the np of s is 'there. ] ➤
 Remove the np of s from s.
 Attach 2nd to s as np. ]
```

This rule takes q 'There was a jar broken' and 1) deletes the 'there' (which has already been parsed as subject by the time this rule goes to work) and 2) makes the np following the verb into the new subject.

7.5 Verbs and verb phrases

```
[rule: passive-by in vp-pool
 [ = pp ] [ test: The prep of 1st is 'by. ] [ test: The v of c is passive. ] ➤
 Attach the np of 1st to s as np.
 Delete 1st from buffer. ]
```

In parsing 'Bill was hit by Jack' the 'by Jack' will first be parsed as a pp, but rather than attaching it as a pp, we take the np and make it into the subject of the sentence. We then destroy the pp we have just created.

```
[rule: dative-movement in (vp ➤ vl   vp ➤ vl + np)
 [ = np ] [ test: The v of c is +dative. ]
 [ test: 1st semantically goes with c as dative. ]
 [ test: c does not have a pp. ] ➤
 Insert 'to into buffer. ]
```

This is the infamous rule of dative movement. As preceding discussion has brought out, it has a lot of problems. I would eventually like to see a rule which looked something like this:

(rule dative-movement in vp → vl
[= np] [= np] →
Attach 1st to c as dative.)

[rule: anything-insertion in (vp → v2   vp → v2 + np)
 [not= np not= pronoun] [test: c may have an optional np.] →
 Insert 'anything into buffer.]

This rule is used to insert missing arguments to verbs which according to my dictionary 'require' them. At the moment I have not investigated principled ways of distinguishing this case from that of optional arguments. The not= pronoun *is to prevent us from having this rule apply twice (or n times) in a row.*

7.6 Verb complement rules

[rule: lowering in vp → vl + n
 [=* to] [= tnsless] [test: The v of c is +lowering.] →
 Insert the np of c into buffer.]

This rule is the untransformational version of the standard rule of raising. It takes 'Jack believes Bill to have hit George' and lowers 'Bill' into the complement, giving us 'Jack believes (that) Bill hit George'. Note that 'Bill' will have already been parsed as the object before this rule goes to work.

[rule: equi-np-insertion in (vp → vl   vp → v2 + np)
 [=* to] [tnsless] [test: The v of c is +equi.] →
 Insert a copy of the np of s.]

Standard untransformational version of equi-np-deletion. Takes 'Jack wants to die' and makes it into 'Jack wants Jack to die'. This rule does not really make a copy, but rather a bound trace.

[rule: object-equi in vp → v2 + np
 [=* to] [= tnsless] [test: The v of c is +objequi.] →
 Insert a copy of the np of c.]

Standard untransformational version of object-equi-np-deletion. Takes 'Jack persuaded Bill to kill Fred' and makes it into 'Jack persuaded Bill (Bill kill Fred)'.

[rule: insert-to-be in vp → vl
 [= en] [test: The v of c is +tobeinsert.] →
 Insert 'be into buffer.
 Insert 'to into buffer.]

Transforms 'Jack seems shaken' into 'Jack seems to be shaken'.

[rule: subject-to-subject-lowering in vp → v1
  [=* to] [= tnsless] [test: The v of c is +subjsubjlowering.] →
  Detach the np of s into 1st.]

*Transforms 'Jack seems to be shaken' into '*seems Jack to be shaken'. This is almost the standard subject-to-subject-raising rule of TG except that normally the result is a sentential subject, and this rule creates a sentential object, with no subject. This could be fixed, I suppose, but I have not given it much thought.*

[rule: insert-to in v → v1 + np
  [= tnsless] [test: The v of c is +toinsert.] →
  Insert 'to into buffer.]

This rule was discussed in the text. Covers the case of 'Jack helped Bill die' and transforms it into 'Jack helped Bill to die'.

[rule: that-s-start in (vp → v1 vp → v2 + np)
  [= np] [= v not= tnsless] [test: The v of c is +thatinsert.] →
  Insert 'that into buffer.]

'Jack said Bill is here' becomes 'Jack said that Bill is here'.

7.7 Noun phrases

[rule: reduced-relative in np → det + noun
  [= np] [= v] [test: c has a noun] →
  Insert 'wh into buffer.]

Standard rule for taking 'The boy Fred hit' and transforming it into 'The boy who Fred hit'.

[rule: det-noun-agreement in np → det
  [= noun not= +neutral] [test: Either c has a det or 1st is plural.] →
  Label 1st +neutral.]

A clearly inadequate rule for requiring that singular nps have determiners. For example, this does not yet ensure that if there is a determiner it has the same number feature as the noun. The requirement not= +neutral is to prevent the rule from operating directly on its own output. Some better way ought to exist to prevent this.

[end-of-grammar]

This simply says that there are no more rules, so special processing on the grammar may begin.

ACKNOWLEDGEMENTS

My thanks to Graeme Hirst, who commented on an earlier draft. This research was supported in part by the Office of Naval Research under contract N00014-79-C-0592, and in part by the National Science Foundation under contract IST-8013689.

NOTES

1. We will be using a version of transformational grammar which was current in the late sixties. The primary reason for this choice is its familiarity. It should not be assumed that Paragram must necessarily use a grammar of this type.
2. Unless we explicitly indicate to the contrary, this and all other examples in this paper can be handled by Paragram. When an example is ungrammatical, Paragram will recognize it as such, but produce a reasonable 'deep structure' anyway. Furthermore it will indicate what in the sentence it did not like.
3. Even worse, not only will ATN parsers be unable to parse ungrammatical sentences, but the time it takes them to decide that the sentence is ungrammatical should go up roughly exponentially with the number of words. For some reason, those who tout ATNs as a model of human performance do not draw much attention to this 'prediction'.
4. In Parsifal the buffer is limited in two ways. First, any rule may only look at three places within the buffer, thus giving limited look-ahead. Second, the total size of the buffer is limited to five places. These two limitations are independent, due to so-called 'attention shifting' rules, to be mentioned shortly. Paragram currently obeys the first of these restrictions, but not the second. This has no theoretical importance. Only laziness has prevented the implementation of the features included in Parsifal which make total buffer-size limits possible.
5. This rule also illustrates the explicit activation and deactivation of packets, here used to tell the parser that we are done parsing the subject and should start on the auxiliary.
6. There is still the possibility of ties. In practice this has not come up, and a little thought should convince you that, for grammatical sentences at least, ties should not be a problem. If the sentence is grammatical then the rules which do not fit the current sentence will have a very low score, and hence cannot compete with those which do fit. If there is more than one which fits, it means that we most likely have a case where we have two rules, one more specific than the other. But, as we have already noted, this will not result

in a tie. The one remaining possibility is that neither case is really a more specific case of the other. This could indeed give a tie, but the problem would not be with ties, but rather with the entire notion of deterministic parsing itself, since this would be saying that we might have two rules, doing very different things, and we cannot decide between them. Finally, ties might come up in ungrammatical sentences, but here an arbitrary tie braking mechanism seems as reasonable as anything else.

7. The footing here is tricky, since this analysis is based on an ATN grammar which is presented, but not explained, in the cited paper. Furthermore, the grammar has terms and features which are not explained in the paper. Nevertheless, it is unlikely that things are not substantially as presented here.

8. Stylistically this ain't so hot, but presumably it is grammatical. At any rate, the ATN grammar has a rule to handle it.

9. It is important, however, to keep in mind the distinction between limitations in the parser and limitations in the particular grammar. It is possible that a more clever grammar writer might have avoided this problem. Indeed Woods has claimed (personal communication) that Parisfal is simply one kind of ATN. This may be so, but only in the uninteresting sense that both are one kind of Turing machine. In particular, the only ways I can see of simulating Parsifal with an ATN would completely ignore all of the built-in features that make ATNs what they are. At any rate, if it is true that Parsifal is one kind of ATN, then it must surely be the case that any improvement in Parsifal's grammar over a particular ATN grammar must only indicate deficiencies in the ATN grammar.

10. He also notes that Shipman (1979) has 'studied' making phrase structure rules part of the actual grammar. However, I have not seen Shipman's unpublished paper.

11. There is one exception here, a rule for attaching *pp*s. This is an artifact of the way in which we handle dative movement, a problem to be mentioned in section 5.

12. Wh-movement can move things other than *np*s as in these examples:

> Jack is in the garden.
> Jack is where.
> Where is Jack.

However, we will ignore this complication.

13. The italicized sections are simplified from the original.

14. Some find this ungrammatical, preferring instead the use of 'whom' or 'to whom'. This would remove the difficulty. On the other hand, the sentence is probably okay for at least colloquial speech.

15. This is a simplification. In the right context we would not object to a location as direct object to 'phone'. We will return to this point later.

16. Of course, we will now need a rule to create a dummy direct object if one is not given at the surface level, but this rule is needed elsewhere, so it cannot be considered a 'replacement' for *insert-to-1*.

17. Of the three examples, two deal with *wh-movement* and will be discussed when we talk about current problems with Paragram. The other is due to the fact that Paragram does not yet handle 'that' when used as a determiner, as in 'that boy'. Parsifal needs several rules to distinguish this usage from that in sentential complements. It is not clear at this point how to avoid these rules.

18. This does not include time for garbage collection, since that figure can be made as high or low as one wishes, depending on how one sets the garbage collection parameters. A reasonable figure for garbage collection would be another 0.05 seconds per word.

19. Even here, it is not clear where the time is going, since the actual actions performed by the parser are so simple. One possible time sink is the morphology component, which could be optimized quite a bit, and also could be operating in parallel with the rest of the grammar, further reducing the time needed for the parallel version.

20. Here I am concerned with alternatives which use these results to challenge the role of syntax in general. I do not wish to discuss the possibility that syntax is fine, but that the passive transformation is all wrong, as claimed by Bresnan (1978).

21. Although, interestingly enough, even the blackboard systems do not seem to actually do this. The system described in Erman et al. (1980) only allows semantic processing on the output of the syntactic phase.

8

Context Free Parsing and the Adequacy of Context-free Grammars

G. R. Sampson

The ideas I shall discuss in this chapter are associated most centrally with Gerald Gazdar (of the University of Sussex), though several other linguists are working along similar lines. The main reference is Gazdar (1982); see also Gazdar (1980a, 1980b, 1981). I begin with a consideration of why, from the parsing point of view, it would be good if context-free grammar could be shown to be adequate for the description of natural languages, and then proceed to an examination of Gazdar's arguments that it is indeed adequate.

Let us take it as a fact that one of the things users of a language have to do in order to comprehend utterances that they encounter is to parse them (into *some* structure, which will almost certainly be some sort of tree or notationally equivalent to some sort of tree). Clearly this is not a wholly uncontroversial assumption, but I imagine that most readers of this book will be convinced that the assumption is correct. Now, some of the people who try to draw implications for linguistic theory from the fact of parsing use, as their premiss, simply the observation that there must exist some algorithm guaranteed to succeed (at least with respect to the utterances on which human hearers do as a matter of fact succeed). This is the case with Marcus, for instance (cf. chapter 6): he notices that hearers grasp the structure of most sentences straight off (the exceptions being the garden-paths), he assumes for *a priori* reasons that the processing machinery will be deterministic (whatever exactly that means), and he argues that only if general linguistic theory constrains the grammars of individual languages in certain ways will a deterministic parser be able to get the right answers in the non-garden-path cases. Gazdar, on the other hand, is interested not so much in the mere fact that we manage to parse somehow as in the fact that we can parse very *quickly*. Part of what he wants to suggest is that general linguistic theory must be wrong if it assigns grammars to individual languages for which the only parsing algorithms are relatively slow, inefficient ones. And of course there is an obvious relevance here for people who work in the field of artificial language-processing, who want their processing algorithms to work rapidly and therefore cheaply: it should be worthwhile for them to investigate a theory which implies that the correct parsings of natural sentences (unlike the ones standardly but wrongly believed to be correct) are ones which can be produced relatively quickly.

Gazdar himself is a theoretician with no particular interest in the practical computing issues just alluded to. Why is it that he feels entitled to use as a premiss the notion that human parsing is very fast? Here Gazdar is relying on the psycho-linguistic findings of William Marslen-Wilson, and the first thing to do, for the benefit of readers unfamiliar with the material, is to look at what Marslen-Wilson has discovered.

Marslen-Wilson has done experiments in what he calls 'shadowing', where a speech stimulus is played to a subject who is asked to repeat what he is hearing after as short a delay as possible. (Details of the experimental findings are in Marslen-Wilson (1975); for discussion of the theoretical implications, see Marslen-Wilson (1976), and more recently Marslen-Wilson and Welsh (1978), Marslen-Wilson and Tyler (1980).) Different subjects vary in their shadowing 'latency', i.e. the minimum time between occurrence of a phoneme in the stimulus and occurrence of the corresponding phoneme in the repetition of the same words by the shadower: average subjects can reliably shadow normal prose with a delay of about two to three syllables, 'close' shadowers can get the delay down to as little as one syllable. What is interesting is what happens when there is some abnormality in the speech stimulus, or when the shadower makes a mistake in repeating normal prose.

What predictions would a linguist working in the 'generativist', M.I.T. tradition be likely to make about mistakes in shadowing, whether or not triggered by incongruities in the stimulus to be shadowed? Marslen-Wilson argues that generative linguists assume, at least implicitly, a model of language-processing which is essentially serial; and he quotes writings by generativists which make this explicit: Miller (1962); Fodor *et al.* (1974) (note the tacit implications of the separation of parts 1 and 2 of chapter 6, and see especially pp. 343-44 – though see also p. 280); Bever and Hurtig (1975). That is, it is supposed that the raw sounds are first analysed phonologically; after enough phonemes to make up a word or so have been detected they are offered to a lexical processing system which decides what word is being heard; and after several words have been registered they are offered to a syntactic processor which parses them into a sentence structure; after which the sentence can be examined from the semantic and pragmatic point of view. In particular, quite a lot of words have to be identified before any syntactic processing can occur, because it is in the nature of transformational theories of grammar to operate in a relatively global rather than local fashion: in generating a sentence a given transformational rule will refer to items at different places in a structure and do things to one item that will depend on the nature of other, fairly distant items, and this means that in parsing one cannot analyse any single word or small contiguous group of words without having a fairly large context available.

I think myself that Marslen-Wilson exaggerates the extent to which generativists are committed to *each* of the notionally separate speech-analysis processes as happening in series; for instance Chomsky and Halle (1968, Section 2.2) make it fairly clear that they believe analysis of 'higher levels' of a speech stimulus will crucially influence one's perception of its phonemic composition, which is contrary to the serial processing idea (admittedly Chomsky and Halle give no clue about any specific mechanism by which this reverse influence could be implemented). With respect to the question whether you need to know what the words are before you can start to do syntactic (and, *a fortiori*, semantic) processing, though, Marslen-Wilson seems to me wholly right. If the claim that transformational theory is 'correct' means anything, it surely means something which implies that in this respect speech-analysis must be serial.

But then that in turn implies that if a shadower makes a spontaneous error (i.e. a failure to replicate the stimulus that is not triggered by an oddity in the stimulus) there should be no reason for the mistake to be syntactically and/or semantically congruent with the context, if the mistake occurs at an early stage in a clause before enough words have been accumulated to start syntactic processing. Furthermore, suppose the experimenter deliberately introduces mispronounced words into the stimulus (Marslen-Wilson used trisyllables in which one syllable was changed, e.g. *tomorrane, compsiny* for *tomorrow, company*), in such a way that in some cases the 'restored' word would be syntactically/semantically congruent with the context while in other cases the result would be a nonsense sentence: then the hypothesis of serial processing predicts that the probability of a mispronounced stimulus word being restored in the shadower's performance should be independent of the question of the congruence in context of the restored word (since, on that hypothesis, you do not begin to parse the words you have until you have decided what words they are).

Both of these predictions were thoroughly rebutted by Marslen-Wilson's data (and I think few of us will find this intuitively very surprising – but the point is that theoretically it is really rather awkward). Shadower's 'spontaneous' errors were syntactically and semantically congruent (with what had preceded – obviously they did not have second sight into what was about to turn up in parts of the tape they had not yet heard) in over 97% of cases, looking at subjects with all latencies including the shortest; and this was not merely because few spontaneous errors of any kind (and hence few non-congruent errors) were made early in clauses: just as many errors were made early in clauses as later, yet still the errors were overwhelmingly congruent. Furthermore, when the stimulus included mispronounced words, the frequency of restoration was very heavily correlated with whether the restored word was congruent, and this was just as true with 'close' shadowers (who had been physically exposed to only one syllable beyond the one they were uttering at a given moment) as it was with distant shadowers. There are many further detailed findings; all tend to go in the same general direction, so I shall not take the space to go into them further.

The conclusions Marslen-Wilson draws from these findings are twofold: one to do with the nature of our processing system, the other with the nature of its output. On the matter of processing Marslen-Wilson suggests (1976: 212) that, contrary to the serial model,

> each word [*sic*, see below] ... enters into the processing system at all levels of description, and is interpreted at all these levels in the light of whatever information is available at that point in the processing of the sentence. ... instead of the hierarchical and stratified relationship between different forms of analysis presupposed in the serial model, it is more natural to think of an on-line interactive system as being heterarchically organized, with no strict chain of informational command.

(and in connexion with 'heterarchical organization' Marslen-Wilson refers to Winograd (1975)).

One has to say, of course, that this idea is less clear than the one Marslen-Wilson is criticizing. In the first place, if he wants to say that phonological and grammatical analysis are all mixed up together, then it seems odd to talk about *words* entering the processing system: you have not got words until you have done phonological and lexical processing of the raw stimulus. But this may be just a slip: perhaps Marslen-Wilson meant to say something like 'each stretch of sound ...'. Then he would seem to be suggesting a picture roughly like this:

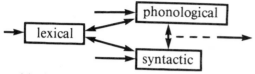

But this is still unclear to me. If the input arrows are raw sound in each case, in what sense are the lower boxes not phonological processors (at least *inter alia*); and if their input arrows represent something 'higher' than raw sound , in what sense is the model not a serial one? Also, who decides what finally gets handed over to the output arrow, if the system is genuinely non-hierarchical? (On this question see Marslen-Wilson and Welsh (1978).)

Personally I suspect that Marslen-Wilson's use of the term 'processing' may imply that he has retained some unexamined M.I.T. baggage, namely the assumption that speech-comprehension is an essentially passive affair – you wait for the speech-signal to tell you what it is, and the hearer's only contribution is his (admittedly very subtle) knowledge of the *language-system as a whole*. I would myself be inclined to favour a more Popperian model, in which the hearer is actively propounding guesses about what he is hearing, and using input to eliminate wrong guesses rather than to force the right guess. This would remove the problem about the different input arrows (the system would make guesses about the message-contents which would lead to guesses about its syntax and about the lexical items slotted into it, which would in turn engender guesses about the phonetics which would be checked, scrupulously or perfunctorily, against the raw stimulus as it came in), and at the same time it would be compatible with the congruence-findings (an intelligent system would guess sense rather than nonsense; shadowers' errors, whether spontaneous or triggered by mispronunciations, would represent failure on the part of the system to check its guesses adequately against input data). Of course a Popperian approach in turn raises a problem about how one can never understand the first remark that a companion makes after a long silence: there is such an infinity of diverse things she *might* say that it seems one could never hope to guess right. But I shall not pursue this question, since it is fairly irrelevant to our overall theme.

As for the output of our parsing machinery: Marslen-Wilson argues that his data cast doubt on the idea that this is a Chomskyan 'deep structure'. The theoretical function of the surface/deep syntax distinction in generative linguistics, Marslen-Wilson suggests, is to mediate between the actual syntax of sentences as they are spoken and the meanings of the sentences. (Chomsky might, I think, question whether that is the *only* function of the distinction; he has justified it also on the ground that a grammar including transformations – and hence a deep/surface distinction – as well as phrase-structure rules is, overall, a *simpler* definition of the set of strings constituting a natural language than would be a definition that tries to do the job with phrase-structure rules alone. We shall return to this point later. But right from the early, *Syntactic Structures* days, this argument for transformations has been very much overlaid by arguments appealing to semantics, so Marslen-Wilson's point seems broadly fair.) Yet, if deep structures are justified in terms of mediating between surface syntax and meaning, then we again have a serial relationship: shadowers should not be able to behave in semantics-influenced ways until after they have got the surface syntax straight. And that is untrue:

> I found no examples of [shadowing] errors that were syntactically normal but semantically inappropriate. The insertion of semantic anomalies ... affected the immediate shadowing performance of even the closest shadowers. ... Contact between the input and stored linguistic knowledge is apparently possible without the construction of an intermediate deep syntactic representation (Marslen-Wilson, 1976: 219).

In which case, what justifies the postulation of such a representation in linguistic theory?

Gazdar uses these ideas of Marslen-Wilson's to support the claim that we ought to define natural languages not in terms of Chomskyan transformational grammars but in terms of context-free grammars.

Let me briefly recap the definition of 'context-free grammar'. Context-free grammars are one variety of 'phrase-structure' grammars (the other variety are 'context-sensitive' grammars). A context-free grammar is a finite set of rules each of the form '$A \rightarrow \varphi$', where A is a single symbol drawn from a set of 'non-terminal symbols' (i.e. symbols invented for use in the formal grammar) and φ is a finite sequence of symbols which may include non-terminals and/or 'terminal symbols' (i.e. elements of the vocabulary of the language to be defined). One non-terminal is distinguished as the 'initial symbol', usually S for 'sentence'. Thus '$S \rightarrow NP\ VP$', '$NP \rightarrow NP$'s N', '$N \rightarrow dog$' would be examples of context-free rules. Beginning with the initial symbol, one continues to write symbols as permitted by the rules until one is left with a string containing only terminal symbols; the set of all and only the strings which it is possible to reach from the initial symbol in this way is the language defined by a particular context-free grammar. Any sentence permitted by a context-free grammar will be associated with a tree-structure in a fairly obvious way: each node of the tree, with the branches below it, will correspond to one application of a rule.

(A grammar is context-*sensitive* if at least one of its rules refers to symbols that are required to occur to the left and/or right of the rewritten symbol to make the rule applicable; an example of such a rule would be '$V \rightarrow terrify\ /\ \_\_\ NP$', i.e. '$V$ may be rewritten as *terrify* but only if an *NP* follows', which is one way of formally expressing the fact – if it is a fact – that *terrify* is exclusively a transitive verb. Clearly context-free grammar is a more restrictive formalism than context-sensitive; a context-free grammar is a context-sensitive grammar in which the number of rules mentioning context happens to be zero.)

It is ironic that one of the main currents in recent linguistic theory involves an argument that transformational grammars should be replaced by context-free grammars, because the way that modern generative linguistics got started, via Chomsky's book 'Syntactic Structures' (1957), was with an argument that phrase-structure grammars (even context-sensitive, and *a fortiori* context-free) are inadequate to capture the properties of natural languages: Chomsky invented transformational grammar precisely in order to remedy these inadequacies. A transformational grammar, at least in its simplest form (many complications have been proposed by various linguists), consists of two parts, of which one is a phrase-structure grammar (either context-free or context-sensitive), and the other is a sequence of 'transformational rules' – which are essentially functions from sets of tree-structures into sets of tree-structures. A sentence is in the language defined by a transformational grammar if there is some tree defined by the phrase-structure grammar (the 'base component') which, when successively modified by those of the transformational rules which are applicable, emerges as a tree whose leaf-sequence is labelled with the sentence in question. Again it is clear that phrase-structure grammar (context-sensitive or context-free) is a more restrictive formalism than transformational grammar with the respective type of base component: a phrase-structure grammar is a transformational grammar in which the number of transformational rules happens to be zero.

Let me defer temporarily an examination of why Gazdar (and a number of other, mainly British linguists of his generation) believe, contrary to 'Syntactic Structures', that context-free notation is after all adequate to describe natural languages. In the next paragraphs I want to focus on why Gazdar would *like* it to be adequate.

One important motive is a question of pure linguistic theory having nothing to do with the psychological considerations mentioned already with reference to Marslen-Wilson. This is that, for *a priori*, methodological reasons, and also because they want to account for the empirical observation that children always succeed in learning the language which surrounds them, theoretical linguists want their general linguistic theory to be as restrictive (in Popperian terms, as 'strong') as possible. A strong theory is a contentful theory, one which succeeds in telling us something substantial about its subject-matter; and in the case of linguistics it seems that the narrower the range of 'possible human languages', the easier it should be to explain how a child manages to pick out the one member of that range which corresponds to the language he is hearing. (This way of describing what children do embodies controversial assumptions, but I shall leave these unexamined here.) Much of the thrust of M.I.T. linguistics consists of searching for the narrowest possible range of 'potential languages' such that all actual human languages are contained in it: this is how the subject makes empirical claims about universals of natural language. For instance, various proposals have been made about limitations on the kind of functions from trees to trees that may occur as transformations in actual languages. And, as we have seen, context-free grammar represents a very restrictive theory indeed: more restrictive than transformational grammar no matter how narrowly transformations are constrained, since context-free grammar involves no transformations of any kind, and more restrictive even than context-sensitive grammar. Because Chomsky became famous in connexion with the idea of 'transformations', people outside linguistics often do not realize that, from his own point of view, the move from phrase-structure to transformational grammar was not a triumphant theoretical advance but more of an unfortunate (though, he believed, empirically necessary) retreat. Much of Chomsky's recent research in grammatical theory has been concerned with greatly reducing the content of the transformational component of grammars; part of his 'trace theory' (cf. chapter 9) involves the claim that languages have only one or two transformations rather than dozens as was believed until recently. (However, the one or two transformations would be used very heavily, so that individual sentences are still subject to a great deal of transforming.) Gazdar is going one better in a direction that all linguists would gladly move in, if they thought they could: he is saying that we do not need even one or two transformations.

The other motive for rehabilitating context-free grammars, though, is that they are parsable in ways that, Gazdar feels, are more compatible with Marslen-Wilson's findings than the parsing of transformational grammar is.

Gazdar quotes an unpublished paper of P. S. Peters, according to whom 'for transformational grammars, it is not known that processing time can be any less than a doubly exponential function of sentence length'. By 'doubly exponential', I take it that Peters means that as the number of words in the sentence to be parsed increases to n, the number of elementary operations carried out by the most efficient known parsing algorithm increases to k^{n^n} for some constant k. (Here and below, I assume that the time an algorithm takes to do something is roughly proportional to the number of elementary operations performed, though it should be said that parallel-processing techniques might make this assumption inappropriate.) In fact it is not clear to me how it can be guaranteed that there always *is* an algorithm available at all, particularly in view of the problems posed by deletion transformations (cf. chapter 2); and even if there is an algorithm for recovering all deletions that can occur in some class of transformational grammars, one might think that the possibility of deletions would imply that a short surface sentence would not necessarily have a simple parsing so that complexity of parsing would not be a function of length. But perhaps Peters (whose article I have not seen) is assuming some theory of transformational grammar in which deletion is severely restricted; and he is saying that, even within such a restricted theory, processing time explodes as sentences increase in length. No great surprise, of course; but no less relevant for that.

Context-free parsing times, on the other hand, are given by much more modest functions of sentence-length. The basic reference here is Earley (1970). Earley gives an algorithm which, in the worst cases, parses sentences of length n in kn^3 operations, but on many context-free languages it is much more efficient: there is a large class of context-free languages (which it is hard to describe in intuitively-comprehensible terms, unfortunately) on which the algorithm needs only kn operations. This class includes plenty of ambiguous languages (i.e. ones whose grammars assign the same string two or more different parsings in some cases) – not merely unambiguous context-free languages, which would make the point fairly irrelevant for human language. For instance, Earley gives a context-free grammar for the propositional calculus, obviously very relevant to natural languages and quite ambiguous, on which his algorithm functions in linear (kn) time.

(Incidentally, an attractive feature of Earley's algorithm is that it can easily be modified to parse co-ordinate structures of unlimited breadth. Such structures seem to exist in the logical forms of natural sentences: one gets phrases like 'A and B and C and D and ...', in which none of the elements group into intermediate-sized constituents smaller than the whole co-ordination; yet phrase-structure grammars cannot produce them, and even if transformational grammars could – which is questionable – that would be irrelevant since the lack of internal structure is a feature of the underlying logic of such phrases, hence of their 'deep structure' before it has been affected by transformational rules. I return to this point below.)

Valiant (1975) offers an algorithm which gets the 'worst-case' processing time down to $kn^{2.81}$. Sheil (1976) gives a depth-first algorithm with worst-case processing time of kn^3 which has the perhaps surprising property that, if all one demands is *a* valid parse rather than *all* valid parses of a structurally-ambiguous sentence (which is reasonable if we are thinking of modelling human language-processing), then the more ambiguous the grammar the faster parsing will occur.

Without going into the details of these algorithms, then, it does seem that if human languages are context-free there is some possibility that human hearers would be able to understand their sentences within some limited time, as we know they do, while if human languages are correctly described by transformational grammars then one would expect that any sentence more than a few words long would take years of hearer's time to be parsed.

I am not entirely sure whether Marslen-Wilson would regard these considerations about the speed of context-free parsing as engaging with his worries about the seriality assumption underlying generative language-processing theories; clearly it is in general true that the faster we can parse the less likely it is that our errors in a shadowing experiment will be uncorrelated with the syntax and semantics of the stimulus, but fast parsing itself does nothing to explain why syntactic/semantic congruence obtains just as much in shadowing errors at the beginnings of clauses as in those which occur at ends of clauses. But the other point about context-free grammar, which Gazdar does not discuss so explicitly but which is also motivating his enthusiasm for it, is that it is a kind of grammar in which syntactic and semantic relationships are essentially local, rather than global as they are in transformational grammar. If a couple of adjacent words have a given parsing, within a context-free grammar, then normally that parsing will remain valid independently of what comes next. There are of course 'garden-path' type exceptions: thus, given a grammar containing the rules:

1. $A \rightarrow j\ B$
    $B \rightarrow k\ l$
    $C \rightarrow j\ k$

an input *jkl* might be misparsed as beginning with a *C* constituent before the item *l* was read. But such examples verge on the pathological. In a transformational grammar, on the other hand, it is the norm for the parsing of any small part of a sentence to have implications for – and conversely to depend for its validity on – the nature of other items quite distant in the sentence. Therefore the notion that we have to wait for a clauseful of words before we can start working out how the words go together, which Marslen-Wilson finds to be deeply-rooted in the thinking of transformational linguists, would be a gratuitous and implausible assumption if the correct theory of grammar is context-free grammar, with the structures relevant for semantic processing being identical to the 'surface' tree-structures recoverable from input strings. (I shall not discuss the semantic aspect of Gazdar's theory of grammar; but for Gazdar it is crucial that the 'context-freeness' of language extends to semantics – it is not merely that context-free grammars succeed in generating the set of surface strings while assigning them structures which have somehow to be related to quite different logical forms, rather the surface structures *are* the logical forms.)

It is clear, then, that there are good reasons for hoping that natural languages are context-free. I turn now to the question of whether this hope can be fulfilled.

As I suggested above, the shape of Chomsky's and his followers' arguments in the early days of generative linguistics was essentially this: 'Our predecessors tacitly assumed, without making the concept explicit, that natural languages can be described by phrase-structure – and probably by context-free phrase-structure – grammars. [This historical aspect of the claims of the M.I.T. school was particularly salient in Postal (1964); for a critique see Sampson (1979).] But phrase-structure grammars, and especially context-free grammars, are demonstrably inadequate, so our predecessors' theories should be abandoned pretty well wholesale.'

Accordingly, the obvious questions to ask when confronting Gazdar are, why did people twenty years ago believe phrase-structure grammar to be inadequate, and what is Gazdar's response to the various points that were made?

The inadequacies that were brought forward fell into several categories:

1) For some constructions it was claimed to be mathematically impossible for *any* context-free phrase-structure grammar to generate the correct set of sentences viewed simply as strings of words, without prejudices about what their structure should be. If the constructions in question are actually found in natural languages, this is the most damning possible objection to context-free grammar. (It was not made against context-sensitive grammar; the stringsets which cannot be defined by context-sensitive grammars are quite recherché and their properties seem to have little to do with anything found in natural languages.)

2) For other constructions it was argued that, while phrase-structure or even context-free grammars could be devised that would generate the correct surface strings, such grammars would be unreasonably cumbersome and ungeneral – the constructions could be described much more straightforwardly if one allowed oneself to go outside phrase-structure formalism.

3) For other constructions again it was said that the *structure* assigned by any phrase-structure grammar to a given sentence would be misleading as a representation of the logical form of the sentence, even though considered merely as strings of words sentences containing the construction in question might be generated quite efficiently. And

4) it was said that phrase-structure grammars necessarily failed to make formally explicit the semantic relationships between different grammatical constructions, whereas by the use of transformational rules this could be done (e.g. active/passive pairs could be derived from a common deep structure with the aid of an optional Passive transformation).

I think all the objections to (context-free) phrase-structure grammar that were made can be brought under these four headings.

Although cases of type (1) form the strongest possible evidence against context-free grammar, the claims that such cases exist were never pushed as hard as some of the other anti-context-free claims, and the claims that *were* made under this heading fared rather badly long before Gazdar published. A type of grammatical phenomenon which cannot possibly be defined in context-free notation is 'unlimited overlapping dependencies'. There is a 'dependency' between two items in a sentence if the nature of either one of them is constrained by the nature of the other: e.g. they might have to be the same word, or if one of them is a noun of a given gender the other might have to inflect into that particular gender, and so forth. If any such dependencies overlap like this:

and provided there is no particular limit to the number of such overlappings in a single sentence, then context-free description is out of the question. (Thus, a very simple example of a non-context free 'language' would be the language each of whose sentences is an arbitrary sequence of *a*s and *b*s followed by the identical sequence: e.g. *aa*, *bbabba, abaaabaa* are grammatical but **ab, *bbaabb* are ungrammatical.)

Several subparts of real languages were cited as cases of overlapping dependencies; Chomsky (1963: 378) gave a list. For instance, P. M. Postal argued in his doctoral thesis that Mohawk had an exotic construction, involving overlapping dependencies; but Floyd Lounsbury, Postal's thesis supervisor, suggested that the Mohawk data were incorrect (Reich 1969: 833-34). Then again Chomsky said that the English word *respectively* is used to set up overlapping dependencies, as in:

2. John and Mary wrote to his and her parents, respectively.

However, there are two problems about this example. In the first place this particular sentence seems to contain no true grammatical 'dependencies' – the phrase *his and her* could be replaced by *her and his* without loss of grammaticality, to indicate that the two people wrote to one another's parents. (This point was made at Lugano by Yorick Wilks.) That objection might be circumvented by replacing Chomsky's example with, say:

3. John and Mary addressed letters to himself and herself respectively.

– in which, provided *John and Mary* are taken to be male and female, re-ordering of the reflexive pronouns would produce ungrammaticality. But, secondly, constructions of these kinds become very artificial as soon as one multiplies the number of overlapping relationships beyond

Chomsky's two. I doubt whether anyone but a linguist would ever say e.g.:

4. John, Mary, their daughter Suzanne, and the family gerbil drank his beer, her sherry, her milk and its water respectively.

– surely we would in practice say something like ... *drank their beer, sherry, milk, and water respectively*, in which case the overlapping relationships disappear? A case which is not quite so easy to dismiss is the *and so did* construction: when we tack on *and so did N* to a declarative we usually suppress a restatement of what N did, but if we do spell it out it has to be a copy of what the subject of the preceding clause did:

5a. John saw the play and so did Bill see the play. [a good sentence]
 b.*John saw the play and so did Bill read the book. [unacceptable]

So far as I have read, Gazdar does not discuss this case. But a view which I would myself favour, and which is broadly in harmony with things that Gazdar says about somewhat comparable examples, is that the 'badness' of the starred sentence is not really a matter of grammar. It is a fact about the semantics of *so did* that the words used after it must be interpreted as referring to the same activity as that of the previous predicate: this does not mean that the words necessarily have to be the same words, thus the following is also (I suggest) acceptable:

6. John told the torturers what they wanted to know and so did Bill crack.

But the starred sentence is bad because one cannot find any way to understand *saw the play* and *read the book* as phrases which both refer to a single activity. In other words, the sentence is *contradictory*, like *The red wine is white*. But a contradictory sentence is grammatical.
 Gazdar does make a novel point about the last case listed by Chomsky as a type of language that mathematically cannot be generated by a context-free grammar. This is a language in which sentences have two parts which are related not in that they are required to be the *same* as one another, or to show some correlation such as gender-agreement between their elements, but rather that they are required to be *different* from one another. Chomsky (loc. cit.) claimed, without citing a proof, that such languages also are impossible for context-free grammars to generate, and he argued that subparts of English exhibit such phenomena; for instance he argued that we can say:

7. That one is wider than this one is DEEP

(with contrastive stress on *deep*), but not:

8.*That one is wider than this one is WIDE

(and Chomsky argued that, by using more complex syntax in the compared clauses, one can make the set of 'unrepeatable' elements, and the set of constituents that can occur in the second clause, each unboundedly numerous.) Gazdar (1980a: 165-66) says that Chomsky seems, judging by remarks in a more recent publication, to have changed his mind about the crucial grammaticality-judgments subsequently. More interestingly, he also claims that Chomsky is just wrong to say that languages having the formal property just described are necessarily non-context-free. For instance, Gazdar says (giving P.S. Peters as his authority) that the language consisting of all strings xcy where x and y are any sequences of a's and b's but x differs from y is a context-free language. Gazdar gives no proof to back up this surprising claim; but at Lugano, Mats Carlsson of Uppsala University constructed the following context-free grammar which does indeed appear to generate the language in question:

9.   S   → D b U, F a U, H
     D → a U c, X D X
     F → b U c, X F X
     H → c X U, X U c, X H X
     U → X U, ε
     X → a, b

I take this as a useful lesson in the unreliability of intuition in mathematical linguistics !

So much for objections of type (1) above. Among objections of type (2) that were made to context-free grammar, one common one was that nodes of phrase-markers need to be labelled not just with atomic categories (*N*, *V*, *NP*, etc.) but with sets of grammatical 'features' – singular, plural, masculine, feminine, and so forth – to handle matters such as grammatical agreement. Chomsky (1965: 82) suggested that the lowest nodes in a phrase-marker above the vocabulary items themselves will be labelled with what he called 'complex symbols', sets of features such as [+N, -Count, +Abstract]. And he went on to say (op. cit.: 88ff.) that a grammar which generates trees including nodes labelled by complex symbols is not a phrase-structure grammar. Admittedly one could replace such a grammar with a grammar that would get the same results and *would* be a phrase-structure grammar, by replacing each possible combination of features (of which there will only be finitely many) by some single symbol. But then, it was suggested, the grammar will be unreasonably cumbersome and will miss generalizations. For instance it will no longer be the case that there is one rule saying that predicate follows subject, with rules specifying that nouns are either singular or plural, in French either masculine or feminine, and rules requiring verbs to agree with subjects in number and gender – rather, there will be four separate and unrelated rules, 'Mascsingpred follows Mascsingsubj', 'Femsingpred follows Femsingsubj', and so on (with 'Mascsingsubj', etc., being single unanalysed symbols); rather than 'NP → Det N (S)' we must have 'Mascsingsubj → Mascsingdet Mascsingnoun (S)', 'Femsingsubj → Femsingdet Femsingnoun (S)', etc.

Gazdar's response to this (in Gazdar (1982) – all future references to Gazdar are to this article) may be summarized as follows. He suggests that Chomsky is unreasonable in defining the term 'phrase-structure grammar' so narrowly as to exclude the use of complex symbols, since admitting them not merely does not increase the *weak* generative capacity of such grammars (as we have seen), but does not even significantly broaden the classes of structures that can be assigned to sentences or increase the difficulty of parsing (as the admission of transformational rules certainly does). If the term 'phrase-structure grammar' is to be used in order to pick out a 'natural class' of grammars, the use of complex symbols ought not to be excluded. Furthermore, while it is true that generalizations are missed if all the phrase-structure rules which refer to features of complex symbols are written out separately, this merely indicates the need for a new notation for abbreviating sets of partially-similar phrase-structure rules, to add to the abbreviatory conventions we already take for granted. A formula such as :

10. A → B ($\{$ C, D, E $\}$)

is not in itself a phrase-structure rule, but 'phrase-structure grammars' standardly include such formulae because they can be expanded into sets of items which individually *are* phrase-structure rules – in this case, the four rules:

11. A → B
   A → B C
   A → B D
   A → B E

At the same time we do not complain that the grammar in question misses a generalization because these four separate phrase-structure rules are partly alike; the whole point of the abbreviatory devices (round brackets, curly brackets, commas) is to capture generalizations that exist implicitly in sets of phrase-structure rules written out separately. The convention has already been established (by Chomsky (1965: 42ff.) as much as by anyone) that what counts in deciding whether a grammar belongs to a given category of grammars is its 'expanded', non-abbreviated form, but that what counts in deciding whether it satisfactorily captures linguistic generalizations is the shorter version in which rules are collapsed together using various standard abbreviatory devices. Accordingly, Gazdar proposes further abbreviatory conventions which allow one to write the single formula:

12. S → NP   VP
         [α]   [α]

with 'α' ranging over combinations of agreement features, to abbreviate as many separate phrase-structure rules as there are possible values of α. Together with certain conventions about features 'trickling down' from higher nodes to lower nodes, which do not need to be stated explicitly in grammars of individual languages because they are universal, these conventions permit all the generalizations for which syntactic features and complex symbols are needed to be stated in very brief, elegant formulae, all of which can nevertheless be 'unpacked' into sets of context-free rules of a standard type (with the processing advantages that that implies).

(Incidentally, Gazdar uses 'X-bar' categories (Jackendoff 1977), so that the symbols S, NP, VP never actually appear in his paper; but this is for current purposes an irrelevance, I mention it only in order to avert misunderstandings. In writing this chapter I have endeavoured to replace Gazdar's notation with more familiar notation wherever possible, in order to bring Gazdar's substantial theoretical innovations more clearly into focus.)

The concept of inventing new ways of abbreviating sets of partially-similar context-free rules so as to capture various kinds of generalization without going outside the limitations of context-free grammar is a powerful one. It can also be used to achieve some of the things standardly achieved by transformational rules. Gazdar's example is yes-no questions in English, which have the first auxiliary verb in front of the subject: *Has John been seen?* as compared to *John has been seen.*

The standard transformational treatment says that yes-no questions have the same deep-structure order as declaratives, but a transformation moves the first auxiliary, whichever it may be, in front of the subject. (There are complications connected with the fact that *do* is used if the declarative has no auxiliary, but let us ignore this point: my aim in this chapter is merely to explain the general way in which Gazdar claims to be able to dispense with transformations, rather than to demonstrate that he has accounted for every detail in this particular case.) A transformational grammarian would concede that in principle it would be possible to write separate sets of phrase-structure rules for declaratives and for yes-no questions, but he would say that this would be unnecessarily cumbersome because all the complex information about the various possible sequences of auxiliaries that can precede a main verb would have to be stated twice: once in a set of rules which has those sequences occurring without interruption after the subject, and all over again in a set of rules which use the subject to split the first auxiliary off from the others.

But, Gazdar says, suppose that the various rules for producing auxiliary-sequences in declarative sentences all have the general form:

13. VP → v VP
    [abc]   [efg]

where 'v' is some auxiliary verb, and '[abc]' and '[efg]' are some sets of grammatical features. This seems plausible: it is a way of adding auxiliaries such as modals, the perfect, the progressive, the passive, one by one, each time changing the features of the daughter *VP* node so as to change the range of auxiliaries which will be acceptable when that *VP* in turn is expanded, and so as to ensure that the next verb in the *VP* is inflected appropriately for the verb just generated (e.g. it must be a past participle if 'v' is the perfective *have*. Then our grammar can include the following 'metarule':

14. 'VP → V VP' ⇒ 'S → V S'
    [d]

That is: for each rule already in the grammar that expands *VP* with certain features into some verb followed by *VP*, the metarule tells you that there is also a rule that expands *S* having the same features together with [d] into the same verb followed by *S* (it being understood automatically that if the right-hand *VP* to the left of the double-shafted arrow has features [*efg*] then the right-hand *S* will likewise be assigned [*efg*] – so that the same auxiliary-sequences can occur in each).

This, as Gazdar is at pains to explain, is not a transformational rule (despite the perhaps slightly cheeky use of a double-shafted arrow). It is not a rule which takes a tree generated by phrase-structure rules and changes it into a differently-shaped tree; it is a rule which creates extra phrase-structure rules in a systematic way on the basis of phrase-structure rules which already exist. Yet it captures just the same syntactic generalization which was previously thought to be expressible only by means of a transformational rule.

(Of course, a transformationalist might reply that the virtues of the yes-no question transformation were not only that it enabled the syntactic constraints on auxiliary-sequences to be stated once rather than twice, but also that it derived questions from underlying structures that were better representations of their 'logical form' – i.e. it removed a surface-structure distortion of semantics. But Gazdar responds by showing how his metarules can be augmented to deal in an appropriately general way not only with the syntax but also the semantics of the constructions they are used to handle. As already suggested, I shall not follow him into this domain but refer the reader to Gazdar's own paper.)

Under heading (3), that phrase-structure grammar assigns the wrong structure to some constructions which it can generate if they are considered merely as surface strings, the case usually discussed is co-ordination. It is easy for a context-free grammar to generate co-ordinations of any number of (say) noun-phrases, by recursive use of rules such as:

15. NP → NP *and* NP

But such a rule implies that wherever we have a many-unit co-ordination the units must be linked by a number of binary conjunctions, and often that it is quite alien to the logic of the utterance. *One and two and three and four are digits*, logically speaking, has a 'flat' co-ordination of four noun-phrases not grouped together into twos or threes; to see the difference, contrast this co-ordination with *Charles and Diana and Anne and Mark are married*. Commonly linguists slide over this difficulty by including in their phrase-structure base component a rule such as:

16. NP → *and* $(NP)^n$, $n \geqslant 2$

and writing a transformation to get *and* in the right place(s), without taking explicit notice of the fact that this 'rule' is not a phrase-structure rule (which obviously it is not), nor even an abbreviation of a *finite* set of phrase-structure rules since no particular upper bound can be stated for *n*. (See e.g. Lakoff and Peters (1966: 114); cf. the passage quoted from D.T. Langendoen in Johnson and Postal (1980: 673).)

I suppose it might be said that what Gazdar does is to slide over the difficulty in an equally slippery way; but he at least makes it explicit what he is doing. He suggests that, rather than defining the notion 'context-free rule' as a formula containing a symbol followed by an arrow followed by a finite *string* of terminal and/or non-terminal symbols, we define it so that what follows the arrow is a *regular expression* (see e.g. Nelson 1968b: 297) over the union of terminal and non-terminal vocabularies. This can be shown not to enlarge the class of languages generated; and it now becomes possible to write:

17. NP → NP* *and* NP

as a single 'context-free' rule permitting an *NP* node to immediately-dominate any finite number of conjuncts. My own reaction to this proposal is that it seems, at least at first blush, a rather large extension of the notion of context-free grammar to make merely because of the single problem of co-ordination, and that it is odd that Gazdar does not feel any need to discuss whether the parsability findings referred to earlier remain true with respect to this version of the theory. But one of the points I mentioned briefly in connexion with Earley's work suggests that the latter issue may not be too problematic. As for the other issue, it is notorious that co-ordination is the death of all attempts to reduce linguistic structure to a neat, limited formal framework, so perhaps it should be no surprise that co-ordination gives Gazdar's unusually austere theory a hiccough.

The fourth heading in my list of categories of standard objections to phrase-structure grammar was that such grammars do not make explicit the logical relationships between pairs of superficially-different constructions – e.g. the sameness of meaning as between actives and passives. But this was always a highly questionable argument for transformational grammar, though a very influential one. The general logic relationship of implication between sentences taken as premisses and sentences which are their consequences is not supposed by any writers to be something that should somehow be directly reflected in the 'underlying structures' of the respective sentences; if we want to state such relationships, we must define inference rules enabling us to move from one sentence to another, as logicians do for the artificial 'sentences' of their symbolic logics. The paraphrase-relationship between actives and passives is only a special case of implication (in which the implication holds equally in either direction): so why is it felt that there is some obligation to do more than write inference rules allowing one to move from active to corresponding passive and vice versa? Why is there assumed to be a special virtue in saying that (at a certain, 'underlying' level) *A verbed B* and *B was verbed by A* are actually the *same* sentence, rather than different sentences with a particular mutual relationship? No good reason has ever been given. And if one supposes that the advantage of a Passive transformation is that it permits a relatively economical definition of the set of surface strings, irrespective of their meanings and the relationships between their meanings, Gazdar will deny this: he captures the passive construction in an equally general fashion using his context-free 'metarules' instead of transformations.

As linguistics became an increasingly fashionable subject in the 1960s and early 1970s, it became decreasingly common for people who got involved with M.I.T. linguistics to feel obliged to get to grips with the fairly rigorous, mathematical ideas from which M.I.T. linguistics had sprung. It seems likely that a number of people who in recent years have discussed the 'inadequacy of context-free [or, phrase-structure] grammar' have had only a rather vague idea of what 'context-free' and 'phrase-structure' mean. Accordingly, some of the objections to (context-free) phrase-structure grammar which Gazdar discusses merely rest on misunderstandings. Thus, he quotes a remarkable statement by Joan Bresnan to the effect that unbound syntactic dependencies 'cannot be adequately described even by context-sensitive phrase structure rules, for the possible context is not correctly describable as a finite string of phrases' (Bresnan 1978: 38). This appears to mean that no construction generated by a phrase-structure grammar can include a dependency between two items unless there is a finite bound to the length of the possible intervening material. That is obviously false, and I can only imagine that Joan Bresnan meant 'finite state' when she wrote 'context-sensitive phrase structure'. Gazdar spends several pages on this sort of 'objection', which I find rather generous of him.

The above exposition has dealt fairly ruthlessly with the finer details of Gazdar's theory of context-free grammar. In particular, Gazdar says a great deal about the precise interpretation of his 'metarules' which I have ignored or even, possibly, distorted in this account. But I hope that what I have written will suffice to explain why Gazdar's attempt is worth making, and to show the broad strategy he uses in going about it. Whether Gazdar is. fully successful in executing the task he has undertaken is, ultimately, a question that the reader must answer for himself by reference to Gazdar's own writings.

9

Trace Theory
Parsing
and Constraints

S. G. Pulman

It might be useful to begin by pointing out some of the ways in which recent versions of the Extended Standard Theory, of which Trace Theory is one component, differ from the Standard Theory: the theory which is presented in Chomsky (1965) and which is still to be found in most introductory books on transformational grammar.

The first striking difference is in the coverage of the syntactic part of the theory for a particular language. Whereas the advertised intention of the Standard Theory was, in principle, to characterize correctly the set of grammatical sentences of the language, ignoring only a few marginal or stylistically marked constructions, in more recent theories the domain of the syntactic component of the grammar has become much more restricted. In part this is because many aspects of Trace Theory make the always theory-laden distinction between syntax and semantics more than usually arbitrary, but also because it has become possible to discern that certain types of superficially distinct constructions share various properties, or that superficially similar constructions in fact behave quite differently. Many phenomena which appeared to be a matter of syntax now seem not to be appropriately treated by syntactic rules at all. For example, the construction described in Standard Theory by a transformational rule of VP-deletion:

1. John will leave early, but Bill won't __ .

is, in recent work, variously described by a semantic rule interpreting 'missing' elements (Wasow 1972), by a rule of 'logical form' (Sag 1976), and has even been claimed to be a phenomenon which is not part of sentence grammar at all, but of a level of 'discourse grammar', operating across sentence boundaries (Williams 1977).

A second difference is the resulting 'modular' nature of the Extended Standard Theory. In Standard Theory the syntax consisted of a context-free phrase structure grammar with a lexicon, and a large set of fairly complex but relatively homogeneous transformational rules which generated structures to be submitted for semantic and phonological interpretation. Mechanisms like constraints on rules (the A over A principle (Chomsky 1964: 73, 1972: 51)) or filters (the # filter on relative clauses (Chomsky 1965: 138)) were envisaged but did not play a central role. In contrast to this monolithic system, the mechanisms of the Extended Standard Theory are both simpler and more differentiated. The syntactic component consists of just a few simple rules which interact with a few constraints on their application. The interpretation of the resulting structures – where this depends on purely linguistic elements, at least – likewise results from the interaction of various subsystems, each of which is simple in itself, but when operating along with the other subsystems produces the complexity found in a language.

The third and perhaps the most profound difference is much more difficult to describe succinctly. It concerns the level of idealization at which grammatical descriptions and principles are pitched. Whereas in the Standard Theory framework it was taken to be a matter of definition that a grammatical statement could not be descriptively, much less explanatorily adequate unless it was also observationally adequate, (see e.g. Chomsky 1964: 62-76) in Chomsky's recent work he has taken the more realistic position that a grammatical principle which unites a range of different phenomena in a satisfying way should not be taken to be refuted by the fact that it may say something false about a particular language at a particular point. Thus a statement may be explanatorily adequate, in principle, without being observationally adequate. [1]

The latter point in particular means that the person with purely practical concerns who is looking for an off-the-shelf grammar for some parsing algorithm to consult will find that Trace Theory is not likely to satisfy his requirements. On the other hand, the person who is interested in elaborating a theory of (human) parsing of natural language and who makes the reasonable assumption that this will connect at some point with universal principles of language structure, will find much interest in Trace Theory. With these sorts of interest in mind, we will give a brief sketch of how the various components of a recent version of the Extended Standard Theory interact, in those areas of grammar which are most obviously relevant to problems of parsing: namely, the location and interpretation of various 'understood' elements – elements which are missing or displaced in an actual sentence.

The syntactic component of the grammar consists of a lexicon, a categorial component and a transformational component. The lexicon contains phonetic, syntactic and semantic information. Syntactic information is in the form of subcategorization restrictions, (mostly) concerning the range of complements the major syntactic categories (N, A, V, P) can take, as well as information about various exceptional properties an item might have. Thus *hit* has the feature [+ _ NP], *believe* is [+ _ $\{\frac{\bar{S}}{NP}\}$], *seem* is [+ _ (PP) $\bar{S}$] etc. The categorial component is a context-free phrase structure grammar, though in fact apart from some aspects of word order such rules largely restate information implicit in the lexicon. The lexicon and the categorial component generate a range of *D-structures*–the basic canonical structures of the language. They are of the general form:

2. [$_{\bar{S}}$ COMP [$_S$ NP INFL VP ...]]

where INFL is either Tense or *to*. Lexical items are optionally inserted into such structures in accordance with subcategorization restrictions.

The Transformational component is severely restricted, containing only one major rule, *Move* α – i.e. move any category – with perhaps a few minor movement rules (e.g. rules moving verbal affixes and some 'root' transformations operating, roughly speaking, only in main clauses). *Move* α, by a general principle of linguistic theory, can only move an α to another α position which is empty (recall that lexical insertion is optional) or to COMP, in the case of wh-phrases (and perhaps some other phrases). A moved item leaves behind an empty category *e* which bears the same referential index as the moved element. An empty category with such an index is a *trace*.[2] Referential indices signal 'intended reference'. Two NPs are coreferential if they have the same index.

COMP is perhaps better regarded as a position than as a constituent, though it can in subordinate clauses contain actual complementisers: *that* for tensed sentences (where INFL = Tense), *for* for untensed sentences (INFL = to), *whether* or *if* for indirect yes-no questions, and possibly one or two others. It is the position to which wh-words are moved but can be null in main clauses unless filled in this way by *Move* α.

The transformational component maps D-structures into S-structures. S-structures are then mapped into what Chomsky calls 'logical form', in which coreference, anaphoric, and quantifier-variable relations are explicitly represented. S-structures are eventually, after deletions, etc., also interpreted phonetically. Thus S-structures are still quite abstract and not to be identified with representations of actual sentences or the 'surface structures' of Standard Theory.

Elements which are 'understood' in actual sentences are represented at S-structure in two ways: as empty categories, resulting from the optionality of lexical insertion or from the application of *Move* α, or as PRO, an abstract pronoun which is 'controlled' (i.e. interpreted) in various ways. Since the syntax proper will distribute *e* and PRO fairly liberally, many of the S-structures generated will not correspond to actual sentences. But in the overall grammar this will be harmless, for each structure must obey a set of constraints and filters, at both the level of syntax and of logical form. These constraints are primarily concerned with defining legitimate positions and interpretations for the various abstract elements, as well as for some overt items like ordinary pronouns, reflexives, 'each other' phrases, quantifiers and so on.

It is these constraints which are regarded as the most important and revealing subsystems of the Extended Standard Theory. They might vary within fairly narrow limits in the form which they assume in different languages, but they are assumed to be part of the system of Universal Grammar with which we are endowed: in fact, Chomsky regards them as the best direct evidence for the existence of such a system. In order to approach a statement of some of these constraints we need some preliminary metatheoretical definitions and conventions.[3]

i) A category α *c-commands* β if (neither dominates the other and) the first branching category dominating α dominates β. So in

3.

NP_1 and Tense c-command each other, they both c-command VP, V, NP_2, V c-commands NP_2 etc. V does not c-command NP_1 or Tense, and VP does not c-command NP_2 or V.

ii) α *governs* β if α c-commands β and no major category ($\bar{S}$, (not S) NP, VP, PP etc.) or major category boundary appears between them. Thus NP_1 governs and is governed by Tense, Tense governs VP, NP_2 is governed by V etc. Provisionally, the possible values of α are restricted to Tense, V, Adj, P.

iii) Case is assigned to an NP (and hence to its head N) in the following situations:

NP Tense... $\longrightarrow$ $NP_{+nominative}$
(where V is not intransitive)...V (P) NP... $\longrightarrow$ $NP_{+objective}$
...P NP... $\longrightarrow$ $NP_{/+oblique}$

There is a corresponding Case filter which requires that all lexical N receive Case. The notion of Case used here is a grammatical one, which in English shows up morphologically only in pronouns (*he* vs. *him* etc.), and it is not to be confused with Fillmore's (1968) notion.

Notice that the rules for assigning Case in (iii) will not assign any case to the subject of an infinitive: i.e. the NP in a configuration ...[$_{\bar{S}}$ NP to VP]. (In the case of a *for* complementiser, the *for* is assumed both to govern and to assign Case as *for* does when a preposition). Since the Case filter requires every lexical N to have Case, this ought to mean that sentences like:

4. John believed [$_{\bar{S}}$ Bill/him to be incompetent].

should be unacceptable. This is where the question of the appropriate level of idealization becomes relevant: Chomsky argues that structures like 4 are relatively unusual – they are not possible in French or German, for example – and that a straightforward theory of Case assignment is correct in regarding 4 as unacceptable. But they are acceptable in English because verbs like *believe* can 'exceptionally' govern and assign Case across an $\bar{S}$ boundary: they are thus a 'marked' or unusual construction in that they depart from the normal or expected linguistic patterns to be found in a language.

For the purposes of stating some of the constraints on linguistic structures, we can distinguish three types of NP: (i) lexical NP and pronominals, abstract or not: this treats PRO as an ordinary pronoun like *he, she, it* etc. (ii) lexical anaphors: *each other, himself,* etc. (iii) empty NP – either from optional lexical insertion, or the trace of *Move* α , where α = wh or NP.

We say that an NP is 'bound' if it is c-commanded by an NP with the same index; this can happen either by rules relating lexical anaphors to their antecedents or by the operation of *Move* α, which carries indices along. An NP which is not bound is 'free'. The 'governing category' for an item is the 'smallest' NP or S in which it is governed.

The principles which are supposed to filter out unwanted structures are these

A) Type (i) NPs must be free in their governing category
B) Type (ii) NPs must be bound in their governing category
C) Type (iii) NPs (β) must have an antecedent α such that (a) α governs β or (b) α c-commands β and there exists a lexical category X such that X governs β and α is contained in some 'projection' of X.

Principle A requires that lexical NP and non-anaphoric pronouns must not have an antecedent within their governing category. Principle B is the counterpart of this, that lexical anaphors must have an antecedent in their governing category. We will come to principle C (which is known as the Empty Category Principle) later. Roughly speaking, C is intended to ensure that traces are 'properly bound'. Meanwhile, let us see how the first two principles interact to derive the correct results for the following familiar range of examples:

5a. $[_S$ John $[_{VP}$ likes him]]. (irrelevant structural detail omitted)
  b. John likes himself.
  c.*Himself likes John.

6a. $[_S$ We expected $[_{\bar{S}}$ $[_S$ you to win] $_{\bar{S}}$].
  b. We expected $\left\{\begin{matrix} \text{each other} \\ \text{ourselves} \end{matrix}\right\}$ to win.

  c. $[_S$ We expected $[_{\bar{S}}$ that $[_S$ you would win]]].
  d.*We expected that $\left\{\begin{matrix} \text{each other} \\ \text{ourselves} \end{matrix}\right\}$ would win.

  e. We expected that we would win.

7a. $[_S$ It is unclear $[_{\bar{S}}$ what $[_X$ to do]]].
  b. John asked $[_{\bar{S}}$ what $[_X$ to do]]].

8a. $[_S$ NP seems $[_{\bar{S}}$ that [John likes Bill]]].
  b. John seems $[_S$ NP to like Bill].
  c. John seems $[_S$ Bill to like NP].

In 5a, *John* and *him* cannot have the same index (i.e. be coreferential) because by A, *him* must be free of its governing category, which is S. But in 5b *himself* must be bound in its governing category, since it is an anaphor: the only interpretation of this sentence is that *himself* refers to John. In 5c the same requirement holds, but here, John cannot be coindexed with *himself*, binding it, because *John* does not c-command *himself*. In 6a *you* is not assigned Case within the subordinate S, for it is the subject of an infinitive. But *expect* is a verb like *believe* which can both govern through an $\bar{\text{S}}$ and assign Case through an $\bar{\text{S}}$, and so *you* is assigned objective Case by *expect*. Thus the governing category for *you* is not the lower S, but the matrix, or highest S, in which it is free, as required. The same remarks apply to 6b except that these anaphors are bound within the matrix S, as required. In 6c *you* is assigned Case by the Tense (*would=will+past*) and so its governing category is the lower S this time: *you* is free in this S as required. This means that if the number and gender permit, it may refer to an NP outside that S, as in 6e where it refers to the matrix *we*. On the other hand, if the subject of the lower S had been an anaphor, as in 6d, the sentence would be ungrammatical, for *each other/ourselves* are assigned Case by the Tense, thus their governing category is the lower S and they are not bound in that S, contrary to the requirement B.

In 7, on Chomsky's assumptions, we have the following at S-structure and so X = S:

9. It is unclear [$_{\bar{S}}$ [$_C$ what] [$_S$ NP to do NP]].

There are only 2 possibilities for the empty NP positions, if we assume, as Chomsky does, that one of them must be the trace left by the movement of *what* to COMP position:

10a. ... what$_i$ [$_S$ e$_i$ to do PRO]
  b. ... what$_i$ [$_S$ PRO to do e$_i$]

Although structure (a) is derivable from the syntactic rules it is declared unacceptable by the Case filter, since *what* has not been assigned Case (it was the subject of an infinitive). Thus 10b is the only possibility: trace is governed by the lexical category V-*do*, as required by principle C to be discussed below: PRO has no Case but since it is not a lexical NP it is not subject to the Case filter: it is free in S, (though as PRO is not actually governed by anything in S, S does not technically count as its governing category. See Chomsky (1981: 225 fn.35) for relevant discussion and a reformulation).

In 7b, the same reasoning leaves us with:

11. John asked [$_{\bar{S}}$ [$_{COMP}$ what] [$_S$ PRO to do e]].

as the only possible structure. Here PRO is free in S, but it is controlled by *John* (i.e. interpreted as referring to John) outside S. (generally speaking, control of PRO in such structures is by the nearest matrix NP:

12a. John pleaded with Bill PRO to leave.
  b. John told Bill PRO to leave.
  c. John tried PRO to leave.

but *promise*, the indirect question sense of *ask* etc. are well known exceptions here which have to be lexically stipulated).

In 8b the underlying structure is assumed to be 8a with NP = e:

13. [[$_{NP}$ e] seems [$_{\bar{S}}$ [$_S$ John to like Bill]]].

If no NP movement (*Move α*) occurs the structure would be ungrammatical on two counts: there is an empty NP without an antecedent (principle C), and there is a lexical NP (John) with no Case. *Move α* 'rescues' the structure leaving:

14. John$_i$ seems [$_{\bar{S}}$ [$_S$ e$_i$ to like Bill]].

The trace of *John* is not governed in the lower S. Chomsky assumes that *seem*, *appear* – the 'raising' verbs – are like *expect* etc. in that they govern across $\bar{S}$, though they do not assign Case (since they are intransitive verbs). So *seems* governs the trace of *John*, even though not assigning Case to it, and so the trace is properly bound by *John*, as required by principle C. However, in 8c, which has the structure:

15. John seems [$_{\bar{S}}$ [$_S$ Bill to like e]].

although *e* is governed by *like*, *Bill* is a lexical NP which, since it is subject of an infinitive, has no case; and so the structure is declared unacceptable by the Case Filter.

When we come on to discuss Wh-movement structures we need the notion of percolation-projection (p-projection) developed by Kayne (1981). A category is a 'projection' of a lexical category (N, V, P, Adj) if it is a phrasal category of the same type (NP, VP, PP, AdjP: in fact this notion is only properly expressible within the $\overline{X}$ theory of phrase structure rules: see Jackendoff (1977)). For simplicity, we will assume that S and $\overline{S}$ are projections of V (as in Jackendoff, although see Kayne: fn 17, Chomsky 1981: 300). The basic idea of p-projection is that a category α can be counted as a p-projection of another category β if α is either a projection of β, or α governs something which is a projection, or a p-projection of β. The Empty Category Principle, repeated below, in effect requires that a trace must be directly governed by its antecedent, or that there should be a route from the antecedent to the trace via the relation of p-projection.

ECP An empty category β must have an antecedent α such that (1) α governs β or (2) α c-commands β and there exists a lexical category X such that X governs β and α is contained in some p-projection of X.

Though complicated to express in detail, the idea is quite simple and can be illustrated graphically: thus the following is a legitimate structure:

16.

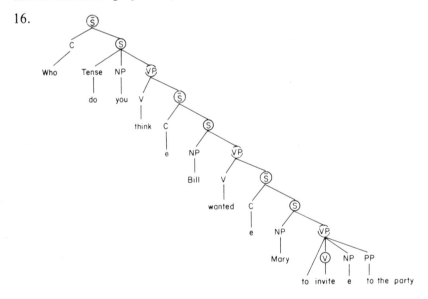

Who is α and c-commands β, which is the lowest [$_{NP}$ e]. *Invite* is the relevant lexical category governing β and the circled nodes represent the p-projections of *invite*. *Who* is contained in the topmost p-projection, $\bar{\text{S}}$, and so structure 16 satisfies the second clause of the ECP.

The ECP makes some surprising predictions: structures like those in 17 ought to be unacceptable, since *e* is governed by P, but VP is not a p-projection of PP.

17.

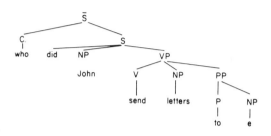

However, Hornstein and Weinberg (1981) argue that in such structures, the VP up to the empty category has been reanalysed as a complex V: $[_V$ send letters to $]$ – somewhat analogous to the way that certain combinations of V with NP or P seem to be regarded as honorary Vs for the purposes of passivisation:

(i) All these people have been written to by the school.
(ii) They were taken advantage of by the children.

In all these cases, the empty category is directly governed by V after reanalysis, allowing the government requirement of the ECP to be satisfied in the letter if not in the spirit.

Notice that the ECP mentions government by 'lexical categories': this is understood to exclude Tense from being a governor. But Kayne (1981) argues that not all lexical categories govern: in particular, N does not govern in the same way as V. If Kayne's arguments are correct (they are too lengthy to be repeated here) then the ECP captures the effect of the Complex Noun Phrase Constraint (CNPC) (See Ross 1967).

18.

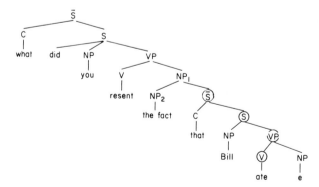

The p-projection route goes from V (*ate*) to its $\bar{\text{S}}$ p-projection. But since NP is not a projection of $\bar{S}$ it can go no further by that clause of the definition of p-projection: nor can it percolate via the part of the definition involving government, for since N is not a governing category in this configuration it will not govern anything in $\bar{S}$. Thus e, though governed by *ate*, does not have an antecedent in a legitimate position. In general the only acceptable structures of the form

19.

where S contains e, will be those in which the antecedent of e is in COMP.

The ECP also captures the effects of Ross's Left Branch Constraint (LBC)

20.

Read does not govern e, since a major category boundary (NP) intervenes: ...*read* $[_{NP} [_{Det} [_{NP} e]$ ... and so the trace of *whose* does not have an appropriate antecedent.

The exclusion of Tense as a governing category for the ECP means that there is an asymmetry between subject and non-subject positions with respect to empty NPs. An e in subject position will not be governed by a lexical category within its S. For structures like

21.

this presents no problem since e is governed by its antecedent *who*, thus falling under the first part of ECP. But in

22.

the antecedent does not directly govern the lowest e, e_2. Kayne's suggestion is that *believe* can exceptionally govern an empty NP across an S̄ just as it can a lexical NP, as in the earlier examples. Since the empty NP in COMP governs the (coindexed) empty subject NP, then assuming that the relation of government in this instance at least can be regarded as transitive, the subject [$_{NP}$ e] is governed by a lexical category (*believe*) which contains the antecedent of e in its p-projection, and so the ECP is satisfied.

These assumptions enable the ECP to account for the contrast between

23a. Who do you believe __ left.
  b. *Who do you believe that __ left.

a contrast which in alternative treatments is described by a different constraint (the 'complementiser constraint on variables', Bresnan 1977, or the '*that-t*' filter in Chomsky and Lasnik 1977). The structure for a is

  ...believe [$_S$ [$_C$ *e*] [$_S$ [$_{NP}$ *e*]] *left*]]

which is analogous to 22 in all relevant respects, and is acceptable. But in b, the structure in more detail, is

24.

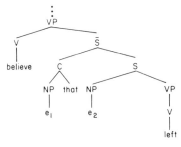

Although *believe* can exceptionally govern e$_1$ across S̄, as before, this e$_1$ does not govern the lower subject e$_2$, for now the first branching category above e$_1$ is COMP, and COMP does not dominate e$_2$. So e$_1$ does not c-command e$_2$ and therefore cannot govern it.

Of course, there is much more to be said about ECP and the other principles described here. It is likely that alternative principles will emerge in the near future and provide a more satisfying account of the phenomena just described. Nevertheless, the approach we have just sketched is full enough for us to go on to pose the question of how these constraints might connect up with theories of parsing – if they do.

II. Various attempts have been made recently to show that there is a fairly direct connection between parsing and constraints, a connection which leads to a functional account of syntactic constraints; an account which attempts to show not only why they exist, but even why they take the particular form that they do. The general form of at least some of these accounts is as follows: firstly, a mechanism for parsing well-formed examples of certain constructions is set up, either suggested directly by existing linguistic accounts (e.g. Marcus (1980) on the CNPC) or proposed as the simplest computational mechanism for the job which is not obviously implausible as a psychological model (as in Winograd's (1972) account of the Coordinate Structure Constraint (CSC), or Ritchie's (1980) account of CNPC). (ii) It is then shown that this mechanism operates in such a way as to automatically fail to parse examples which violate the various constraints, needing no extra stipulation to distinguish these cases, which are thus implicitly defined as ungrammatical. For example, Winograd's programme regards a coordinate conjunction, syntactically speaking, as an instruction to parse a constituent of the same type as the one which has just ended. So in:

25. Pick up the red block and put it on the blue one.

an S is found after the conjunction; in

26. Pick up the red block and the blue block.

an NP is found. He points out that such a procedure will fail when encountering examples like:

27a. Who did you see ___ and John.
  b. Who did you see John and ___ .

since the program will not find any matching pair of constituents surrounding the conjunction. Ignoring the question of whether such a treatment actually is generally adequate or psychologically plausible (see Dresher and Hornstein 1976), Winograd's account can be seen as a simple paradigm example of the kind of thing attempted by Ritchie, or on a larger scale, by Marcus.

As a pattern of explanation this kind of approach is extremely appealing. Competence – the grammar – is sharply distinguished from performance – the parsing algorithm, and its description is simplified, since syntactic constraints are no longer regarded as a matter of competence. Instead they are shown to be consequences of the interaction of two components of the language faculty. Examples involving violations of constraints are to be regarded as grammatical, but unparsable structures.

However, there are several problems that the proponents of this pattern of explanation must face. First, there is the problem that the constraints themselves may not be quite as rigid as such an account might be taken to imply: there are English examples which appear to violate the CNPC:

28. This is the only tune that we've had a request for the band to play.

and it is well known that some Scandinavian languages allow structures which seem to be CNPC violations; e.g. in Danish it is possible to say the equivalent of

29. Which sort of cakes do you have an aunt who bakes __ .

The CSC seems more resistant to violation but even here some languages have been claimed to provide counterexamples: in Fe' Fe' it is apparently possible to find the equivalent of

30. Who did he cut meat and thank __ . (Smith and Wilson 1979: 258)

It may be that these are only apparent violations and that these constructions should not be analysed as analogous to their English translation, but the general point is valid: if a constraint is supposed to be the result of general principles of the operation of the human parsing mechanism, assuming this to be universal, then while language specific constraints might not be a problem, constraints which operate in some areas but not other apparently analogous areas are a problem (they are a problem for the syntactic theorist too).

It is of course possible at this point to respond that no claim for the universality of the parsing principles is being made. While this is logically tenable – different parsing mechanisms might be required for different (types of) languages – it is a much weaker assumption to make and the attractiveness of the explanatory programme diminishes proportionally.

The second difficulty is in motivating the specific principles of the parser's operation which are responsible for the explanation of the constraints. For example, Ritchie's explanation for the wh-island subset of CNPC phenomena relies on the fact that the register in which a fronted wh-word is stored behaves as a 'local variable': i.e., it takes on a new value each time it is invoked. Thus the contents of one incarnation of this register are inaccessible to any of the others:

31. [Wh-1 ...... [wh-2 ......] ......]

This has the effect that the only legitimate wh-word-gap associations will be nested within each other: they cannot overlap.

32. W1   W2   G2   G1   W1   W2   G1   G2

(See Fodor (1978) for discussion of other such phenomena). As Ritchie says, this is a simple and natural computational mechanism. But there are several other equally simple and equally natural computational mechanisms envisageable: what is the evidence that these are not the ones that are involved? It seems likely, as Fodor (1980) points out, that the existence of the constraints themselves in treatments such as this is actually the only direct evidence that the parser works in the way suggested. This would not be viciously circular if it could be shown that the principles involved extended also to other areas: that other types of observation could be accomodated by similar mechanisms. But in fact this often does not seem to be the case: as regards the principle in question, there are examples where dependencies of other types appear to overlap without resulting in any noticeable difficulty in parsing:

33a. *John* asked Bill *what* to do.

  b. *How long* does that film last tonight *which has Julie Andrews in it.*

  c. *Who* did John give the book to *that you lent me.*

And the 'local variable' principle of sentential level grammatical registers would, if extended, seem to imply that self-embedding should be easier to cope with than it is:

34a. The rat the cat the dog chased bit died.

  b. That for Bill to leave would be a nuisance is obvious.

Grammatical registers like *subject* would be created anew as each level of embedding is encountered: since no register needs access to any others of a different level such sentences ought to be easy to process. But in Ritchie's treatment multiple self-embeddings like 34a are only ruled out by a stipulation on depth of processing (p.92-3).

A less direct functional motivation for syntactic constraints is attempted by Fodor (1980, 1981). She suggests that in general terms it is correct to see the constraints as concerned to limit the positions of missing constituents in sentences. But the most obvious functional interpretation of such a claim, that the constraints rule out holes or gaps which are difficult for a parser to detect, is not tenable, she points out. There is no difficulty in locating gaps in:

35a.*Peanuts, I don't like either __ or cashews.

  b.*Who do you think that __ left.

Fodor's suggestion is that syntactic constraints are the product of negotiations between two separate components of the language faculty which have conflicting concerns. One component – the expressor – is concerned with the expression of information over and above that conveyed by the predicate+argument or verb+thematic role structure of a sentence: namely, information about scope, emphasis, given and new, focus and such like. There are various devices by which such information is conveyed: stress, reordering, and the use of deletions, ellipsis or proforms. To some extent also, various grammatical constructions – *extraposition, clefting, passive, there-insertion* – can be seen as fulfilling such a role, as has often been observed.

The ideal state of affairs from the point of view of the expressor, we assume, would be one in which it had complete freedom to use any of the devices it possesses: to reorder, delete, or emphasise wherever it liked. The parser, on the other hand, is concerned to process input as quickly and as accurately as possible, in order to assemble interpretable constituents and package them off to wherever it is they go to. When it is processing grammatical input we can safely assume that the parser wants to know as quickly as possible what type of constituent it is on. When it is processing input which is either ungrammatical *per se* or ungrammatical on the current parsing hypothesis – a garden path – then it likewise needs to know this as quickly as possible.

Fodor points out that some of the devices available to the expressor, in particular, reordering and deletion, actually conflict quite squarely with these demands of the parser. For example, if reordering were completely free, then in a sentence like:

36. John thought Harry that Bill didn't like.

with a topicalisation out of a subordinate sentence, the parser would not be able to tell until the very end of the sentence that *Harry* was in fact a reordered object of the lower sentence, rather than an intruding constituent signalling ungrammaticality, as in

37. John thought Harry that Bill liked Fred.

Mutatis mutandis, the same is true of gaps: if the parser does not have sufficient information to recognise that a particular configuration, say ... *put off until tomorrow* ... could contain a gap, then it would not be able to distinguish constituents containing gaps from constituents which were ill-formed. This suggests that a restriction on the possibilities for reordering and for missing elements would be to the advantage of the parser, since it would limit or possibly even remove any local uncertainty of this type. Such a restriction would be apparently to the detriment of the expressor, however, for some of its freedom would be sacrificed. Not all of the possible options for rearrangement and deletion would be available to it. Fodor argues that in general it turns out that these restrictions are not fatal or even particularly damaging to the expressor; that it in effect only agrees to forego options that it can afford to do without.

The ideal outcome of such a negotiation between expressor and parser would be a situation in which reordered constituents – fillers – would never be confusable with grammatical errors in the form of missing constituents. General properties of the grammar of English and other languages go quite a long way towards meeting this ideal, in fact: most fillers are to be found in sentence initial position, where they can be recognised as potential fillers as quickly as possible, or if in initial position of a subordinate clause they have their status as fillers clearly marked by the presence of a wh-element.[4] But legitimate positions for gaps have to be stipulated by constraints, certain gaps being regarded as illegitimate: the parser can then regard these as a genuine 'mistake'. This would account for the asymmetry between gaps and resumptive pronouns: as is well known, constructions analoguous to those with gaps but in which a pronoun appears, in general are interpreted as if they do not obey the constraints:

38a.*Peanuts, I don't like either __ or cashews.
   b. As for peanuts, I don't like either them or cashews.

Pronouns are overt constituents appearing in normal positions and thus are not liable to be misconstrued as a mistake.

Thus syntactic constraints are regarded as the product of a contract between the expressor and the parser. Notice that this somewhat picturesque and metaphorical pattern of 'explanation' is quite different from that which tries to explain the constraints as a redescription of the direct consequences of a particular parsing mechanism. For whereas in the first the constraints could be dispensed with as a separate statement, emerging instead as the by-product of the interaction between grammar and parser, in Fodor's theory the constraints, though the outcome of trading between the expressor and the parser, are still a separate component of grammatical description to which it must be assumed that the parser has access. Notice also that although on Fodor's account constraints on the positions of empty nodes and PRO might be given a functional motivation in terms of parsing, it is not immediately obvious how constraints on the *interpretation* of empty – or overt – elements could be accounted for in similar terms. This does not rule out the possibility that some analogous account in terms of a trade-off between semantic processing routines and the expressor might be formulated, but there are no plausible candidates for such processing routines in view.

However, the main question which we must now pose is how, on Fodor's theory, constraints like the ECP might be motivated. In general terms the definition of the ECP in terms of p-projection distinguishes a set of permissible 'paths' from filler to gaps. The path is stated in terms of structural information (c-command and government) which, we assume, has been implicitly computed by the parser anyway in the course of building a tree: it thus seems to require no extra computation to be able to use such constraints during parsing. We can see immediately how information about such permissible paths would be of value to a parser, for it would be able at once, on encountering something which could be construed as a gap, to know whether this was a possible gap or a mistake. If there is no moved constituent to relate to the gap, then it is a mistake: if it is not on a legitimate path from the antecedent it is also a mistake; otherwise it is a possible gap. But the other side of the bargain is not so clear: why does the path pick out just these positions? What, if anything, is the expressor giving up by agreeing that these positions should be illegitimate? (In what follows, although we will draw heavily on Fodor's work, and although the general approach is the same, this should not be taken to be committing her to the particular conclusions reached here).

In order to begin answering this question we need to make some prior assumptions. We will follow Fodor in assuming that the rules that a parser has access to define directly something like the full class of well-formed sentences of English. It has usually been assumed (e.g. by Kimball 1973, 1975) that (a) these rules will be at least partly context free, and that (b) they must generate VP or $\overline{\text{VP}}$ directly as complements to verbs exactly as they appear to be on the surface. [5] Fodor makes the further assumption that all these rules will be context free, and of the form proposed by Gazdar (1981) (see also Chapter 8), and therefore able to mention 'slashed' categories: categories with a hole or a gap in them. [6] We will henceforth assume, then, that the type of structure being built by the parser for a sentence is that made available by Gazdar's 'generalised phrase structure grammar'. For obvious reasons, this will make it difficult to address directly the possibility of a parsing motivation for the ECP, since there is no direct equivalent in Gazdar's framework. We can approach it indirectly, though, by pointing to (at least some of) the effects of the ECP for a language like English, and asking what the parsing motivation would be for a constraint having the same effect, but formulated in terms of a generalised phrase structure grammar framework.

Fodor points out that among the slashed categories available for English in Gazdar's account, one – S/NP – is particularly significant, for one of its realizations corresponds to an already existing unslashed category. If the NP hole in S/NP is in the subject position, the resulting configuration (in a generalised phrase structure grammar at least) is superficially indistinguishable from a $\overline{\text{VP}}$. This enables Fodor to explain a difference between two sorts of 'fillers', in the most general sense.

In the preceding discussion we have limited our attention to fillers which have been fronted constituents and recognizable as fillers by that fact. But in fact the semantic relation between such a constituent and its associated gap is almost exactly the same as the relation between a controlling NP and its associated PRO as far as the parser is concerned – the one needs to be linked to the other, even though within the version of trace theory that we sketched, the first type of path is described by the ECP and the second by principles of control. In a sentence like:

39. John promised Bill [$_\text{S}$ PRO to leave].

the PRO can be regarded as a 'gap' for which a filler is required: *John* in this case. The only difference is that the filler is in a canonical NP position, unlike fronted constituents: it is a 'structure preserving' filler, in Fodor's terminology. However, this in turn means that at the point at which it is encountered there is no syntactic indication in the string to tell us that *John* is a filler: this information is actually associated lexically with the verb *promise*. Since there is no syntactically displaced constituent, to regard ... *to leave* as a subjectless sentence is therefore redundant: there is no syntactic filler and so no need for a syntactic gap. The information which for overt fillers and gaps is obtained via the reconstruction of a syntactic relationship ('moving' the filler into its gap) here can be directly read off from the lexical information associated with particular verbs, as in part it must be anyway. (As we pointed out earlier, control of PRO is lexically governed). In other words, if the expressor agreed to a restriction which was roughly of the form 'there are no sentences of the form $[_S [_{NP} e]$ to VP $]$' it would lose absolutely nothing: anything that can be done syntactically by such a construction (where $[_{NP} e]$ is PRO) can be done by $\overline{\text{VP}}$, and the semantic information about the understood subject of the infinitive conveyed by such a structure along with principles of control can be recovered from the lexicon, where it appears to belong most naturally anyway.

Fodor suggests that this makes sense of the fact that structure preserving fillers are only found in constructions which are lexically governed: either Equi verbs like *promise* and *persuade*; *too/enough* and *ready* constructions, or *tough* movement:

40a. John tried to leave.
  b. He is ready to eat.
  c. He is too big to eat.
  d. This fish is difficult to get hold of.

Either, like Equi verbs, their gap is a subject one, and they are subcategorized $\overline{\text{VP}}$, or like Tough movement constructions, the gap is any non-subject NP, and hence they can be subcategorized (when with a lexical subject) as $+\_\overline{\text{VP}}/\text{NP}$, (as in effect is done in Gazdar's framework), or like the others, both of these possibilities are available. Either way, the route from filler to gap is recoverable from lexical information to which the parser must already have access. Infinitive constructions, then, can be regarded as $\overline{\text{VP}}$s rather than as sentences with empty subjects, and in a grammar, directly generated as such.

What does the parser get out of this bargain? A plausible suggestion is that it enables the parser to be sure that when it is processing something which looks like a $\overline{\text{VP}}$ (to VP), it can, given the restriction on empty subjects, actually be sure that it is a $\overline{\text{VP}}$ it is processing and not something which is later going to turn out to be an S with a missing syntactic subject, requiring expensive recomputation. (See Gazdar 1981: fn 17) While the benefits from this bargain might seem in this instance rather marginal, it can in fact be seen as an instance of a more general strategy, as we will argue below.

But how could such an explanation extend to the data accounted for by the ECP? Notice that the definition of ECP in effect excludes Tense as a governing category for the ECP (though it does count as a governing category for the assignment of Case). In the simplest cases this stipulates an asymmetry between subject and non-subject position with respect to empty nodes: empty nodes in non-subject positions will (almost) always be properly governed and thus admissible, but empty nodes in subject position require the quite complicated conditions on legitimate antecedents stated in part (b) of the ECP. Let us ignore part (b) of the ECP for the time being and ask why the expressor might consent to a restriction such as that given in (a), namely, prohibiting empty nodes in subject position. The answer we could give to this is presumably the same as before: anything that can be achieved syntactically via [[$_{NP}$ e] VP], where VP is tensed (at surface structure the tensed element is of course no longer outside VP), can equally well be achieved by VP. To put it as before, as far as the parser is concerned, a subjectless sentence is indistinguishable from a VP. It would thus be to the advantage of the parser that something which looks like a tensed VP always is one, and that it will not need to be recomputed as a sentence with a missing subject.

The expressor loses little by this restriction on empty subjects, except in one case. Since within the framework of trace theory there are no verbs in English which are subcategorized to take a tensed VP, the only structures where the difference between a subjectless tensed sentence and a VP could show up is in the case of movement rules. Consider simple cases of Wh-movement from subject position; in a structure like

41.

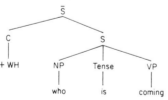

We have, in Chomsky's treatment, Wh-movement to COMP position, and subject auxiliary inversion. But the final result is exactly the same as regards the order of the overt elements:

42a. Who is coming?
  b. Who e is coming?
  c. Who is e coming?

It is not clear whether to regard the parser as 'undoing' subject auxiliary inversion in such structures, but whether it does or not it is clear that the computation of a gap in such a structure is redundant. Exactly that information which computation of a gap leads to – that *who* is a subject – could be got by treating the sentences as actually having the form that they appear to have:

43a.   rather than   b.

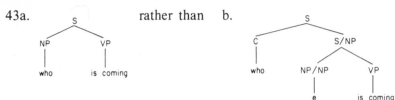

In Gazdar's treatment, this is exactly what happens. He imposes a 'Generalized Left Branch Constraint', (GLBC) which prohibits NP/NP nodes on left branches of larger constituents. This constraint achieves the effect of Ross's original Left Branch Constraint, and his Sentential Subject Constraint. It also, of course, singles out subject positions in tensed sentences as not being possible gap positions, as does the ECP. But Gazdar's treatment makes explicit the parallellism between VP and $[_S [_{NP} e] VP]$ by invoking a metarule to replace the latter structures with the former. This metarule can be seen as a way of escaping the effects of the GLBC in these cases, (just as clause (b) of the ECP can be seen as a way of rescuing some empty subject positions). 43b would violate the GLBC, but the structure which actually results is 43a, via the meta-rule just mentioned. The same thing applies equally to other types of wh-movement, though this necessitates regarding *that* as a relative pronoun rather than a complementiser. Thus it is clear that in these instances the expressor loses nothing by consenting to a restriction on empty nodes in subject position.

If we were to maintain that the restriction was quite simply that there can be no structures of the form $[_S [_{NP} e] X]$, where X is either VP or $\overline{VP}$, then both cases fall together. This would also account straightforwardly for the fact that sentences like these are ungrammatical:

44a.*Who did you arrange for __ to leave.
  b.*Who did you think that __ had left.

There is no possibility of parsing *for __ to leave* or *that __ had left* as a $\overline{VP}$. However, we have to account for the fact that these are acceptable:

45a. Who did you expect __ to leave.
  b. Who did you think __ had left.

In Gazdar's treatment this is again achieved via the metarule ruling out subjectless sentences as illegitimate. Thus both examples in 45 have the structure:[7]

46.

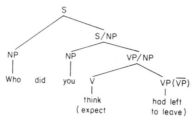

Notice that this means that if our parser is consulting such a grammar no syntactic gap is computed in these structures: the slashed nodes do not 'cancel out' anywhere: we never reach the trace, NP/NP. Thus the relation between *who* and *had left* has to be reconstructed semantically rather than syntactically. (These examples are treated as lexically marked exceptions in Kayne's treatment too: see above).

It might be objected that this analysis involves giving up a generalization about English syntax, that a tensed sentence always has an overt subject, though not necessarily in the subject position of that sentence. But in fact there are other constructions, discussed in Bresnan (1977), where there is also no overt subject, as in:

47a. There were as many people as __ could fit into the bus.
  b. More men were angry than __ were amused.

Nevertheless, it is certainly true that such constructions are not straightforward: many people have pointed out that even where acceptable, subject gaps are more awkward than non-subject gaps. For example, Fodor (p.54) contrasts:

48a. Who does John think saw Mary.
  b. Who does John think Mary saw.

and Chomsky (1981: 159, see also p.246-7) contrasts the degrees of unacceptability between:

49a. This book, I wonder how well John understands.
  b. John, I wonder how well understands this book.

In the framework here proposed this difference in complexity might plausibly be attributed precisely to the fact that fillers in these constructions can only be interpreted by associating them with the VP (which is not part of an S and therefore for which no syntactic (empty) subject has already been computed) by some mechanism other than that associating fillers and gaps, perhaps analoguous to that associating controlling NPs with their V̄P in Equi constructions (except that it is not directly lexically governed). In this respect it might be accurate to regard them as, though acceptable, a marked or possibly even ungrammatical construction.

Although we can provide in the terms above a reasonable functional motivation for the asymmetry between subjects and non-subjects described by both ECP and the GLBC + metarule of Gazdar, we have still to provide a similar motivation for the other structures ruled out by these constraints. Both constraints will characterize sentences like:

50a. Whose did you drink __ beer.

   b. The president's, they shot __ father.

as ungrammatical. What properties do these structures share with those in which a subject is missing? I suggest that in both cases there is a situation which results in what we might call 'accidental constructional homonymity'. That is, in both cases, a gap results in a structure which is parsable as a complete constituent: in the cases above, a $\overline{\text{VP}}$ or VP, here, a noun phrase. In particular, in the case of 50a and b there is no indication in the later portion of the surface string that a gap is present: ... *did you drink beer*, and ... *they shot father* are both well formed substrings. (In cases like:

51. Whose did you read __ book.

then there is a substring which is not wholly well-formed: ... *did you read book*, but failure of agreement is not the kind of ungrammaticality which elsewhere signals that a gap is present.)

We can perhaps see the GLBC and, to some extent, the ECP, then, as the result of a general tendency to rule as inadmissible empty nodes in positions where the resulting overt structure is syntactically homonymous or confusable with some other structure which could legitimately appear in that position. The restriction on questioning of objects in constructions like:

52. Who did Fred buy __ books.

discussed in Fodor (1978) might also be regarded as a case of the same type. In all these cases the restrictions conspire to reduce local ambiguity, and to avoid the need for any revision or backtracking during parsing. However, this principle needs stating with some care. For example, an empty node in the structure

results in a structure homonymous to

but such empty nodes are nevertheless permitted. Presumably the difference is that unlike the case of empty nodes at the beginning of constituents, here there is enough information available at the time via subcategorization to work out that there could in fact be a gap. In the cases we have been looking at, however, this information comes too late, if it comes at all, to avoid having to change a structure already built by the parser.

While it seems that the attempt to provide a functional motivation for syntactic constraints along the lines suggested by Fodor is fairly promising, there are many problems to be faced, both of principle and of substance. Among the first type is the fact that in many respects this whole pattern of teleological explanation is rather problematic. In particular there is the objection that, as Bever (1975) puts it 'functional explanations require independently motivated functional theories' – we have no such theory in the case of parsing, beyond a few prima facie plausible assumptions about what a parser might find easy or difficult. We have assumed throughout, for example, that it is difficult for the parser to change decisions it has already made. But without independent justification of this there is a danger of the kind of circularity of which we accused proponents of the 'direct functional' approach earlier.

Secondly, there is at least one problem of substance, again analogous to one raised earlier for the Ritchie-Marcus type of explanation for syntactic constraints. For while we can provide a seemingly plausible account of a contract between parser and expressor to motivate the exclusion of subject gaps in English, it is a well known fact that there are languages such as Spanish or Italian for which no such constraint holds, and in which such sentences as the following are grammatical:

53a. Hemos trabajado todo el dia.
    (we) have worked all day.
  b. Quien dijiste que __ salio temprano?
    who did you say that __ left early?

(from Perlmutter 1971: 103)
Within the framework of the ECP, such facts could be taken to indicate that Tense is a governing category for these languages. (Chomsky 1981 describes this parameter rather differently). But if we take the contract account of the ECP seriously, then we should be able to point to some factor which makes it worthwile for the parser to strike a 'no missing subject' bargain in some languages but not in others.

One possibility might be to point to the fact that in the languages that allow missing subjects, the overt verbal morphology is generally far richer than English, enabling the number and gender, at least, of the missing subject to be determined. Perlmutter, who was the first to discuss this phenomenon in detail within a transformational framework, in fact rejected this kind of explanation on the grounds that French, which ought if this were correct to always allow empty subjects, in many instances:

54. *Avons travaillé toute la journée.

does not, even where the subject is clear: conversely, there are cases in which deletion is allowed where the subject is not uniquely recoverable, as in Italian

55. Sono qui = *I am here* or *they are here.*

Nevertheless, it is still the case that the correlation between the possibility of empty subjects and overt agreement is impressive if not exact. As Chomsky puts it in his (different) treatment of these facts:

> The intuitive idea is that where there is overt agreement, the subject can be dropped, since the deletion is recoverable ... The correlation with overt inflection need not be exact. We expect at most a tendency in this direction. (1981: 241)

The motivation in these terms for the difference between languages in this respect might be something like this: in languages with a sufficiently rich inflectional morphology, a main clause S of the form $[_S [_{NP} e] VP]$ presents no difficulty since the parser is aware from the outset not only that it is parsing a subjectless sentence rather than a VP, but also what the content of the missing subject is, up to the level of specificity conveyed by pronouns. Presumably it is only the fact that the subject is recoverable in this way that allows the expressor to eliminate what it considers to be redundant material. If it were not recoverable, it would not be redundant. Thus the parser would gain no great benefit by extracting a 'no missing subjects' contract from the expressor. In languages with poor morphology, on the other hand, main clause structures like $[[_{NP} e] VP]$ would violate recoverability – there would not, we assume, always be sufficient information for the parser (or perhaps the semantic routines) to recover the missing subject. Thus such structures will be ruled out. If they are ruled out by a general 'no missing subjects' constraint applying in subordinate clauses too, then the parser will gain the added advantage that we mentioned before, namely, it can be sure that anything that looks like a VP actually is a VP and not $[_S [_{NP} e] VP]$. What is surprising from this point of view is not that in these languages, like English, structures like

56.*Who do you think that __ left.

should be ungrammatical, but that

57. Who do you think __ left.

should be apparently grammatical.

ACKNOWLEDGEMENTS

Thanks to Louis Des Tombe, Hanne Ruus and Erich Werhli for discussion and examples, and Graeme Ritchie for many helpful comments and suggestions over presentation.

NOTES

1. This rather exaggerates the extent of the shift, in fact: see Chomsky (1964: 62 fn 8).
2. This is variously represented as *e*, or *t*, when with an index.
3. Like the principles A, B and C below, these represent something of a hybrid, being culled from various sources: Chomsky (1979, 1980) and Kayne (1981). Alternative definitions can be found in Chomsky (1981), as well as discussion of interactions with other subsystems not described at all here.
4. Where there is no overt filler, as for some relative clauses, presumably the configuration ...NP NP... is sufficient to indicate that a relative clause is being started. It is not clear whether to regard the parser as creating a copy of the head NP, treating it as a filler, or as simply looking for a gap to associate the head NP with.
5. We will henceforth assume that $\overline{\text{VP}}$ is the node dominating *to VP* in structures built up during a parse. Notice that this is different from the structure implied by Chomsky's analysis.
6. Rules mentioning slashed categories, in a grammar, are themselves mostly derived via a schema. If a grammar contains categories S and NP, for example, it will also contain categories S/NP, NP/NP etc. If a grammar contains a rule S → NP VP, then it will also contain rules S/NP → NP VP/NP, S/NP → NP/NP VP. Given a 'linking' rule to introduce a derived category into a tree, e.g. S → NP S/NP, then slashed categories can be passed down a tree, via the mechanism for replacing rules like VP → V NP by VP/NP → V NP/NP. When a category like NP/NP is arrived at it is interpreted as a trace, or an 'NP hole'. This mechanism allows Gazdar to generate unbounded dependencies without using transformations. The trees induced by such rules are exemplified by

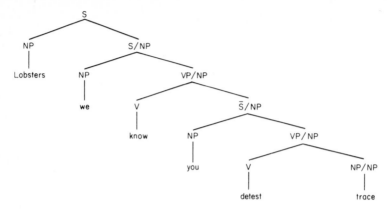

7. In fact this structure is not quite correct, for Gazdar does not regard interrogatives as dominated by S.

Section III

Parsing and Semantics
Introduction

One reaction to some of the difficulties encountered in early work in parsing was to argue that it was a fundamental error to concentrate on analysis of the syntactic structure of the text, neglecting its semantic content completely or, at best, leaving semantic interpretation as a final stage to be done after syntactic analysis and working only on the results of the latter. Historically, this reaction often went to an extreme, and a number of attempts were made to produce parsers which were mainly or entirely based on a semantic analysis of the text. In more recent years, at least within the computational world, a truce has reigned between the extreme parties, with the syntax enthusiasts conceding that semantics has an important role to play in the parsing process, and the semantics enthusiasts conceding that a certain amount of syntax is useful.

This state of affairs is reflected in this final Section, which consists for the most part in a consideration of the precise role to be played by semantics. Chapter 10, indeed, confronts the issue directly, examining different ways in which semantic methods can be integrated into parsing, exemplifying the various proposals and discussing the difficulties raised by each of them.

In parallel with the syntax/semantics distinction, a different distinction has often been made, opposing parsers which rely on surface characteristics of text, functioning mainly as pattern-matchers working on features immediately present with very little detailed analysis of any sort, to parsers aiming at going directly to a semantic representation. This opposition is challenged in chapter 11, where it is argued that the two types of parser in fact have much more in common than at first appears.

Chapter 12 describes a parser based on the idea that the elementary units of the text – its words – can be used to trigger a semantics based analysis, and thus to construct higher level units, rather than trying to construct the higher level units first and then find a semantic interpretation for them. It is interesting to note the close connection between this chapter and the preceding one. Starting from extremely superficial characteristics of the text, the parser described here moves directly to a deep semantic representation. It is interesting too to note a connection between the idea of an essentially lexicon-based parser and recent developments in linguistics which regard the lexicon as having considerably more importance than was previously thought.

10

Semantics in Parsing

G. Ritchie

1. SYNTAX AND SEMANTICS

If a natural language understanding system is to serve either as a model of human linguistic ability or as a practical front-end for an intelligent computer system, it must, at some stage, deal with the 'meaning' of sentences, as well as the surface syntax. (This requirement does not apply to systems like ELIZA (Weizenbaum 1966, 1967) or PARRY (see Chapter 11 in this volume)). In this chapter we will be looking at some of the issues that arise in handling the semantic structure for sentences, and at some of the techniques that have been proposed to deal with this.

Computational approaches to sentence-analysis can be roughly classed into three categories, according to the way in which they handle syntax and semantics:

A) Sentence-final : a first pass builds a full syntactic structure for the sentence, and a second pass converts this to a semantic representation.
B) Homogeneous : there is no syntax/semantics distinction, and a semantic structure is built directly from the input string.
C) Interleaved : the conversion from syntactic structure to semantic representation is carried out throughout the parsing process, using partial syntactic structures.

We will look at these approaches in turn.

2. SENTENCE-FINAL SEMANTIC INTERACTION

The main advantage of this approach is the simplicity of design of the program. Separate 'syntax' and 'semantics' modules can be implemented, without a need for a complex control structure between them. The disadvantages are that this organization is implausible as a model of human sentence-processing, and that the syntactic parser cannot use semantic information to guide its structure building. This latter point can be illustrated by the following. Consider the sentences in 1.

1a. Boris hit the boy with the cricket bat.
 b. Boris hit the boy with the red hair.
 c. Boris hit the swan with the cricket bat.

Sentence 1a is structurally ambiguous, since the adjunct 'with the cricket bat' can be either a modifier of 'the boy' (as in 1b) or an instrumental modifier of the verb (as in 1c). If a parser has only syntactic information, it is likely to find 1b and 1c ambiguous in exactly the same way, since the disambiguation (or 'preference' for a particular reading) comes from semantic (or real-world) information. Hence, a parser which builds an entire syntactic tree before performing any semantic processing will have to build both trees to avoid discarding the 'correct' structure. (Alternatively, it could build one complete version, retain the state of the parser, form the semantic interpretation, and cause the parser to 'backtrack' completely if the interpretation proved unsuitable). A parser with 'feed-back' from the semantic component during parsing might be able to choose the appropriate version and build only the structure corresponding to that meaning.

2.1 The LUNAR question answering system

Perhaps the best known 'sentence-final' program was the question-answering system of Woods et al. (1972), in which the parser and interpretive rules formed totally separate programs. The parser built a syntactic structure similar to the 'deep structure' of Chomsky (1965), and semantic interpretive rules converted this to a piece of program which would access a data-base. The interpretive rules consisted of a pair of a 'test' and an 'action' (cf. Chapter 4 in this volume), and were defined in terms of nodes in the syntax tree. That is, the 'test' in a rule described the sort of node to which it was applicable, and the 'action' stated what semantic processing was to be carried out if the node passed the 'test'. When a semantic rule was applied to a node, it could 'call' other rules to process the daughter nodes, and in this way a flow of rule-application would emanate from the application of rules to the top node in the tree. Woods has argued (Woods 1973) that, from an engineering point of view, this approach is more efficient than complex interleaved semantics, since semantic processing is more costly than syntactic parsing, and it therefore does not matter, from a practical point of view, if some extra syntactic work is done by the parser. Also, the syntactic component may be able to eliminate some possibilities, thus avoiding the need to interpret them semantically.

A later version of this program incorporated a certain amount of 'interleaved' semantic processing specifically to deal with the kind of problems illustrated in 1 above. The parser, when about to complete a potential prepositional modifier, checked to see if there were several candidates for attachment, and assessed their suitability on semantic grounds. It is not reported (in Woods 1973) how well this facility ('Selective Modifier Placement') worked in practice.

3. HOMOGENEOUS ANALYSERS

Throughout the 1960s, there was an emphasis on purely syntactic parsers (e.g. Kuno 1965, Thorne et al. 1968), but this was followed, in the early 1970s, by a desire to design 'wholly semantic' sentence-analysers. One motivation for this was the fact that people can understand sentences as they go along (i.e. partial meanings can be constructed as the sentence is processed left-to-right). There was also an intuitive belief (e.g. Schank 1972) that syntactic structure was an invention of linguists, with no real relevance to sentence- understanding. At about this time, there were one or two proposals for 'non-syntactic' analysers, and more recently 'semantic grammars' have received attention as a way of building natural language front-ends for intelligent systems. As will be argued below, it is rather misleading to term such systems 'non-syntactic' or 'wholly semantic', since they actually use a mixture of syntactic and semantic constructs. Their main distinguishing feature is the lack of a formal separation between these constructs – all grammatical information is treated as being qualitatively the same.

3.1 Riesbeck's Conceptual Dependency Analyser

One of the best known of the proposals for so-called 'non-syntactic' analysers was that of Riesbeck (1974, 1975a,b). This system built a 'conceptual dependency' structure (Schank 1972, 1975) while scanning a sentence from left-to-right. Riesbeck's main claims were that no traditional syntax was needed to achieve this, and that conceptual predictions would facilitate understanding (particularly of word-sense ambiguity). The control structure was essentially as follows. The processing rules were in the form of 'requests', which were pairs of a 'test' and an 'action' (cf. Chapter 3 of this volume), and each word had a set of requests stored in its lexical entry. The analyser, in scanning a sentence, maintained a list of 'active requests', and the requests of each input word were added to this list as the words were encountered. Whenever the 'test' of an active request was found to be true, the resulting action was executed. The disambiguating effect comes from the fact that the only sense of a word which will be seen by the analyser is that for which some currently active request (activated by the previous context) is testing. Hence, if only one particular meaning is 'predicted' on conceptual grounds, it alone will cause active requests to fire.

The much-quoted example of this predictive disambiguation is 3.

3. John shot five bucks.

In Riesbeck's dialect (and, apparently, in that of Groucho Marx), this can mean 'John spent five dollars', as well as the more conventional meaning of 'John shot five male deer'. He proposes that 3, preceded by 4, would be automatically disambiguated by the conceptual prediction mechanism, since the 'hunting' context would establish requests looking for the correct meaning of 'buck'.

4. John went hunting.

As Hayes (1975) has pointed out, this crude technique breaks down on sentences like 5:

5. John went hunting with five bucks in his pocket.

Of course, 5 could be disambiguated by inferences about the relative sizes of deer and pockets, etc., but that would not even be possible in Riesbeck's proposed system, since he claims that the conceptual predictions will cause the analyser to find only one sense as soon as the word is encountered, so the 'dollar' sense would not even be available for further inference. For those who find the 'buck' example implausible, there is the following example (from the author's own experience) of a 'conceptual context' predicting the wrong sense. Several people are discussing cooking, recipes, ideas for meals, etc., and one participant says 6:

6. I've run out of ideas for meals – I'll have to grill my aunt the next time I see her.

The ambiguity of 'grill' ('cook' or 'interrogate') was not noticed by the speaker or his listeners, and the intended sense was not that associated with the conceptual context. These arguments against Riesbeck's idea might be irrelevant if his proposals were put forward simply as a 'quick trick' which might make a natural language front-end more efficient. However, Riesbeck is not working within that methodological framework – his declared subject matter is 'cognitive mechanics', and so counter-examples from human sentence processing are relevant.

The other half of Riesbeck's claim (i.e. that his analyser avoids the need for syntactic information) is simply false. Inspection of his example 'requests' reveals the presence of much traditional syntax – e.g. tests such as 'Is input an NP?'. Also, there are syntactic nesting devices for analysing noun phrases, and registers labelled 'SUBJ' and 'OBJ' for holding surface subject and object.(See Ritchie (1980: Section 2.8) and Wilks (1975a, and Chapter 11 in this volume) for further discussion).

3.2 Wilks' Preference Semantics

Another supposedly non-syntactic analyser was that of Wilks (1973a, 1975b), which was part of a machine-translation system at Stanford University in the early 1970s. This system used a large number (several hundred) of 'primitives', which were atomic symbols such as 'MAN', 'FOLK', 'PART'. These items, when grouped into trees, made 'formulae', and each word-sense had a formula to represent its meaning, as for example,in 7:

7.

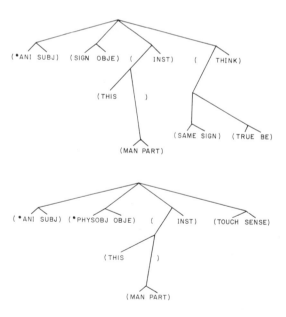

This (from Wilks 1978) shows two senses of the verb 'grasp' (namely, understanding an idea, and taking hold of a physical object). The items marked with a '•' are a short-hand device indicating a finite set of atomic primitives – MAN falls within *ANI, for example. The top-right primitive in the formula ('THINK' and 'SENSE' respectively in the above formulae) is called the 'head' of the formula.

The processing rules include 'templates', which are patterns, usually of three primitives. The input sentence is passed through an initial 'fragmenter' which clusters the words into small phrases or groups. A template matcher then tries to find, for each fragment, a template (or several) which will match it, in the sense that three words in the fragment have formulae whose heads match those in the bare template. The resulting structure (i.e. template plus matching formulae) is a 'filled template', and the semantic representation of the string is given, at this stage, by the sequence of filled templates thus constructed. Further routines then try to find links between these filled templates in various ways, using (among other things) rules called 'paraplates' which specify how adjuncts may be fitted into case-slots (to use conventional terminology for a moment).

The essential characteristic of this system (other than its lack of emphasis on syntax) is the use of semantic 'preference'. Whereas many systems (e.g. Winograd 1972) use the linguistic notion of 'selectional restrictions' (Katz and Fodor 1963) to reject semantically anomalous constructions (see Section 5.4 below), Wilks' analyser merely *prefers* some combinations to others. In this way, slightly non-standard subjects and objects may be allowed (e.g. 'My car drinks gasoline'), but ambiguity is resolved by selecting the most preferred reading. This assessment is done after the filled templates have been constructed, by checking how many of the 'preferences' specified in the formulae have been satisfied by the neighbouring items (e.g. the formulae in 7 above indicate a preference for a SUBJ which is '*ANI').

As in the case of Riesbeck's work, the system cannot be said to be non-syntactic, since both the fragmenting and the later 'tying together' routines use a large amount of syntactic information. In particular, the fragmenting (which is wholly syntactic) occurs before the semantic template matching, and there is no facility for 'feed- back' (i.e. revoking fragmentation decisions). Neither Wilks' program nor that of Riesbeck deals with questions of reference (see Sections 5.2, 5.3 below). Further details of 'preference semantics' can be found in Chapter 11 of this volume, and Boguraev (1980) describes an extension of Wilks' work, together with some constructive criticism of the original version.

3.3 Semantic ATNs

The ATN grammar mechanism (see Chapter 4 of this volume) was originally introduced for the writing of syntactic recognition grammars, but the idea of using this kind of grammar for semantic processing was proposed in the mid-1970s, mainly by workers at BBN (Burton 1976, Woods et al. 1976). In this approach, the arc and state labels in the ATN grammar are no longer simply syntactic categories, but include semantic categories indicating the items which the words and phrases may refer to. For example, Woods et al. give this example of a semantic ATN sub-network.

8.

A grammar like this is supposed to have various advantages. There is no need to build a separate 'syntactic structure', and semantic checking can be embedded directly in the grammar, with the result that only semantically well-formed input is accepted.

There are two main drawbacks to this way of designing parsers. The grammar is appropriate only for one subject matter, and cannot be used on any other domain (since categories like 'trip', 'meeting' are embedded in it). A complete new grammar is needed for a separate subject area. Also, it is not clear how the various sub-networks for different semantic categories are to be designed. Is the sub-network for parsing a 'trip' radically different from that for parsing a 'meeting'? The range of ways of expressing these referential items are roughly the same (traditional noun phrases, in fact). This gives the grammar-writer three options:

A) build separate networks for each such category, even though they may be essentially the same.
B) restrict the allowable ways of expressing the different categories so that there are genuinely different sub-networks.
C) have the same sub-network for several labels (an old-style 'NP' network, probably), possibly with semantic tests at its conclusion.

None of these are particularly elegant, but the proponents of semantic ATNs do not claim to have a theoretically general linguistic mechanism – they put it forward as a technique for programming specific systems in a fast, efficient way. (See Ritchie 1978a for a more detailed discussion).

4. LIMITS OF SEMANTIC PREDICTION

Both Riesbeck's CD analyser and Burton's semantic ATNs are limited (from the point of view of a general theory of parsing) by their (claimed) dependence on semantic categories (and predictions) for organizing processing. At the lower levels of sentence-processing, the parser (or 'analyser') has to handle words, grouping them into phrases, etc., and most of the structuring at this level is not predictable (during a left-to-right scan) from semantic information, nor do there seem to be natural semantic categories round which processing units can be organized.

Consider the question of high-level semantic (or conceptual) prediction. After a parser has executed a phrase like 9, it may be able to make various predictions about what is to come, as summarized A-C

9. John swallowed....

A) Surface abstract syntax: an item to be the surface object.
B) Deep abstract syntax: an item to fill the 'patient' case role.
C) Referential semantics: an item which can refer to an 'ingestible' material.

(This terminology is elaborated in Ritchie 1978a, b, 1980). Notice that there is no valid prediction of the concrete syntax of the item (i.e. the low-level structure which the item will have). The object phrase could take any of several forms:

10a. ... a biscuit.
  b. ... what he had in his hand.
  c. ... the contents of the bag.

Hence, although predictions like those in A - C may activate certain checking routines, it is unrealistic to expect them to start up specific low-level parsing processes. There will have to be a concrete syntactic parse (possibly bottom-up) before these top-down expectations can take effect. This is a generalization of the criticism made earlier of semantic ATNs – low-level processing units (i.e. phrase sub-networks) do not fall naturally into semantic categories.(See Ritchie 1978b for a fuller argument).

5. INTERLEAVED SEMANTIC PROCESSING

Various systems, including the SHRDLU program (Winograd 1972), have included a degree of interleaved processing. There were two main aims behind this. Firstly, it was thought that allowing semantic 'feed-back' to the parser would avoid unnecessary structure-building or searching (as discussed at the start of Section 2 above). In fact, it is very difficult to find many convincing examples of this although we shall discuss one or two below. Secondly, performing semantic processing as early as possible in the left-to-right scan was felt to be a more plausible model of human linguistic behaviour, in view of psychol-inguistic evidence (cf. comments in Section 3 above).

In this section, we shall look at the general problem of how to carry out useful semantic processing at an early stage, not confining attention simply to the notion of 'feed-back' to a syntactic parser. Hence, much of the discussion will apply equally to a 'non-syntactic' (or 'homogeneous') analyser, since we will often be addressing the general question of whether there is enough information locally available, during the scan of the string, to allow full semantic processing to proceed.

5.1 Compatibility checks

The SHRDLU program (Winograd 1972) associated a list of 'semantic markers' with each semantic structure that it built during parsing, and the idea was that the internal composition of this list could be checked for consistency while the structure was being built. Thus, for example, a phrase like 11 would (presumably) be classed as semantically anomalous, since it has two conflicting 'colour' markers.

11.*a green red block

In fact, it is extremely hard to find illustrative examples from Winograd's BLOCKS world, since the range of semantic combinations is so limited (and none are included in the published sample dialogue, which is taken as defining SHRDLU's performance), but the notion is clear in principle, being a direct adoption of the suggestions of Katz and Fodor(1963).

There are two main problems with this as a practical aid to parsing. Firstly, it is quite hard to define formally the criteria for 'semantic consistency'. If each 'object semantic structure' (Winograd's term for a noun-group meaning) has a fixed set of possible attributes (colour, size, etc.) and can have at most one value for each attribute, then this check is fairly straightforward. The range of natural language meanings for which this is a reasonable approximation is quite small. What makes it difficult to apply this arrangement widely is the tendency for adjectives to have relative meanings, rather than indicating absolute values on a scale. For example, it has often been observed that 'a small elephant' is larger than 'a large flea', since an adjective like 'small' means 'small for the class of things being described'. Thus phrases like those marked in 12a and b are quite acceptable, and 12c is valid in the author's idiolect.

12a. He is a *tall midget*.
  b. The land was ruled by a *benevolent tyrant*.
  c. The Ford Fiesta is quite a *large small car*.

The second difficulty with this form of semantic checking is its *local* nature, within the sentence or context. A phrase or clause which seems to violate this simple form of semantic consistency when considered in isolation, may function perfectly smoothly in context. This point was argued at some length (within the framework of transformational grammar) by McCawley (1968), as part of a criticism of the original Katz and Fodor version. McCawley observes that a seemingly 'ill-formed' clause or phrase may occur in a well-formed sentence:

13a. It is nonsense to speak of a rock having diabetes.
  b. He says that he poured his mother into an inkwell.

It might be argued that this deficiency can be patched up by incorporating the provision that various embedding constructions (e.g. 'It is nonsense....') switch off the semantic checking, but the relevant construction may not appear until after the questionable phrase has been parsed :

14. A round square is a puzzling idea.

Even if we assume that some coherent way can be devised for the embedding construction to disable the semantic checking (and this is not trivial), the fact that it may occur after the checks have been carried out means that it is difficult to perform such checks at a purely local level while parsing.

It might be possible to use such semantic consistency-checking if the result was not a simple success/failure judgement, but was some kind of 'rating' of the 'plausibility' of the item (as, for example, in the 'preference semantics' of Wilks, mentioned in Section 3.2 above). Even then, computing preferences on a local basis may lead to problems (see Ritchie 1980: Section 8.3 for a brief discussion).

5.2 Sense and reference

Before proceeding to discuss some of the other devices which have been proposed for early semantic processing, it is necessary to explain an analogy between computational approaches to meaning and certain ideas from philosophical logic.

Frege expounded the difference between two notions of meaning – 'sense' and 'reference' (Geach and Black 1960). The 'sense' of a phrase was what we would call its 'semantic structure', and retained some of the way in which the meaning was expressed in the original phrase.

The 'reference' was what the phrase (and its 'sense') referred to in the real world (now often called the 'referent' of the phrase). Frege's example was 'the morning star' and 'the evening star' (which are both old-fashioned locutions for a particular bright spot which appears in the sky at sunrise and sunset). These phrases mean different things (they have different 'senses') but in fact the object they refer to (the planet Venus) is the same (they have a single 'referent'). This distinction is not only intuitively satisfying, it allows a systematic treatment of certain language phenomena which are not amenable to an approach based only on 'reference' as a theory of meaning. Modern intensional logic includes sophisticated developments of this simple insight, in which 'senses' can have different 'referents' in different 'states of the world' (e.g. Montague 1972).

Much of recent work in artificial intelligence uses programs (or complex data structures) to represent 'meanings', and often these items can be 'evaluated', in a given context, to produce a result which is the object referred to by the 'meaning'. There is an analogy here with the traditional Fregean ideas – the 'sense' corresponds to the procedural meaning structure and the 'referent' corresponds to the result of evaluating the procedure in a particular environment. Evaluating the procedure in different environments (states of the world) can give rise to different results (referents) for the same procedural 'sense'. (See Davies and Isard 1972, Winograd 1976 and Ritchie 1980: Chapter 6 for a fuller discussion of these concepts). This comparison will be central to the arguments presented in Section 5.3 below.

5.3 Reference evaluation

One part of the dialogue in Winograd (1972) which is sometimes cited as exemplifying the use of semantic (or 'real-world') knowledge during parsing is the following:

PUT THE BLUE PYRAMID ON THE BLOCK IN THE BOX

This is syntactically ambiguous, but is understood without ambiguity since the parsing corresponding to 'put the blue pyramid which is on the block in the box' does not make sense in the current scene, while 'put the blue pyramid on the block which is in the box' does. (Winograd 1972).

The rest of the published account of SHRDLU does not give a detailed explanation of how this particular effect is achieved. Marcus (1980) suggests that the mechanism involves the comparison, during parsing, of two alternative syntactic structures and their BLOCKS-world interpretations, but this does not seem to fit in with the rest of the Winograd account, in which parsing proceeds depth-first. The rule implied by the above quotation seems to be as follows:

15. After building an object-semantic structure, use it at once to locate a BLOCKS world object. If none can be found, cause this parse to fail.

This rule (which is how Woods (1973) interprets Winograd's proposal) certainly does not generalize to ordinary language use, since it is commonplace to use phrases for which the hearer may not have a referent already:

16. The *principal of our university* lives in *a beautiful detached house.*

Winograd (1972: 156) mentions this kind of example, but does not comment on their relationship to the implied rule 15. To amend 15 to cover just those examples in which lack of a referent does lead to semantic anomaly is quite complex, since the set of expressions to which it must apply is not simply those which are syntactically 'definite' (see Ritchie 1980: Chapter 6 for a fuller discussion of this).

Let us assume for the moment that the relevant re-formulation of 15 can be found (e.g. 17), and examine whether this rule can in fact be applied on a local basis (i.e. during parsing).

17. For those noun phrases which have an 'assumed referent', try to compute this referent as soon as the phrase is complete. If none can be found, cause the parse to fail.

As mentioned in Section 5.2 above, the process of running a procedure-meaning to compute a result-referent will have different effects depending on the environment (state of the world). A phrase like 'the man sitting on the table' could refer to someone sitting on the table now, or to someone sitting on the table at some other time, as Winograd (1972: 146) points out. The context of the utterance should make it clear what the relevant time-point is. In trying to use 17 (or something like it) during parsing, the question arises of whether the relevant information (i.e. an indication of the appropriate environment) will be available when the phrase has just been completed. The contextual clues to the intended 'state of the world' are often conveyed by time adjuncts (or tense-markers – see Isard 1974), and these may occur some distance after the noun phrase under consideration.

18a. The president of the United States was shot in 1963.
  b. The king of France lived at Versailles for some years.

The relevant 'environment' for reference evaluation is therefore not always available as soon as the noun phrase is completed, and reference-evaluation may have to be postponed until it is. This undermines the usefulness of a rule like 17 for local processing. (See Ritchie (1976) for further discussion, and Bien (1976) for other issues involving reference-environments).

5.4 Selectional restrictions

It has frequently been observed, in both AI and linguistics, that most English verbs are restricted in the range of items that they may take as subjects, objects, etc. For example, the verb 'marry' requires an underlying subject which is 'HUMAN', and the verb 'flow' should have a subject which is 'LIQUID' (see Hayes 1975 for a discussion). This kind of information can sometimes be useful to eliminate possible structural ambiguity during parsing. The form 'NP V-ed' at the start of an English clause, is ambiguous between a past tense Subject + Main Verb combination (as in 19a), or a Subject + Passive Modifier (as in 19b).

19a. The army attacked the fort.
  b. The army attacked by Napoleon was crushed.

In 19a and b, the selectional restrictions of 'attack' give no clue to the parser (when it has scanned just 'The army attacked...'), since 'army' is an equally plausible subject or object for 'attack'.
In 20, the ambiguity is resolved, if we assume that the verb 'paint' cannot take 'landscape' as its subject.

20. The landscape painted...

The preferred structure here is that corresponding to 19b. This technique is of limited application, since many verbs do not have sufficiently constrained selectional restrictions to make the choice (as in 19). Also, as Wilks has often observed (see Section 3.2 above) selectional restrictions are freely violated in fairly ordinary English. Another obstacle to using this kind of information is the fact that it requires the phrases in question to display their semantic properties in a useable way. That is, a simple phrase like 'the landscape' may have semantic features that are fairly easy for the parser to access, but other phrases may be more complex (e.g. 'what was lying on the floor') or simply uninformative (e.g. 'something'). It might be possible to alleviate this difficulty by using some extra tricks to compute the semantic characteristics of an item from those of its parts, so that 'what he saw' is computed to be 'VISIBLE'. The necessary rules would not be wholly trivial, since modifiers can have a marked effect on the semantic features of the head of an item – a 'dead cat' is not 'ANIMATE'. Although this idea was suggested (in a rather casual fashion) in Ritchie (1976), it has not been properly explored.
  Another possibility that might allow access to an item's inherent semantic properties is reference evaluation. That is, although a phrase like 'what is on the table' may not overtly display semantic details, if the hearer (or program) can immediately compute the intended referent, that may provide richer information. It is not at all obvious

that there are realistic examples in which this approach would actually resolve structural ambiguity, and it introduces the various problems of immediate reference evaluation that were discussed in Section 5.3 above. It is mentioned here only because it would appear to be a possibility, on the basis of the formal structure of the problem.

5.5 General inference

So far (Sections 5.1 to 5.4) we have considered specific devices that might be incorporated into parsing and/or semantic interpretation rules in order to allow semantic information to be used during parsing. There is, of course, the wider approach, in which a system of world knowledge is assumed to be available during parsing, together with some form of inference rules which carry out arbitrarily complex reasoning. The results of these inferences may then influence the parser.

It is remarkably hard to construct examples in which this kind of information can be used to guide parsing (in the sense of using the 'feed-back' to resolve structural attachment within a syntax tree). Even examples of the use of world knowledge to resolve ambiguity (which are often cited within AI and linguistics) rarely involve semantic processing *during parsing*

This can be illustrated with some typical examples. The sentence 21 includes a lexical ambiguity – the verb 'ran' could mean 'moved quickly on foot' or 'organized'.

21. My uncle ran the London Marathon.

This ambiguity might be resolvable by the hearer, if he knew more about the referent of the subject phrase. If he knew that the 'uncle' in question was a young athlete, he might prefer the first interpretation; if he knew that the 'uncle' was an elderly administrator with the Greater London Council, the second reading would probably dominate. Notice that nothing in the structural part of the parsing depends on this decision, so it is not pertinent to the question of 'feed-back' aiding a syntactic parser. Even in terms of the broader question of performing 'early' semantic processing (as a generally desirable way of organizing an analyser), there are few convincing examples of inference being able to provide useful information *at intermediate stages of the analysis*. The resolution of 21 requires the whole clause, as do the following examples, borrowed from Winograd and Wilks respectively.

22a. The council refused a permit to the protesters because they feared civil disorder. ('they' = 'council').
  b. The council refused a permit to the protesters because they advocated civil disorder. ('they' = 'protesters').

23a. The soldiers fired at the women and some of them fell. ('them' = 'women').

b. The soldiers fired at the women and some of them missed. ('them' = 'soldiers').

6. SOME PROPOSALS FOR INTERLEAVED SEMANTICS

6.1 Semantic rule trees

One of the motivations for some of the 'non-syntactic' approaches (e.g. Riesbeck's) seems to be the intuition that traditional syntax trees are a redundant construct for a program whose prime aim is the computation of meaning. Surface structure trees, at first glance, do not have anything directly to do with meaning. This appearance is deceptive, in that the hierarchical grouping of linguistic constituents is a useful preliminary step to applying hierarchically organized semantic rules (as in Woods et al. 1972 – see Section 2.1 above). Coupling syntactic and semantic rules around a tree-structure is a common theme in many approaches to language (e.g. Katz and Fodor 1963, Winograd 1972, Montague 1968, ordinary predicate logic), and could, in principle, be used as the basis for interleaved semantics.

The program described in Ritchie (1977) (see Ritchie 1980 for a less detailed summary) worked in the following way. An ATN-based parser scanned sentences from left to right, building a surface structure tree as it went. Each non-terminal node of the tree had an attached 'combining rule' (placed there by the parser) which specified how the semantic structures of the daughter nodes were to be merged to form the 'meaning' for that node. (cf. the rule-trees of Montague 1968). Each rule was executed as soon as all its arguments (i.e. the daughter nodes) were available, and the result was stored at that point in the tree, so that the rule at the next node up the tree could use it. This meant that the semantic structure for each constituent (subtree) was built as soon as possible.

Unfortunately, since all daughter nodes (arguments) had to be ready before applying a rule, a large subtree might remain unprocessed if any of its subtrees were incomplete. In this way, lack of an item low down the tree might hold up the semantic processing of quite a large part of the input. To try to avoid this, it might be possible to divide each combining rule into 'components', one for each argument-place. On obtaining the nth argument, the nth component could be executed. The only place where this seemed to produce benefit was in the placement of subjects, objects, etc., into their appropriate roles around the verb (the case frame, to use the usual Fillmore terminology). If a constituent could be slotted into the verb frame as soon as it was built, then any selectional restrictions that were attached to the slot could be checked immediately. For other constructions, the use of 'rule components' was less successful, since very few semantic combinations of constituents allowed this kind of subdivision in a useful way. There was the additional problem that the consequences of applying the first component of a rule (thus building a partial semantic structure) would not usually allow the effects to propagate up the rule tree, unless the next rule (further up the tree) could accept the partial structure.

Although the use of a semantic rule tree, in which each node was evaluated as soon as possible, was quite elegant and theoretically attractive, the grammar written for that program did not provide any convincing examples of real benefits from this form of early semantic processing.

6.2 Psi-Klone

Bobrow and Webber (1980a, b) outline a system in which semantic interpretation is carried out at frequent intermediate stages of the syntactic parsing. The parser is based on an ATN grammar, and performs structure-building by executing arc-actions which pass messages to a semantic component. The semantic component tries to carry out the structure-building requested by the parser, and either performs it or passes back a 'fail' message. The receipt of a 'fail' message causes that arc to fail, and the ATN parser backs up in the normal way. This arrangement gains most of the advantages of separating syntax and semantics (modular design, portability of syntactic rules to different domains), but allows a large amount of semantic checking to occur, by having every proposed structure considered for its semantic effect. (The mechanism is described as being a form of 'cascaded ATN grammar' (Woods 1980), but the use of ATNs for the semantic processing is not described in detail in the papers cited; it is not clear how the strict left-right ordering imposed by an ATN is adapted for the less order-dependent constructs at the semantic level).

The 'messages' passed from the parser to the semantic component are of the form

24. *(M, L, C)*

where M (the 'matrix') is some half-built constituent, C is a constituent of some kind, and L is a label naming some syntactic relation. A triple like this is to be interpreted as a proposal that C be attached to M by a link labelled L. If the semantic component allows this, it passes back a symbolic name which the parser can then use to refer to the result of this structure-building (i.e. the updated matrix) in later messages. The semantic component processes one of these *(M, L, C)* messages using 'relation-mapping rules' (RMRULES), which are applied on receipt of a message from the parser, and which determine what semantic relation would correspond to *L*. Each RMRULE has three patterns, which describe the range of *(M, L, C)* triples it applies to (one pattern for each of *M*, *L* and *C*). If the patterns match the message, then the rest of the RMRULE supplies the semantic relation that *L* should be mapped into. These relations are like roles or cases in other systems. Once all the constituents of a particular matrix have been attached in this way, there are other interpretive rules (IRULES), attached to the various semantic relations, which are applied to convert this case-frame-like structure into a full semantic item for the matrix.

The RMRULES are like the 'rule-components' in the previous section, but have a restricted area of responsibility – instead of trying to build part of the final semantic structure, they merely compute a suitable case-label and use this to attach the 'daughter' item. This is presumably something which can be done reliably on a local basis. The IRULES pick up the arguments which have been set out by the RMRULES and combine them suitably, with the choice of IRULES being determined by the semantic roles assigned by the RMRULES and by the semantic category of the matrix.

Bobrow and Webber also outline a special technique for attaching prepositional modifiers (see Section 2 above), in which the longest modifier to be found is tried, semantically, in all possible attachments before re-parsing to find shorter possible modifiers. It is quite hard to assess these proposals on the basis of the summary given in the cited papers, but the overall scheme seems attractive; its empirical usefulness remains to be proven (cf. comments in 6.1 above).

6.3 Reference evaluation by constraint satisfaction

Mellish (1980, 1981) has developed an approach to semantic processing in which the semantic structures are built as soon as possible during parsing, but where uncertainties are left unresolved until there is sufficient information to determine the correct analysis. It is not feasible to outline the whole system here, but we will briefly consider Mellish's elegant mechanism for reference evaluation. The program acts as a front-end to a large program which reads in and solves elementary mechanics problems such as are found in a school textbook (Bundy et al. 1979). Hence most of the sentences which the analyser has to process are declarative statements, from which the system has to build up a small 'world model' of physical objects. For example,

25a. A bridge sixty feet long is supported by a pier at each end.
  b. Small blocks, each of mass m, are clamped at the ends and at the centre of a light rod.
  c. One painter stands on the scaffold four feet from the end.

This means that the set of possible referents for any noun phrase is typically small, and sometimes directly listable, thus simplifying slightly the processes of reference evaluation and pronoun disambiguation.

Noun phrases are initially interpreted into symbolic referents ('ref(1)', 'ref(2)', etc.), and the actual referents for these are computed using any information that is available to the analyser (including general inferences about blocks, pulleys, etc.). The information conveyed by the noun phrase itself, the enclosing sentence, and the general context, can all contribute 'constraints' which limit what the phrase refers to. In this way, the accumulation of information during sentence analysis can be seen as the gradual imposition of more constraints until the set of possible referents (or referent sets) is sufficiently reduced. Since these constraints do not apply simply to single items in isolation, but may express a relation between two items (e.g. SUPPORT(ref(1), ref(3))), elimination of possible referents for one referring expression may, via the constraints, reduce the allowable sets for some other referring expressions. This leads to a formal similarity with Waltz' procedure for labelling line-drawings (Waltz 1975), and so Waltz' highly efficient constraint-satisfaction algorithm can be used here. The following simple example illustrates this procedure. (This example merely demonstrates the process of referent selection by constraint satisfaction – it does not illustrate the use of this technique at stages throughout a clause. Also, the whole process has been greatly simplified for the purposes of exposition, and the interested reader should consult Mellish (1981) for details). Consider the sentence:

26. A uniform rod is supported by a string attached to its ends.

The word 'its' could, from a syntactic point of view, refer to either the rod or the string; a human reader normally takes the referent to be the rod. The reasoning behind this pronoun resolution can be mechanised quite neatly using a system of constraints.

We will assume that, at the stage where we are trying to determine the reference of 'its', that there are three symbolic expressions under consideration – ref(1) ('it'), ref(2) and ref(3) (the 'ends'). There are also six world objects (ROD1, STRING1, and the ends of these two objects) which provide candidates for ref(1), ref(2) and ref(3). The pertinent information available is as follows:

A) left-end(ref(1), ref(2)): by definition of ref(1) and ref(2)
B) right-end(ref(1), ref(3)): by definition of ref(1) and ref(3)

C) attached(ref(2), STRING1): from phrase
   'a string attached to its ends'
D) attached(ref(3), STRING1): from phrase
   'a string attached to its ends'

As mentioned earlier, the analyser has full access to a general inference system which embodies knowledge of the world model so far built, and which has various general rules about the possible configurations of objects within such worlds. One such rule expresses the fact that an object cannot be attached to its own ends. Hence, for the new information conveyed by C and D to make sense, there must be the following pre-conditions:

E) separate(ref(2), STRING1)
F) separate(ref(3), STRING1)

That is, the various assertions involved derive from three kinds of source – 'given' information (e.g. A and B), 'new' information (e.g. C and D), and prerequisites (e.g. E, F). Now this information has consequences for the candidate sets of certain symbolic referents. Constraints E and A mean, using a fairly simple inference, that STRING1 cannot be in the candidate set for ref(1); hence, the only candidate for ref(1) is ROD1. Although this resolves the pronoun reference, the constraint checking can be continued to ensure that a consistent interpretation has been found.

The fact that ref(1) is ROD1, together with constraint A, implies that ref(2) must be an end of ROD1 and similarly ref(3) is an end of ROD1. These are both compatible with all the constraints.

7. A DIFFICULT PROBLEM

Two main issues have been examined in this chapter – whether sentence-analysers can be organized around semantic constructs (rather than syntactic units), and the extent to which semantic processing can be carried out locally as the sentence is parsed. The answer proposed to the first question has been negative, (a view which has been reflected in the recent trend back to the use of non-trivial syntax, as in Marcus (1980)). The second question (early or immediate semantic processing) is more awkward. Psycholinguistic evidence seems to suggest that people absorb much (or all) of the semantic content of a sentence on a word-by-word basis, but it is very hard to design a clean, systematic, theoretically defensible way of programming such a mechanism.

11

Deep and Superficial Parsing

Y. Wilks

1. INTRODUCTION

In this chapter I will discuss two types of parsing system which I shall distinguish as *deep* and *superficial*. Part of my aim is to show that they are not as different as might appear or as some of their proponents claim. What they have in common from the outset is the desire to avoid conventional syntactic parsing from surface sentences to hierarchical (tree-like) constituents. A number of systems of linguistic syntax, particularly those in the Halliday tradition and, more recently (Hudson 1980) could come under this general heading, but I shall restrict myself to proposals within the AI/psychology tradition.

I shall set out two paradigm cases in a moment, but first give a little further clarification of the terms *deep* and *superficial*.

It is tempting initially to define deep systems as those which aim to parse directly from English to a semantic representation of some kind without passing through any conventional syntax phase. It has sometimes been claimed of such systems that they do not make use of surface information, and this I believe to be false (and *interestingly* false). I use the word 'semantic' as a description of the representation aimed at, but in such a way as to include what Schank and his school intended by 'conceptual'. His choice was motivated by a desire to use a neologism over which he had some control, and thus to avoid the territorial disputes associated with 'semantic'. No difference of substance is at issue there.

I shall refer to two types of deep parsers: (1) the *micro*, producing representations corresponding to clauses using whatever representational machinery is required, which may include frames and scripts; and (2) the *macro*, which aims at representations that are inherently *textual* in some sense. This last distinction will break down in practice, but the latter category is intended to capture systems that it is claimed parse texts *directly* with frames or scripts, and without passing through either a syntactic analyser *or a micro-semantic analyser.*

Deep systems, then, avoid conventional syntax in general and aim for semantic representations without making any direct commitment about method. I will take this definition as excluding most Montague-type systems, because I will take their attachment to hierarchical syntax components as non-dispensible; and also as excluding Generative Semantics because, whatever the differences, its proponents retained a strong committment to the overall transformational paradigm.

Superficial systems, on the other hand, make little commitment about the nature of the representation, but strong commitments on method in that they are all committed to a view of language as (to put it crudely) a flat, linear, phenomenon, rather than a highly structured one.

1.1 Syntax and semantics

But whatever the opposition of deep to superficial parsing is to be taken to mean in this paper, it cannot be identified simply with a form of the syntax-semantics distinction. At one time this might have been a natural confusion because, in both AI and generative linguistics, syntax was associated with 'surfaceness' and semantics with 'depth' (although there were of course 'deep' syntactic structures as well during a long phase of generative grammar). In generative linguistics, a great change has come about in recent years in the role of semantics, and it (like much of syntax itself) is now taken to be a matter of interpretation of the surface. It is most important to remember that within AI, the systems that stressed the role of meaning (and were opposed to the dominant syntactic paradigm in linguistics) in the seventies included both those stressing the role of surface matching (Colby, see below) as well as those who stressed the distance of semantic representations from the surface (Schank, Wilks, see below). The deep-surface opposition has nothing *essentially* to do with the opposition of syntax to semantics.

1.2 The role of linguistic theory

The reaction of some readers may already be to ask why we do not leave the details of dead AI programs and look to the uplands of the linguistic discoveries of recent years. One form of such a reaction, when I argue below that some 'semantically orientated' AI systems were more superficial than their authors realized, would be to say 'Ah, well, the AI guys couldn't go on ignoring linguistic discoveries forever could they?' But that reaction would be, in my view, wholly misguided: 'superficial', in fact, in the worst sense.

On the contrary, the parsing developments within AI have been driven almost entirely by internal considerations. Even the work of Marcus and Woods, which is most often referred to as AI making use of linguistic theory, was in fact the product of procedural considerations and only later tied to linguistic theory: Marcus' notions of a wait-and-see-parser were fairly complete in Marcus (1975) and owed little or nothing to contemporary linguistics. A detailed scholar of these matters might show that Woods' (1970) argument that a transformational grammar had to be augmented by a surface grammar, of the sort an ATN provided (see chapter 4), before it could be relevant to parsing, must have had some influence on the present state of linguistics. If mutual indebtedness between the fields is to be explored, it is not at all clear on what foot the boots will end up.

It is hardly surprising, in retrospect, that linguistic theory should have had so little direct influence on parsing technique for so long a period: parsing is wholly performance, and unashamedly *directional* (i.e. surface *to* structure), the very things that a competence theory was not to be. However, and in spite of all this, there are striking similarities in the drift of change and criticism in the two areas: much of the discussion below on the long-unnoticed surfaceness of semantic and conceptual structures in AI systems, could be paralled in the linguistic history of the period. There were, for example, the well-known problems raised by the survival of English SVO form in deep structures, and the consequences of the appearance of English lexemes in deep structures where something less surfacey, if not downright universal, might have been more plausible.

The role of this brief section is simply to declare, if not justify, the single-minded concentration of this chapter on AI systems so as to discuss the opposition of deep to superficial parsing; whatever linguistic discoveries there may be in this area, they have been won by the same kind of trial and error process as AI discoveries, and have no special merit in terms of scientific status.

1.3 Parsing and expert systems

Another initial thought that may occur to some readers is that what unites much AI research, more widely than questions of natural language, is the belief that structures representing human knowledge – not essentially *of* language, but of how the world works – are essential for human understanding, and that much of our operation of language itself is dependent on such knowledge. It might be thought that, since such knowledge is probably stored in non-linguistic form then, if it constitutes 'deep structures' for language understanding, in any sense, then an AI theory of parsing must be a deep one: in the precise sense of being done by means of, and into, structures that have no discernible relic in them of surface language form.

Suppose, for example, that our understanding of language about liquids is based upon our real knowledge of the behaviour of liquids – what Hayes (1978) has called the 'naive physics' of liquids – then that might be expected to owe nothing whatever to language structure, since it is probably stored in some analogue form: in terms of chemical solution parameters, perhaps. If this example, taken at random, is a good guide to the understanding of human language then it would be hopeless to look for any distinctive theory of human language, for it could be no more than a by-product of our representation of the world and our own expertise. It might, curiously, have the universality sought by Chomskyans (since the representation of liquids may well be the same in all human brains of the same composition and structure), but would have few other features congenial to them.

However, the assumptions just discussed are not necessarily true: it is a matter of the merest speculation what the stored forms of different types of human knowledge are (the present author suspects that much of it may be stored in ways more language-like than many in AI suspect), and what the relation of such knowledge to the representation and analysis of natural language is. It is not even obvious that an expert systems approach will be what we are here calling 'deep parsing': the 'semantic grammar' approach of Burton (chapter 10) is both expertise-based and wholly superficial, in the precise sense that the items of the grammar are technical words arranged on a network and matched directly to text. Whatever may be the technical *power* of any particular example of such a grammar, it is one where a word leads to expectations of other *words* and I shall take that (next section below) as a sufficient condition of being a superficial parsing system. To take a knowledge-or-expertise-based approach to parsing does not, of itself, make a system deep or superficial, and so discussions of expert systems also are independent of our main distinction.

1.4 The fundamental distinction reviewed

All parsers, of whatever type, ultimately tie their structures of representation, by rules, to surface words or other concrete cues. It could not be otherwise, and so that fact alone says nothing about whether a system is deep or superficial. In order to proceed to samples, I shall sum up the discussion so far by suggesting that any of the following be sufficient for calling a parsing system superficial:

A) the structure of representation achieved by the parsing process has either items or order of items that are those of the surface language analysed, and which have no *independent* justification.

B) the parsing process makes important use of partitioning the input text for analysis purposes, by the use of key words, punctuation, or perhaps even word counting.

C) the patterns to be matched against incoming text contain *sequences* of surface items. On this criterion, any system that could recognise a single idiom or lexicalised phrase would be superficial to that degree. Becker's phrasal lexicon (1975) would be some way further down that road, and a system working with a full sentence dictionary (per impossibile, but some working machine translation systems approach this state) would be fully superficial by this criterion.

D) there is no fully recursive treatment of embedded structures. By this criterion, only a full 'competence' grammar treatment of centre-embedding, say, would fail to be superficial. Any system with memory limitations for storing such structures (that is to say, any psychologically plausible system, that can simulate such structures by a finite state system) will be superficial on this count.

E) a variant of (A) above: the criteria used to establish the representation range over word names and not types (however expressed: markers, patterns of markers, inferences on non-word structures etc.).

F) which follows from the above: the representation, and the criteria for establishing it, must be such as to allow interesting generalizations above and beyond what the control structure itself provides (such as the control structure of a production system itself, if that is the parsing mechanism adopted: see below and chapter 3).

These criteria may not serve us well in what follows, and we should turn now to sample systems that have taken sides on the deep vs. superficial issue in a clear way, so as to see if these can help us better to see what the crucial issue is.

2. A PARADIGM SUPERFICIAL SYSTEM: COLBY

Colby (e.g. 1975) developed a well-known dialogue system PARRY which can converse indefinitely in the following vein (in upper case):

Have you been hospitalised before ?
THIS IS THE FIRST TIME.

How long have you been there ?
ABOUT TWO WEEKS.
Any headaches ?
MY HEALTH IS FINE.
Are you having any difficulty with your memory ?
NO.
Then perhaps you can tell me who is the President of the United States ?
NIXON IS PRESIDENT.
What day is it today ?
TODAY IS THURSDAY.
What season is it ?
LET'S GET ON WITH THE INTERVIEW.

Fragility in operation is avoided by having no conventional syntax analyser, and by not even attempting to take account of all the words in the input. This is a considerable aid, since any parser that begins to parse a more than usually polite request such as 'Would you be so kind as to ...' is going to be in trouble. British English speakers arriving in the U.S. quickly learn not to use such phrases, since they cause great confusion to human listeners in stores, etc., who may be presumed to be, like PARRY, seeking the 'give me a hamburger' that follows.

The input text is segmented by a heuristic that breaks it at any occurrence of a range of key words. Patterns are then matched with each segment. There are at present about 1,700 patterns on a list that is stored and matched, not against any syntactic or semantic representations of words (except to deal with contradictions and misspellings), but against the input word string direct, and by a process of sequential deletion. So, for example, 'What is your main problem?' has a root verb 'BE' substituted, and a generic 'YOU' for 'YOUR', to become

WHAT BE YOU MAIN PROBLEM

It is then matched successively against the stored pattern list in the following forms, each of which is formed by deleting one word from the original string in turn:

BE YOU MAIN PROBLEM
WHAT YOU MAIN PROBLEM
WHAT BE MAIN PROBLEM
WHAT BE YOU PROBLEM
WHAT BE YOU MAIN

Only the *penultimate* line exists as one of the stored patterns, and it is therefore matched by what we might call this *minimal parsing procedure*. Stored in the same format as the patterns are rules expressing the consequences for the 'patient' of detecting aggression and over-friendliness in the interviewer's questions and remarks. The matched patterns found are then tied directly, or via these inference rules, to response patterns wich are generated. Enormous ingenuity has gone into the heuristics of this system, as its popularity testified. Its view of language is as a linear sequence of partially instantiated word patterns. It is thus a superficial parser in exactly the sense of our initial criterion C.

Colby's method is, of course, open to the immediate rebuttal that it could match both 'John hit Mary' and 'John was hit by Mary' to the pattern:

JOHN HIT MARY

and so confuse active and passive. True, but a little sophistication of the method would allow both patterns:

JOHN HIT MARY
JOHN HIT BY MARY

in the list. The important question is how far such a simple method can be extended to cope with the complexity of English.

3. A PARADIGM DEEP SYSTEM: RIESBECK

Riesbeck's first parser (1975b and see chapter 10) was part of the MARGIE system and designed to parse English sentences into Schank's conceptual dependency diagrams in the linearised form. The construction of a parser for conceptual dependency notation was certainly no trivial task: although Schank gave procedures for extending the conceptual-isations – case inferences, for example – he did not, in any sense, give procedures for attaching the conceptual structures to natural language, nor did he consider it his task to provide the information to enable this to be done.

Riesbeck's parser is depth-first and becomes top-down almost immediately in the parsing process. Not immediately, because the conceptual structures to be parsed onto the text are 'cued in' by the appearance of the words of the sentence, examined from left to right. Riesbeck describes these structures as *expectations*: expectations, that is, about what else will be said, or has already been said, in the text; and these expectations are concretely expressed as *requests* associated with the appearance of text words. The strongest argument for this approach is that the most appropriate conceptual structures for what appears in a text are utterly unlike the superficial structure, and that these most appropriate structures are best applied as soon as possible in the parsing. The best example for showing this is Riesbeck's 'John gave Mary a beating' which, of course, has little to do with giving.

In Riesbeck's system the proper structure for this sentence is actually attached to 'beating', so that when 'beating' is reached, in going through the sentence, that proper conceptualisation (based on the primitive action PROPEL, and expressing the movement of John's hand) will, as it were, *take over* and supplant the request structures already satisfied during the analysis of the first four words of the sentence.

Below (figure 1) is Riesbeck's sequential table of requests (as input to a standard production system, see chapter 3) with the sentence words, as it is parsed from left to right, and expressed here as a sequence *down* the page.

NP here is the familiar grammar category noun-phrase. The table is quite easy to follow if we remember that the numbered requests in the third column remain active (and are thus passed down the third column) if they are not satisfied. The requests 5 and 6 called 'true' are simply default requests that will be satisfied automatically if nothing above them is.

What happens with the parsing of this sentence, put very roughly, is that the satisfaction of request 2 makes the parser think, as it were, that it is dealing with a sentence like 'John gave Mary a dollar'; hence its expectations about 'to' at step 2. It goes on believing this until requests 3 and 4 are reinstated at step 7 and request 4 is satisfied and not request 3, as would have been the case if Mary had been given a dollar.

The action taken at step 7 is to completely restructure the representation and to base it, not on the Schankian primitive act ATRANS (for 'give'), but on PROPEL (for 'beat'). This same method is applied to more complex sentences, such as those containing prepositional phrases. Let us look at the parsing of a prepositional phrase as in 'John prevented Mary from leaving by locking her in'.

There are three phases in the parsing:

1) 'Prevent' generates requests (expectations) for prepositions FROM and BY1. Let me call these objects *preposition-forms* for the moment. BY1 is what we can think of as a 'sense' of the preposition 'by'. If Riesbeck were using case description, we could say that BY1 is the 'manner case' manifestation of 'by', as opposed to its other case manifestations.

2) FROM itself has very complex requests associated with it such as FROMO:

```
(T(IMBED ← ((MOD QUOTE ((CANNOT)))
  (TIME CHOICE ← TIME)
  (SUBJ CHOICE OBJ))
 ((OR(EQ WORD(QUOTE BY))
 (RESET-ALL)NIL))
 NIL)
```

STEP	WORD READ	REQUESTS WAITING	REQUESTS TRIGGERED	ACTIONS TAKEN
0	none	1 - is there an NP?	none	none
1	John	1 - is there an NP?	1	assume John is subject of the verb to follow.
2	gave	2 - is the current NP a human? 3 - is the current NP an object? 4 - is the current NP an action? 5 - true	5	assume the word 'to', if it appears, introduces the recipient of the 'giving'.
3	Mary	2 - is the current NP a human? 3 - is the current NP an object? 4 - is the current NP an action?	2	assume Mary is the recipient of the 'giving'.
4	a	3 - is the current NP an object? 4 - is the current NP an action? 6 - true	6	save the current list of requests and replace it with: 7 - does the current word end an NP?
5	beating	7 - does the current word end an NP?	none	none
6	period	7 - does the current word end an NP?	7	build the NP 'a beating' and reset the list of requests
7	none	3 - is the current NP an object? 4 - is the current NP an action?	4	assume the NP action is the main action of the clause, the subject (John) is the actor and the recipient (Mary) is the object.

Figure 1

This is clearly a complex object and need not be fully explained to define its role, namely that of tying together two conceptualisations: one for the preventing and one for the leaving. It is written out here so that we can see that this request is seeking the (lexeme) preposition 'by' to follow it (fourth line from bottom).

3) The requests of BY1 are an even more formidable object than that above, but Riesbeck makes clear that it is seeking forms of primitive act to fit a following 'by' phrase should it occur, as it does in fact in the example sentence.

The system is highly superficial in the sense of criteria A and E above: it is *verbs* that seek *prepositions* (if FROMO is a preposition), rather than *basic actions* seeking *cases*. This surface method naturally makes it hard to state 'significant semantic generalizations', and is particularly odd in a parser that claims to be based on Schank who abhored all processing based on surface correlations. So, in that sense, Riesbeck's parser may be more independent of Schank's system than appears initially.

Another general, and related, problem is that Riesbeck wishes to avoid any intermediate structure, whether syntactic or semantic, between text words and the final conceptualisation. To do this he may, in the end, have to associate different requests with a word corresponding not only to different senses of the word, but to its syntactic positions. Riesbeck's request table shows how closely related requests are to syntactic order. That need not be fatal, even if so, but it would clearly make it hard to state any semantic generalizations that should be the heart of the system (criterion F above), and very hard to specify the word-by-word requests for a sentence of any length or complexity.

Part of this comes from general difficulties about uncontrolled expectation as a parsing mechanism, and the question of whether one can have a wholly depth-first parser, like Riesbeck's, if one has no back up. One might say that depth-first parsing, whether semantic or syntactic, requires a notion of failure and backup: that is to say, a notion of when a current structure has become *inapplicable*, and then of where, in the previous choices taken, to go back and try again. But almost all contemporary approaches are weak on failure and backup; indeed, part of the point of a top-down, frames-like, approach is to make backup much less needed. The tension comes in trying to combine this with a wholly depth-first parsing technique as Riesbeck as done. Or, to put this in slogan form, structures of expectation may have to be explored more than one at a time so as to simulate *attention*. Systems that do not attend are like people that do not attend but only expect what to hear. In neither case do they communicate or understand.

Exaggerated expectation involves what one could call the *phenom-*

enological fallacy: when understanding language as human beings we are never conscious of alternative interpretations, the fact that a word we read in context has many senses out of context, etc., therefore a semantic parser should not consider such alternatives either: if it has the right conceptual/semantic/preferential/frame structures in it, it will go directly in a depth-first manner to the correct reading and never consider any other.

The premise of this position is of course true, but the conclusion is totally false, and it is perhaps worth setting out why. Where it is wrong is in its assumption that the correct interpretation fits and the other possible interpretations *do not fit at all*. Hence the first path that can be followed will be the right one. The truth of the matter is that the right interpretation *fits better* than the others, but to see that we necessarily have to see how well the other possibilities fit.

One detailed example Riesbeck discusses is the parsing of 'John gave Mary the book' in which the action 'give' generates requests, one of which is that 'if what follows the verb immediately is human then assume it is RECIPIENT case, otherwise assume it is OBJECT case.' There is nothing in his description that allows any backup to an alternative request should one fail after appearing to succeed and this is consistent with the depth-first no backup position. So, for example, both the following perfectly natural sentences would be wrongly analysed on such a method: 'John gave Mary to the Iman of Oudh' and 'John gave his city his stamp collection'.

There is nothing the least tricky or bizarre about such sentences, and the examples show that simple unfettered expectation is not enough unless one can be sure one has one's criteria right, *or* one has some breadth-first way of considering alternatives *or* one has complex backup.

It could be argued that since Riesbeck has constructed a new parser ELI (see below, and Schank and Riesbeck 1981) therefore this criticism is out of date; to which I reply that although ELI is more bottom up, it is in essence the same system and, in any case, what I intend here is not so much criticism of Riesbeck as presentation of a paradigm. Moreover, it is highly significant, to me, that a parser, billed as deep, turns out, on examination, to rest upon such highly superficial items as *sequences of preposition names* explicitly stored as patterns to be sought after verbs, and without any relation to semantic generality.

4. ANOTHER DEEP SYSTEM: WILKS

This system (see also chapter 10) constructs a semantic representation for small natural texts: the basic representation is applied directly to the text and can then be 'massaged' by various forms of inference to become progressively less like the surface text, so as to perform tasks intended to demonstrate understanding. It is a uniform representation, in that information that might conventionally be considered as syntactic, semantic, factual or inferential is all expressed within a single type of structure. The fundamental unit of this meaning representation is the *template*, which corresponds to an intuitive notion of a basic message of agent-action-object form.

The system ran on-line as a package of LISP, MLISP and MLISP2 programs, the two latter languages being expanded LISP languages that have a command structure and pattern matching capacities. It took as input small paragraphs of English, that could be made up by the user from a vocabulary of about 600 word-senses, and produced a good French translation as output for a considerable range of input texts. This environment provided a pretty clear test of language understanding, because French translations for everyday prose are in general either right or wrong, and can be seen to be so while, at the same time, the major difficulties of understanding programs – word sense ambiguity, case ambiguity, difficult pronoun reference, etc. – can all be represented within a machine translation environment by, for example, choosing the words of an input sentence containing a difficult pronoun reference in such a way that the possible alternative references have different genders in French. In that way the French output makes quite clear whether or not the program has made the correct inferences in order to understand what it is translating.

The program was reasonably robust in actual performance, and would tolerate a certain amount of bad grammar in the input, since it did not perform a syntax analysis in the conventional sense, but sought message forms representable in the semantic structures employed.

The system contained no explicitly snytactic information at all: what it knows about any English word sense is its *formula*. This is a tree structure of semantic primitives, and is to be interpreted formally using dependency relations (examples are given in chapter 10).

Template structures, which actually represent sentences and their parts are built up as networks of formulas. Templates always consist of an agent node, an action node and an object node, and other nodes that may depend on these. So, in building a template for 'John beat the carpet' the whole of the tree-formula for 'beat' would be placed at the action node, another tree structure for 'John' at the agent node and so on. The complexity of the system comes from the way in which the formulas, considered as active entities, dictate how other nodes in the same template should be filled.

Thus, a full template is a complex structure. Here, for example, is one for 'John shut the door':

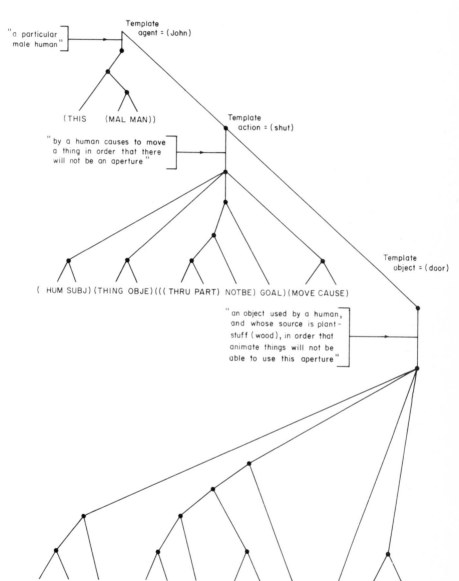

The process of matching such structures onto input text begins with *fragmentation*, a purely superficial process, in the sense of criterion B: the program goes through a sentence breaking it at key words like prepositions etc. This is done only on the basis of the list of key words plus the range of semantic formulas for each (non-key) word. A sentence like: 'The sort of man / that dogs like / is kind' would be fragmented at the two strokes as shown. Even this requires use of the formula semantics, so as to see that the 'that' is a relative that, and not a qualifier as it would be in 'The dog likes that man'.

Next come the procedures for matching templates onto fragments. First the parser goes through the formula combinations (for there will in general be more than one formula for each word, as formulas correspond to word-senses) for a fragment from left to right looking only at the *head* elements of the formulas. It looks for agent, action and object formulas, in that order initially. So, since all qualifier (adjective) formulas have KIND as their head, this procedure would never take a KIND-headed formula as a possible agent. This process is *bare template matching*, and is more complex than I have suggested here because fragments of text do not always have their main items in convenient agent-action-object order. So, there is a scale of preferred head sequences. Again, many fragments do not have all three formula types: 'John left' has no object, naturally enough, and so that node is filled out by a dummy so as to retain a canonical form of template. Finally, prepositions in English are always assigned to the action node, and so will always have corresponding dummy agent nodes.

There are about a thousand of the bare templates in the system: triple patterns of primitives like

<MAN GET THING>

which would match onto an infinite number of clauses like: 'John found a toy'. They are rather like Colby's patterns, but are not superficial in the sense of criterion E above, for they match onto parts of semantic formulas, not surface words. The bare templates are in no sense a representation, only devices by which the full templates, as for 'John shut the door' above can be created by a process of 'preferential expansion'.

In this phase, the contents of formulas are examined in the possible competing template matches for a fragment, and the system looks for those templates where the internal preferences of formulas (for neighbouring formulas) are in fact satisfied: thus a formula for 'drink' as a verb seeks an animate agent and so on. Again, in a template for 'John got a shock' the formula for 'shock' would seek an action indicating suffering rather than receipt, so the preferences are by no means only for verbs seeking noun groups.

Competing templates have their satisfied preferences added up, and the one with the greatest number becomes the structure for that template. This notion of always taking the representation with the greatest 'semantic density' of satisfied connections is the general rule driving the whole parsing. It is, as it were, looking for sentences with, in the extreme case, as little information as 'The shepherd tended his flock' where all default preferences are satisfied, and the sentence conveys almost nothing. This bias in no way prevents the system accepting sentences like 'The meeting broke up for half-an-hour' where such preferences are not satisfied, but no competing interpretation is available either, to supplant the preference-violating one (in the sense in which 'breaking up' does not prefer abstract or human-structure subject like 'meeting'). Such forms, and they are the norm in English, are just noted and accepted, as having ill-fitting templates.

When expanded templates have been constructed, the system then tries to fill any empty slots they may have, again on a preferential basis, and to extend the preference ties to the relationship between templates. The final text representation is a 'semantic block' of templates, with pointers tying anaphoric items and case dependencies between them. Thus, for 'The sort of man dogs like is kind' we should end up with something like:

$$
\left[
\begin{array}{ccc}
\text{the sort of man} & \& & \& \\
\text{dogs} & \text{like} & \& \\
\& & \text{is} & \text{kind}
\end{array}
\right]
$$

where '&' denotes a dummy agent, action or object.

Opting for the most densely packed block of templates as the preferred representation of a text is not arbitrary, for it is argued that this in fact is the representation one would expect on a least effort principle of language understanding. It should also be noted that this semantic block is only an initial representation in the system, one still very close to the input surface form: the next phase is the production of inferences (initially case inferences and the application of inference rules) from the semantic block, which are, although in template form themselves, not isomorphic to anything in the input text. Thus, using a GOAL, or purpose, case the system will infer from 'John aimed at a target' that he hit it. Even though that inference may often be factually false, it is easy to show that it is required for further anaphora and word sense ambiguity resolutions.

This whole approach has highly superficial and linear features:

1) the notion of representing a text as a linear chaining of templates, without any explicit hierarchical structure (though the pointers between templates and their nodes implicitly express one);
2) the fragmentation routine dividing the input at clause and phrase partitions does so mainly by access to formulas, but also has access

to mere lists (such as conjunctions etc.);
3) although there is no separate syntactic component, much of the structure of the formulas could be said to be syntactically motivated: there is, for example, a special primitive formula head GIVTEL for verbs that take indirect objects (i.e. *give*, *tell*, etc.). Thus *say* and *tell* would have their formulas distinguished on what one could call purely syntactic grounds, as would *arms* (head STUFF, in the hardware sense) and *weapons* (head THING). However, this point concerns the embedding of the syntactic information in the semantic codings, and not strictly the issue of depth and superficiality.

The last point indicates a crucial difference between the Riesbeck and Wilks systems: it is just such distinctions that Riesbeck would not allow into his representations because they could be said to reflect nothing about *meaning* (though one could use the whole case grammar tradition to argue that they do). But such matters have to appear *somewhere* in Riesbeck's system, and so they are added on later as an unmotivated sub-theory, like the preposition patterns described earlier.

He cannot reach a final, acceptable, meaning representation by stages of deepening an analysis to show equivalences, as the Wilks system does, because he explicitly rejects all intermediate representations, syntactic or semantic, in the English-to-CD transduction. However, Riesbeck's control structure (left-to-right single-pass) is far more perspicuous and psychologically plausible than Wilks' many-pass combinatorial approach.

I will conclude this section by making some points of contrast between the two systems' approaches to the English indirect object construction, because I believe an interesting moral can be drawn about the superficiality issue. I argued above that Riesbeck's treatment of (among other phenomena) the English indirect object would often go wrong. His system had a firm and unshakeable conviction that, if what followed *give* immediately was ANIMATE, then it was an indirect object, which, as we saw earlier, gets wrong forms like 'John gave Mary to the Imam of Oudh'.

Now it can well be argued that other productions could be added to the system to get this right and that I do not deny (and that has almost certainly been done in later Yale parsers described below). My case remains that the generalizations are then those of production systems themselves which, like old-fashioned TG, can do anything and, as Peters and Ritchie pointed out in the latter case, therefore say nothing specific at all about language (as opposed to, say, the mating habits of pigeons).

One alternative was what I called a 'preference' approach, on which the first item after a verb like *give* was attached directly to, and made dependent on, the verb; while the next appropriate item, if any, was made the object. The 'semantic densities' (found by counting such attachment arcs) were compared in the two cases. If there was no indirect object, as in 'John gave his rabbit', the more dense structure won out as always, because being a direct object counted for more than being an indirect object, because it held principal place in a template pattern. Thus in all cases the correct structure was imposed by a simple, 'greatest density' rule. There was only one problem: there was nothing particularly semantic about the whole business (except that the dictionary codings were uniform in type and in that sense semantic, since some of the information in the codings was indubitably semantic, such as the likely results of actions, etc.). But at bottom, it was all just slot filling and counting.

Relevant psychological evidence is along the following lines (see work by Quinn reported in Steedman and Johnson-Laird (1976)):

The boy gave the girl a toy
The girl gave the toy a boy
The boy gave the woman a man

where the first is understood much the fastest by subjects, and the other two much slower, with the last marginally the worst. If that is roughly how it is, then syntactically motivated approaches, *and* the preference approach just described for these constructions are implausible, because they all get all of them right and in the same way and at the same speed. (Worse still, the middle example is often, in fact, understood wrongly, as having a deleted *to* in it).

So the Wilks system could be said to fail with verbs of this type for quite different reasons from the Riesbeck system: Riesbeck's is (in Chomsky's phrase) observationally inadequate, whereas the Wilks system is observationally adequate but, in psychological terms, descriptively inadequate.

5. A HYBRID SYSTEM: WILENSKY AND ARENS

This system, called PHRAN (Wilensky and Arens 1980), is an interesting hybrid, in terms of the classification we are using: it is deep in that it aims to produce a meaning representation direct from English text without passing through a syntax analysis. In their case the final representation is a fairly standard version of Conceptual Dependency formalism. However, Wilensky and Arens do make claims about how to get to the representation and these involve considerations we have called superficial.

One of their main inspirations is Becker (1975) who argued that many of the constructs in natural language are 'phrasal' (PHRAN is an acronym for PHRasal ANalyzer) in that they are idioms, or clichés of various types: strings whose meaning is not directly computable from representations for the constituent words. A claim like that can seem to be taking on what one could call the Fregean Assumption about meaning representation: that it is a function of the meanings of constituent parts of an utterance. But that clash is merely apparent, of course, because all clichés, idioms, or whatever, have in the last resort to be indexed from the surface words of a sentence, and so the Fregean Assumption is in some sense trivially true. It would be true in the extreme case of a system that assigned a meaning to a sentence of eight words in which the whole meaning structure was indexed from the last word and nothing was indexed from the remaining seven. 'Would you be so kind as to leave' is arguably such an example.

A principle of which Wilensky and Arens make a great deal is that theirs is not a word-based system (they explicitly contrast themselves with Small, see chapter 12) but contains items at a higher level than words. They are quite indifferent as to what these *patterns* are: they can be strings of surface words (as in 'for example'); partial formulas (in Fillmore's phrase), such as 'X in and X out' where X can be replaced by 'night', 'day', 'morning', etc.; or more obviously semantic patterns of features or semantic structures, such as

<PERSON> <active-EAT> <FOOD>

which need not be indexed by any *specific* word in a matching surface string as 'John ate breakfast'. The data base consists of pattern-concept pairs (the latter are sometimes referred to as *conceptual templates*) and the conceptual template for the pattern above would be

(INGEST (ACTOR⟨first term⟩) (OBJECT⟨third term⟩if present, else FOOD))

And it is from this latter conceptual template that the final meaning structure is computed by slot-filling in the standard way. The control structure is one of production rules applied to sentence words inserted one at a time into a buffer, with all active patterns applicable to the buffer until deactivated.

One could thus describe PHRAN as an interesting combination of techniques already mentioned: there are obvious similarities of goals with Riesbeck, but the patterns are not simply word-indexed as all Riesbeck's requests are. In the end however, their treatments of 'John gave Mary a beating' will not be fundamentally different: both will have *two* partially satisfied requests/patterns, one of which will finally supplant the other. In Riesbeck's case the correct pattern will be inserted only when 'beating' is reached, where with PHRAN both will be associated with 'give', and the correct pattern will win on the basis of heuristics that longer patterns and more specific patterns are always preferred to others, though virtually all systems incorporate these heuristics. Like Wilks', and unlike Riesbeck's system, PHRAN can search forward as well as back, and so it is incorrect to describe PHRAN as expectation based.

PHRAN also combines obvious features of Colby and Wilks' systems; indeed it can search for both Colby's superficial and Wilks' semantic patterns within the same control structure, as well as for the intermediate partially filled Fillmorean stereotypes, and that is an obvious advantage. Unlike those two systems it has no clear treatment of phrase/fragment boundaries (within which patterns are to be matched), so that patterns presumably have to be deactivated either by being filled or by being explicitly deactivated by a pattern associated with a boundary marking word. So, in a relative clause sentence like 'John ate greedily which surprised the sandwich seller', the relative clause marker will have to *prevent* the example pattern given earlier completing itself with the appearance of 'sandwich'. While in 'John, who was feeling ill, ate a big breakfast anyway' continuing to fill the pattern across the clause boundary would cause no problem.

In long and serious, rather than little example, sentences this is a fundamental problem. The fragmentation approach of Colby and Wilks is overcrude, but it is not clear exactly what Wilensky and Arens' alternative is.

Wilensky and Arens are not altogether clear about the antecedents of their own system, as their use of the word 'template' makes clear: a template must, to preserve its original craft metaphor, be something that is matched against something else. But in Wilensky and Arens' pattern-concept-pair structure the conceptual template is the *output* obtained by matching a pattern ! The analogue in the Wilks system to the Wilensky and Arens pattern is, of course, the *bare template*: structured items actually matched against what is known about the input words. But Wilensky and Arens have not got this straight, even in generous passages like the following (ibid, p. 72):

In contrast to the systems just described, Wilks' English-French translator does not share several of their shortcomings ...

It produces a representation of the meaning of an utterance, and it attempts to deal with unrestricted natural language. The main difference between Wilks' system and (the one) we describe is that Wilks' patterns are matched against concepts mentioned in a sentence. To recognise these concepts he attaches representations to words in a dictionary.

The problem is that this presupposes that there is a simple correspondence between the form of a concept and the form of a language utterance. However, it is the fact that this correspondence is not simple that leads to the difficulties we are addressing in our work.

Well, one might want to reply that it presupposes no such thing, even in (Wilks 1973b), and had they read on to, say, (Wilks 1975d, 1977a) they would have found the difference much laboured. Of course the Wilks bare templates are matched against concept names occurring in dictionary entries for surface words, just as they are in PHRAN. How otherwise, but from a dictionary entry for 'John' declaring it to be a ⟨PERSON⟩, could the first part of the pattern

⟨PERSON⟩ ⟨active – eat⟩ ⟨FOOD⟩

be matched? The problem is simply that Wilensky and Arens have got muddled up in their terminology and its relation to those of others, and thus think that what they are doing is more different than it is. Let us put this in theory-neutral term:

Wilensky and Arens	which	meaning = output as
Pattern = string of items	matches	CONCEPTUAL
<PERSON><EAT><FOOD>	markers	TEMPLATE
	attached	
	to	
Wilks	surface	meaning = output as
Pattern = string of items	word	FULL
<MAN HAVE THING>	string	TEMPLATE

The full template given earlier for 'John shut the door' (and based on the bare template match of ⟨MAN CAUSE-MOVE THING⟩) happens to be a reasonable representation for it, just as is the PHRAN conceptual template (INGEST (ACTOR JOHN) (OBJECT FOOD)) for 'John ate food' given appropriate conventions in both cases (first item = actor in the Wilks form; first item = action in the Wilensky and Arens form, etc.). In the Wilks system more appropriate representations are achieved by *extraction* and other inferences (mentioned earlier but see further below) which would, for example, produce the more appropriate Riesbeck-style representation for 'John gave Mary a beating', rather than the one based on primitives like GIVE or ATRANS. One of the difficulties in discussing this issue is differing views about where parsing stops, and inference (above and beyond parsing) begins. There is, of course, no clear answer to this, and we shall return to it in the next section.

The clarifications here about the arguments of Wilensky and Arens have not been intended to be merely self-justifying and self-serving; the deeper problem is one that has much exercised formal semanticists, too: what is required of a semantic representation if it is not to be just a surface or syntactic representation in disguise. Thus Wilensky and Arens write of their pattern-concept pair as if they were quite different *types of item*, where it is quite clear from examples like the one given that that is not so, and nothing is gained by pretending it is. In the 'eating' structure given earlier, the right hand side is, in a once fashionable phrase, a simple *transformation* of the left-hand side, and does not suddenly become a *real meaning* as distinct from a mere *surface pattern* on the left. It is part of the argument of this chapter that in recognizing surface to 'semantic parsing' for what it is – a series of appropriate transformations from the surface into a more revealing semantic representation, but without passing through a semantic analysis *nor into* a model theoretic one – we do not fall into traps laid by the salesmen of other disciplines.

What Wilensky and Arens have done, of some considerable value, is to clarify the role of surface collocations in surface to conceptual dependency parsing by, for example, the introduction of a variable surface object 'a piece of x's mind' into the pattern for 'give', so as to parse 'John gave Mary a piece of his mind'. This had been adumbrated in Wilks (1975b), but never set out clearly in the conceptual dependency tradition.

6. FRAME-USING MICRO SYSTEMS

In this section we shall glance at systems that make use of frames or scripts to produce more appropriate representations of clauses (as opposed to using the frame or script as a macro-grammar for a text).

6.1 ELI and SAM

As we mentioned in an earlier section, Riesbeck strengthened his MARGIE parser to yield ELI and MICRO-ELI (see Schank and Riesbeck 1981, Riesbeck and Schank 1976). ELI was a little more bottom-up in detail and content than its predecessor: the number of ways in which additional requests could be added to the stack by 'unexpected' surface was increased beyond the 'beating' example. In response to such criticisms as those of the present author about 'John gave Mary to the Imam of Oudh', the 'to' phrase was allowed to cause the reassignment of case slot fillers, with 'Mary' now going into an OBJECT slot rather than a RECIPIENT.

The system remained a top-down, production rule system though, as (Eisenstadt 1979) showed it could equally well have been expressed as an ATN. It retained surface case frames tied to particular verbs and their associated prepositions (rather than to primitives as Schank had originally envisaged), and the surface syntax component was strengthened by the addition of NPR, a explicit noun-phrase recognition module by Gershman (1979).

The role of ELI was now to be the front-end of SAM (Shank and Riesbeck 1981, and many earlier papers by Cullingford and Lehnert), a Script Applied Mechanism. Scripts, alias frames, have been much discussed since their introduction by Minsky about 1974. For our very limited purposes here we may consider them to be ordered (simply or partially) predicates, where each predicate can have type restricted variables, along with default information. Thus for 'smoking' we might imagine an informal frame:

$$
\begin{aligned}
&\text{CAUSE-MOVE (OBJECT}_1\text{(+plant material, DEFAULT = cigarette))}\\
&\qquad\text{(FROM} \qquad\text{(+container, DEFAULT = packet))}\\
&\qquad\text{(TO} \qquad\text{(+location, DEFAULT = mouth))}\\
&\text{CAUSE-MOVE (OBJECT}_2\text{(+plant material, DEFAULT = match))}\\
&\qquad\text{(FROM} \qquad\text{(+container, DEFAULT = matchbox))}\\
&\qquad\text{(TO} \qquad\text{(OBJECT}_1\text{))}\\
&\text{CHANGE (RESULT} \qquad\text{(lit OBJECT}_1\text{)))}\\
&\qquad\text{(INSTRUMENT} \qquad\text{(OBJECT}_2\text{))}
\end{aligned}
$$

and so on.

There are three kinds of stereotopy here: first, the ordering of the predicates (i.e. lighting the cigarette is *normally* after putting it in the mouth); secondly, the type/feature restrictions, which can also be over-ridden (cigarettes can be lit with a metal poker); thirdly, the default restrictions (again, the poker). A frame or script must be able to contain episodic as well as semantic/stereotypic information: i.e. the fact that in a particular episode, a poker *was* used.

The job of SAM is to use structures of this general type to resolve issues not resolved in the ELI parser. That description is over-general, and deliberately so, because there are many ways in which the tasks to be done could be shared between ELI and SAM. It is for this reason, that it is an arbitrary matter whether we wish to call SAM part of the parser, or to use that word to cover only ELI.

There are two broad types of additional power that the script can add to the parser:

6.1.1 Episodic facts as part of the memory. In a sentence like 'John went to the store for his mother' a decision between interpretation corresponding to

'John went to the store $\begin{cases}\text{(on behalf of)}\\ \text{(to get)}\end{cases}$ his mother'

cannot be made without access to the facts of the particular situation, and it is an assumption of (Riesbeck and Schank 1976), though not of course of MARGIE (1975), that a parser should *never* remain content with 'alternative readings' nor should it choose randomly between them. The information in question might well be contained in a script of general name $MOTHER of which we might imagine a copy has been made for John's-mother, or, and the difference is in no way crucial, the same information could be available in $JOHN, in some area devoted to information about relatives.

6.1.2 Script contextual resolution. One of the main functions of scripts is to provide global semantic resolution. In the classic Schankian example, $RESTAURANT, the restaurant scripts, if called, will resolve the (American English) ambiguity of 'bill' in the sentence 'John paid with a large bill' occurring at the end of a restaurant story, precisely because the system (by means of a cursor moving through the script) will expect John to tender a (money) bill during the paying process, as distinct from congressional bills and (British English) bills claiming payment. Here, too, the script enables decisions to be made that are not made in ELI, but there has been much discussion about whether all, or even many, of such resolutions actually *need* scriptal information. Examples like the one above almost certainly do not (see Wilks 1977a).

6.2 Pseudo-texts

When frames first appeared, I argued (Wilks 1976) that parsing problems would not solved by simply matching these skeletons that would somehow 'appear' in texts to be parsed, and this seems now to be accepted even by enthusiasts. Where they do have a role in parsing (I argued in Wilks 1978) is to deal with the fact that the slot expectations of word semantics are, in real text, violated as often as observed and this is seen as much in 'John ran a mile', an apparently syntactic example (of violation of intransitivity) as in apparently idiomatic examples like 'My car drinks petrol' and 'My car leaks petrol', normally considered a syntactic variant of *Petrol leaks from my car.*

In all these cases, I have argued, it is only by reference to a frame-like structure that shows, at a low level of detail, what is normally associated with such actions, that we can reliably infer the most appropriate representational structure. It is in that sense that I believe that representational structures like frames are fundamental to parsing, while not accepting that access to a story line or plan are in the same sense fundamental.

To this end I proposed that use might be made during parsing of a frame-like structure of information about entities which I called pseudo-texts (Wilks 1978). The reason behind the inelegant name was first, to have a structure of exactly the same format as the semantic structure for texts produced by the parser itself, i.e. in the preference semantics system that is a semantic block of tied templates described earlier and, secondly, as a way of reminding myself and others that knowledge structures may not be as different as some believe without reflection.

The pseudo-text (PT) then, is no more than a semantic block (which might itself have been the result of input in English) that represents information about a concept in addition to its semantic formula. The figure that follows represents quite low level factual information about cars, where the items in each template are primitive structures or are (lower case) the English names or formulas for the items named (they are most certainly not meant to be English lexemes). Prefacing them by '#' indicates that they are higher level concepts, and the * merely stands for 'car' the PTs name. It is left as an exercice to the reader to guess what facts about cars are coded here:

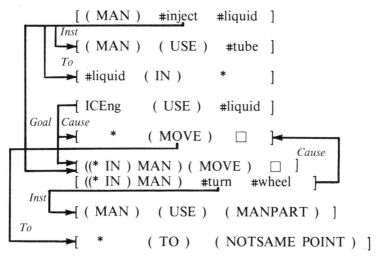

The proposed role of such items in parsing was to suggest that, in templates which were ill-fitting in the sense described earlier (because preferences were broken) there could be a match from such a template to the forms-of-fact in the PT and, under well-defined conditions, a better representation might be found to replace the original template structure. Thus an ill-fitting template for 'My car drinks petrol' could be partially matched with the first and third lines of the PT illustrated via a close match of formulas for 'drink' and 'inject', etc. If such a match can be obtained it was hypothesised that the non-matching parts of the template in the PT could then be *projected* to replace the corresponding parts of the original, but ill-fitting, template. Thus the template for the above sentence would not then be of the structural form ⟨THING CAUSE-MOVE STUFF⟩ but ⟨THING USE STUFF⟩, in virtue of USE in the fourth line of the PT being projected back onto the template, and this latter form is now better fitting (given an appropriate semantics for USE that allows use by non-humans).

All this is no more than a complex system of forms of fact being default structures for surface clauses, better than their actual surface forms, or to put that very crudely, when in doubt about ill-fitting semantic structures, consult forms of fact indicating what is normally done with the real world item in question, etc. The method should work not only for quasi-metaphorical forms like this example, but just as well for 'John ran a mile' which gives rise to an ill-fitting template if 'run' is coded as intransitive. The appropriate PT for 'run' or 'mile', however should indicate precisely the relation of self-movement to distance via some form of 'spatial extension' case. The difficulty in assessing this proposal in terms of our deep/superficial distinction is that how superficial this form of frame-assisted parsing is will depend very much on the relationship of the forms of facts in the PT to their surface equivalents. This may be quite close in the 'car drinks' case, but in the 'John runs' case there will presumably not be a template in the PT of structure ⟨MAN MOVE WHERE-LINE⟩, where the primitive coding WHERE-LINE expresses spatial linear extension. That is because the primitive MOVE is also 'intransitive' and so the linkage to a distance moved will be via a template tied by the appropriate spatial case marker. Then the crude matching techniques use for the 'car drinks' case will have to be modified, and the generalization of the algorithm of matching may be lost. One might then not be all that far from the standard linguistic accounts of such an example, in terms of default cases space and time appearing as pseudo objects of verbs.

We should move finally from the use of frame like structures to aid clause parsing to the claimed use of frames to provide a text structure directly, and to obviate all intermediate representations between input text and such frame structures.

7. MACRO-FRAME SYSTEMS

These, as just noted, are frame systems where (a) it is claimed the frame itself provides the final semantic structure for the text (as in 'text grammar') and (b) no intermediate phase of parsing is required and the frame can itself be the parsing device. The most adventurous and complex suggestion yet is the Yale BORIS system (Lehnert et al. 1981) which aims to give a full parsing meeting those two criteria.

There have also been attempts to use frame-like structures in this way at Yale but to produce only a partial parsing, not including all the information in the text (Schank et al. 1978 and de Jong 1979). For reasons of space I will take a sample from the last set, de Jong's FRUMP.

This system is sometimes called a text skimmer: it employs not full but what he calls 'sketchy scripts', and analyses stories coming off the AP news wire. It aims for no syntactic analysis, no parallel paths and immediate resolution of ambiguities. FRUMP has a strongly top-down methodology, and is armed with sketchy scripts that can be effectively specialized senses of words, inference rules, and what he calls *issue skeletons*.

Thus a sketchy script $NATIONALIZE might contain, in part,

⟷	ATRANS
MANNER	FORCED
ACTOR	POLITY
OBJECT	CONT
TYPE	ECONOMIC
PART	SPEC INDUSTRY
TO	POLITY
FROM	POLITY

We do not need technical explanation to understand roughly what is going on here: POLITY is a public institution of some kind, and the sketchy script is in a KRL predicate-argument type format.

This script is also, in effect, a specialized sense of 'take' in the dictionary, and so is called in the analysis of 'Uganda today took control of a US oil refinery'.

The heart of the method is what de Jong calls Prediction and Substantiation which would be illustrated by :

PREDICTOR: predicting role FROM will be filled with an element from list POLITY.
SUBSTANTIATOR: text analyzer unable to add from – calling inference procedures – predicting (OBJECT PART OWNER) is modifier of word 'oil'.

All this is good old slot filling from context under a new name. One feature to notice is that it is only luck that 'predicting......modifier of word 'oil' gets the appropriate word 'US' as the filler of FROM (i.e. that it was taken from the US). Or perhaps one should say that it is not luck, since the refinery was *not* taken from the US but from an unnamed US company, which may not be a vital distinction in some countries but is in the United States ! The method is fairly clear to inspection: US is the only entity of type POLITY around in the sentence, and so it is chosen. In that sense the inference rules do not seem, on this much inspection at least, to have much to do with frames, text structures and forms of fact: it is good old semantic typing again, of a familiar kind. That suspicion is reinforced by the observation that $NATIONALIZE is not very much like what we have grown to know and love as frames or scripts: it is very like a word sense formula.

One answer to that is always to say that since frames and scripts have never been formally defined, then who is to say what is and is not one? That is true, but the sketchy script does have a rather low level flavour. Indeed a macro-frame claim will not be distinct from earlier claims we have examined if, in fact, the frames offered in connection with the thesis are formula-like (or clausal in surface terms).

In fact more frame-like power is added by '*issue skeletons*':

!TERRORISM (AUTHORITY   TERRORISTS)

TERRORISTS DEMANDS(CDI)
TERRORIST INCIDENT ($HIJACK $TERROCCPY1)
MEDIATION ATTEMPTS (......
AUTHORITY RETALIATIONS (......
OUTCOME (.........

This, of course, is more familiar as a frame-like object, with a notion of causal/temporal order, pointers to other items of the same high-level type etc. Here, if anywhere is FRUMP's scriptal power, but these as we saw, are not matched directly to the text, but only via the much lower level items like $NATIONALIZE. It is quite unclear then that FRUMP does fall within the definition *macro-frame hypothesis*, and as I hinted earlier (and argued in Wilks 1977a) I am not sure that any system, on detailed examination, could do so, except in the most tightly constrained technical areas.

By that last remark, I am making an implicit contrast with the semantic parser of Burton (1976 and chapter 10), which is as clear a case of a superficial system as PARRY (with which Burton draws strong parallels), is highly technically specialized or expert, but which is in some sense a frame-using system, at least it certainly is if FRUMP is allowed to count as a frame using system. Burton's system certainly has stereotypically ordered events in time, and that is very close to being a sufficient condition of being a frame system for many observers.

8. CONCLUSION

I have no very clear conclusions to offer. In the course of the chapter I have shown, to my own satisfaction at least:

1) AI parsers that claim to be semantically driven fall into two types along the deep/superficial divide, at least if divided by their claims.
2) On further inspection, those that claim to be deep have far more features in common with the 'superficial' ones than one might expect, if one examines their target parsing structures.
3) However, the unclarity of that boundary does not correlate in any

clear way with the syntax/semantics distinction: all the systems examined, deep or superficial, have ways of capturing syntactic generalizations or avoiding them, but that issue has nothing to do with (ii) above, for reasons I set out at the beginning.

4) Paradoxically, some of the most blatantly superficial systems also have features deeper than any examined here. By that I mean, for example, that much recent work on belief structures and their role in parsing (see Wilks and Bien, in press) has emphasised that the simple 'match a static semantic structure against an incoming text' view, even if of the deep type, is simply inadequate as a model of language understanding. However, it was Colby's PARRY, with its model of the human interlocutor's emotions and beliefs, however primitive, that incorporated that feature long before its contemporary 'deep' systems.

ACKNOWLEDGEMENT

This research was supported by a grant from the Leverhulme Trust and that is gratefully acknowledged.

12

Parsing as Cooperative Distributed Inference:Understanding through Memory Interactions

S. Small

1. INTRODUCTION

The *Word Expert Parser* (WEP) is a computer program that analyzes fragments of natural language text in order to extract their meaning in context. The system has been developed with particular attention paid to the wide variety of different meaning roles of words when appearing in combination with other words. The character of such lexical relations runs the gamut from the simple direct knowledge that some word sequence represents some remembered concept to the more analytical knowledge that particular kinds of lexical sequences often represent certain classes of conceptual notions.

An underlying perspective of the research about the nature of individual words recasts them in a procedural associative light. Words do not have meaning per se, but rather, contribute to understanding through their effects on the ongoing interactions of memory. Fragments of lexical items mean something only through the interactions *(a)* among experts for their component words; and *(b)* between individual word experts and other memory processes. Lexical relations are thus viewed not as static functions, but as active processes causing words to combine together through a dynamic interrogative and inferential process. Word Expert Parsing converges at their eventual agreement on a mutually acceptable interpretation for a fragment of text.

Note the fundamentally different perspective advanced by WEP compared to traditional computer parsing systems. The interpretation of natural language discourse cannot take place in isolation from other memory processes and have a reasonable chance of success at difficult applications (e.g., ones that can be said to require some sort of understanding to achieve). WEP does not separate comprehension into distinct phases, and the parser operates through constant interaction with other (currently simulated) parallel programs concerned with attention, reference, discourse structure, and reasoning about beliefs. The role of the parser is to participate in this mutual inference process; WEP does not build a syntactic or semantic structure to be used at some later time by some independent computer system. A parsing system is an expert language program which executes at the same time as many other expert programs, and which contributes to understanding by its interactions over time with the other modules. By the time the parser has examined an entire sentence, a large proportion of the effects of reading that sentence should have already been felt by the rest of the overall computer system.

1.1 Linguistic motivations

The evolution of this perspective started with the observation that the understanding of a particular fragment of text depends fundamentally on the disambiguation of the individual words composing it. Knowing the contextual meanings of the words is tantamount to understanding the meaning of the overall fragment. Another way of saying the same thing (Rieger 1976) is that language interpretation can be ultimately viewed as a process of word sense discrimination. Unfortunately, this perspective does not eliminate the classic problems of deciding the nature of a distinct word sense, and the difference between different usages, word senses, and idioms. The solution to these problems comes in realizing that the process of understanding the meaning of words in context does not require reference to those notions at all. The design of a parsing procedure based on determining the meaning roles of individual words in context has led to the orthogonal linguistic notions which are the subject of this paper.

The organization of WEP is founded on the belief that the grouping together of words to form meaningful sequences is an active process which succeeds only because of highly idiosyncratic application of lexical knowledge. That is, we fragment text and understand the meaning of the pieces because we know how the particular words involved interact with each other. Clearly, the first time we see a word, none of these interactions can be idiosyncratic (from the point of view of that word), and the parser must appeal more to general linguistic processing and to hypothesis-driven processing by surrounding word experts than might otherwise have been needed to understand the meaning of the fragment. If many of the words are new, processes to apply general knowledge must do what they can.

Sometimes sequences of two or more words interact together to such an extent that they seem to behave as a single lexical item. Linguists have labelled such sequences *idioms*. The notion to which this definition gives rise, however, causes several problems for linguistic theory. First of all, rarely does such a sequence hold together so tightly that it can be truly treated theoretically as a single lexical item. Secondly, rarely does such a sequence have a unique meaning. More often than not, the meaning of an idiomatic expression must be determined by disambiguation. The sequence must be analyzed in context and be treated by comprehension processes as being either *(a)* a cohesive whole with idiosyncratic meaning, or *(b)* a sequence having meaning through less specific language knowledge. There is no *a priori* way of knowing the meaning of the sequence to be the one or the other.

The notion of *idiom* falls at one end of a spectrum, an idealized end that I claim does not exist. Lexical sequences can be *more or less idiomatic*, in the sense that the process interactions constituting the understanding of them includes greater or fewer idiosyncratic interactions. The WEP way of looking at the most idiomatic sequences is that the special interactions among the participating words take priority over any other potential interactions involving those words. The disambiguation of idiomatic expressions, i.e. the understanding of the sequences as either idioms or non-idioms (to use the popular distinction), generally requires other process interactions besides the strictly word-specific ones. The understanding of an idiom thus differs insignificantly, from the perspective of WEP theory, from comprehension of any other kind (according to whatever classification scheme) of lexical sequence.

The notion that all fragments of language are more or less idiomatic, while radical in some linguistic quarters, has been previously suggested. In his introductory textbook, 'Aspects of Language', Dwight Bolinger asks 'whether everything we say may be in some degree idiomatic; that is, whether there are affinities among words that continue to reflect the attachments the words had when we learned them, within larger groups' (Bolinger 1975). After working within what he calls 'the prevailing reductionism', Bolinger began to suggest a positive answer to his pedagogical question, choosing to take 'an idiomatic rather than an analytical view' (Bolinger 1979) of language. The contribution of artificial intelligence in general, and of *Word Expert Parsing* in particular, is to develop theory from this informal view.

The notion of process, and of process interaction, allows us to begin to do just that.

1.2 Psychological motivations

The Word Expert Parser is being developed as one part of a uniform memory model that represents understanding through interactions among its large number of fairly small distributed elements. These elements are seen as processors, rather than as static structures, and communicate by transmitting among themselves some kind of symbolic messages or signals. While the existing WEP system operates through the transmission of symbol structures (Newell 1980), there seem to be good psychological reasons to restrict word and concept experts to the transmission of activation (Feldman and Ballard 1982). The nature of the human intelligence, as a serial symbol manipulating system or as a highly parallel system of activation propagating connections, must influence profoundly the architecture of computer systems to understand. The work described in this paper consists of a highly distributed system of symbol transmitting connections. As the research proceeds, it will be necessary to decide whether or not the experts should communicate by more than weighted activation levels.

The present research takes a stand on a number of ongoing debates in psycholinguistics. In particular, just as WEP disputes the sharpness of the linguistic notion of idiom, so it argues that the psycholinguistic concept of *function words* does not help understand the phenomena under study. The words of language can be *more or less functional,* in the nature of their effects in directing the language comprehension process. Some words (morphemes) have no roles other than functional ones (e.g. *a*, *-ing*), while others make significant contributions on a number of fronts including functionality (e.g. *deep*, *in*). The representation of function words in WEP does not differ in structure from the representation of typical content words. The difference lies simply in the amount of certain kinds of word expert processing that are performed in each case. It would be interesting to see if neurological evidence (in comprehension, rather than production) supports the WEP contention.

A second psychological question involves the effects of context on the processes of word and sentence interpretation. Are these processes 'of a highly interactive, directable nature' or are they 'basically isolable and autonomous' (Swinney 1979)? This question has been studied often with experiments involving the processing of lexical ambiguities during comprehension. These experiments have tested whether *(a)* context prevents access to inappropriate word senses (the *prior decision hypothesis*); or *(b)* context has its effect only after access to all word senses (the *post decision hypothesis*). The design of WEP has been based on the latter idea, that word sense disambiguation takes place through the application of context after retrieval of all senses. While we considered constraining word experts by prior pruning (Rieger and Small 1979), and even built an early version of WEP to perform that way (on several examples), the parser now operates in accord with the post decision hypothesis.

1.3 Computational motivations

It has been recognized for some time that the most difficult applications of computers in the processing of natural language (e.g. machine translation) require significantly more than syntactic analysis alone. The structure of most natural languages does not lead straightforwardly to simple semantic interpretation of sentences based on their syntax. The unfortunate metaphor that suggests viewing people as Von Neumann computers has led to mistaken approaches to the analysis of natural languages as if they were similar to computer (or logical) languages. While the structure of ALGOL statements or sentences of the first order predicate calculus may lead directly to interpretations of their meaning, this same mechanism just does not work for highly ambiguous, context-dependent sentences of evolved human languages.

It seems further to be the case that the processes of syntactic, semantic, and even pragmatic (general and discourse-specific context) analysis are very much interrelated. There are many feedback situations involving each of these aspects of processing. The body of this paper discusses a variety of these interdependencies as they relate to parsing: how objects mentioned in previous sentences can affect the meaning of the current sentence (even its structural analysis); how knowledge about the actors and objects, apart from that explicitly represented in a text can do the same; how the structure of idiosyncratic fragments often has nothing to do with their meaning. In developing a computer program to participate in dialogues with a person, many analogous feedback situations at the levels of plan recognition (speech actions and overall user goals), plan generation, and language production (Allen and Small 1982) are prevalent.

The only computationally effective way to accomodate these fundamental interactions across the many inferential tasks of natural language comprehension appears to be in modular distributed computer systems. Such systems are both difficult to construct and inherently different in design from those intended to be sequential and non-interacting. The reader will note the fundamental difference on many levels between the Word Expert Parsing system described in this chapter and the parsing systems surveyed in other chapters in this book. While other programs account for the significant feedback cycles in language processing (Riesbeck and Schank 1976), and the procedural deterministic nature of parsing (Marcus 1979), no system yet takes into consideration both of these phenomena and the inherent parallelism and interdependence over time of all comprehension processes. The work described here is intended to be a first step in that direction. Within the next several years, and in conjunction with the work in planning and goal recognition of Allen (1978) and the representation of naive human knowledge about the world (Hayes 1978), an initial prototype of such a computer system should become a reality.

2. THE WORD EXPERT PARSER

The WEP computer system maintains linguistic knowledge across a community of word-based structures called *word experts*, which represent the process of determining the contextual meaning and role of the individual words. A word expert must not be thought of as a representation for the various meanings, roles, and contributions of a word in context, but rather as a declarative representation (a network) of the process (which we shall call *disambiguation*) of determining these things. Certainly, it is the meaning contributions of individual lexical items that we wish to determine. Word experts are both data and process; they can be augmented, examined, and manipulated as data, yet parsing takes place through their interpretation as program by an expert evaluator, similar to the EVAL of Lisp.

The distributed parsing scheme of WEP works as follows. The WEP reader examines a word of text and retrieves its word expert from memory. The word expert starts executing, trying to determine the meaning role of its word in context, i.e., interacting with other word experts and with higher-order system processes to acquire the appropriate contextual knowledge to make the correct inferences. Finally, all the word experts for a particular fragment of text come to mutual agreement on the meaning of the fragment, and the local distributed process terminates. Local, in the sense that as long as there remains input text, the overall parsing process continues, while the disambiguation of individual lexical sequences making up the larger text terminates.

Interaction, between individuals in the world, or between distributed processes in a computer program, requires both *(a)* giving information and *(b)* receiving information. In WEP, the experts exchange two kinds of information, called *concept structures* and *control signals*. Concept structures represent human concepts, such as 'a book', 'going fishing', 'the box of candy I gave Joanie for Valentine's day in 1981', 'some blue physical object', and the like. Control signals represent processing clues, such as 'expect a word that can begin a lexical sequence that can describe concept structure X', 'send me the concept structure representing the agent of concept structure Y or a signal saying you cannot', 'wait a second and you will be sent a concept structure that will help you', and similar things. The representation and use of concepts and signals are described fully in (Small and Rieger 1982), and their significance for distributed cognitive modelling (i.e. for engineering of artificial intelligence programs) is described in Small (1981).

3. LEXICAL INTERACTIONS

I use the term *lexical interaction* to denote the sending and receiving of control signals and concept structures by word experts in WEP. This includes interactions between individual experts, as well as those between a word expert and another kind of model process (e.g. a mechanism inferring the goals of a dialogue participant). This paper discusses lexical interactions by presenting four classes of required interaction, and then arguing for their necessity and giving examples of each. The categorization is by the kind of knowledge exchanged in the communication, and includes the following: *Idiosyncratic Interaction, Linguistic Interaction, Discourse Interaction* and *Logical Interaction.*

The least general class of lexical interactions are considered *idiosyncratic* since they are word-specific and arise through simple recall memory. This type of interaction permits the understanding of idiomatic fragments. General knowledge about the syntax and semantics of some natural language gives rise to *linguistic* interactions, and are of course crucial to the understanding of lexical sequences not previously seen. Sometimes words interact with processes that monitor the development of an entire text (or parts thereof), or the goals of participants in discussion. These *discourse* interactions are often necessary for the meaningful cohesion of lexical fragments. Lastly, but certainly not least important are the logical interactions between words and the most general cognitive processes. Such things as perceptions about the world, beliefs, inference-making skills, and rote memory, are basic to language understanding.

The classification of word fragments into categories such as 'idiom', 'collocation', 'colligation', 'noun phrase', and 'complement', does not make sense in WEP theory. Rather, individual words are viewed as having certain kinds and sequences of interactions with their neighbors to form meaningful pieces of text. Fragments often described as 'idioms' are those that are understood principally through idiosyncratic lexical interactions. A non-idiomatic structure, diagnosed as a 'noun phrase', is one that involves mostly linguistic interactions to understand. A so-called 'noun-noun pair' can be thought of as a lexical sequence comprehended with the help of logical interactions, with recourse to common sense memory and skills.

3.1 Idiosyncratic interaction

Since the emphasis of the WEP research effort is to construct a computer program to understand natural language, we are not qualified to make claims about just how much of human parsing involves idiosyncratic lexical interaction. Suffice it to say that no theory of language analysis can do without such a notion, and that we have come across many examples, both in our own work and in the linguistic literature, where it applies. Furthermore, our conception of idiosyncratic interaction (in conjunction with the other interaction types), provides explanatory adequacy for many linguistic phenomena, observed in diverse camps.

3.1.1 Idioms.   The comprehension of idioms requires both idiosyncratic lexical interactions and context-probing disambiguation (i.e., interactions between lexical processes and higher-order memory processes). As an example, examine the following sentence, which has actually been analyzed by the prototype WEP system described in (Small and Rieger 1982) and which is described with a computer trace later in this paper.

1. The fellow throws in the towel.

Linguistic description of this sentence could take several different routes. The verb in the sentence could be seen to be either one of *(a) throw, (b) throw in,* or *(c) throw in the towel,* depending on the theoretical perspective of the linguistic approach. While WEP does not itself (explicitly) make use of the notion of a verb, if forced to explain its behavior in these terms, I would say that WEP would consider the verb to be either *(a), (b),* or *(c),* depending on the context.

The WEP computer system would behave as follows. The word expert for *throw* would send a message to the *in* expert, consisting of both a control signal and a concept structure. The signal would in effect tell *in* that *throw* would like to pair up with it to form a cohesive fragment. The accompanying concept structure would tell *in* what kind of lexical sequence (or conceptual mapping of one) throw would expect to find to the right of *in* for it to have confidence in such a pairing. Of course, the *in* expert has independent control of its own interactions, and could decide (based on the nature of the input) to reject any suggestions it receives. In the above example, *in* would wait for a signal from the expert on its right (the *the* expert) indicating the formation of a cohesive fragment designating a towel, and then act on this information.

The concept structure sent by *throw* indicates that if the words to the right of *in* are *the towel*, then the words *throw* and *in* should pair up. However, the *in* expert has the prerogative to override this suggestion, and if a query to the processes modelling the focus of discourse attention (see the later section on discourse interactions) determined that some large towel was the location of some active event, would do so, transmitting a signal to *throw* rejecting its advice. (An actual trace of this appears later.) Ordinarily, this would not happen[1], and the *in* expert would signal acceptance to *throw*. The *throw* expert would then query the discourse processes monitoring the activity context to determine if *(a)* someone is actually throwing a towel into some volume, or *(b)* someone is conceding defeat to someone in a game. When this was determined, the understanding of the fragment (in this case a sentence) would be complete.

3.1.2 Collocation and Colligation. What is the nature of the advice given by one word expert to another, as from the *throw* expert to the *in* expert above, and what is its basis? These suggestions, transmitted as control signals and concept structures in WEP, are based on purely idiosyncratic criteria. While the idiomatic meaning of certain lexical sequences cannot be predicted from the parts, certain others have meanings that differ slightly from what might be inferred. These sequences are sometimes called *collocations*, and illustrate the idiosyncracy of lexical pairings and thus the basis for certain interactions in WEP analysis.

In his recent paper, Bolinger (1979) quotes from T.F. Mitchell (1971) about the word *work* and its meaning in various fragments of lexical items: 'Men – specifically cement workers – work *in* cement works; others of different occupation work *on* works of art; others again, or both, *perform* good works. Not only are good works *performed* but cement works are *built* and works of art *produced*' (italics in original). Bolinger goes on to reflect why 'builders do not *produce* a building or authors *invent* a novel.' From the vantage point of the distributed lexical actors of WEP, these particularities form the basis of the inter-expert communications we have been calling *idiosyncratic interactions*.

Let us take Mitchell's example, the ambiguous word *work*, and see how the word experts of WEP can interact to determine its meaning in context. It should be easy to see from the discussion so far how WEP would handle the following fragment.

2. The Ensemble Intercontemporain performed a work.

Without knowing anything about the various entities mentioned in the sentence, it is clear that an ensemble of musicians played a musical piece. Lexical interactions between the word expert for *perform* and that for *work* make clear the meaning of the fragment. The *perform* expert would signal to *work* its expectation of a lexical sequence denoting a conceptual entity that can be 'performed', such as 'a service', 'a musical piece', or 'a series of actions'. It would then be up to *work* to use this (non-binding) advice to contribute to the meaning of the overall fragment in which it participates.

The following fragment can be understood through the same mechanism.

3. Sempe worked on a work.

In this sentence, the interactions between (the first) *work* and *on*, and between *on* and (the second) *work*, make clear the meaning of the second *work* as a piece of art. The WEP analysis of the fragment takes place in a manner similar to the example of *throw in* outlined above. In this case, however, the suggestions communicated by *work* for pairing with *on* are eventually sent as advice to the ambiguous work and used for its disambiguation, just as in the previous example, the *perform* expert guided the work expert *in* inferring that it denoted a musical piece.

3.2 Linguistic interaction

The syntax and semantics of natural language comprise the stuff of most linguistic theory, and their use is the cornerstone of computer parsing programs. However, WEP forces us to perceive the nature and use of this knowledge from an untraditional vantage point, that of the individual word and its active processing to form meaningful fragments of text with its neighbors. From this perspective, the syntax and semantics of a language is that body of knowledge that helps us infer enough about the meaning contributions of new words to understand lexical sequences completely different from ones that we have already seen. After processing some lexical sequence, this linguistic knowledge provides us with certain expectations about upcoming lexical items and the nature of their interactions, thus helping us to fragment those items into pieces and to infer the meaning of the pieces from general information about their component parts.

3.2.1 Noun Phrases.   How can the purely lexical WEP system require no notion of high order structural phenomena, yet still be able to account for them? The following example (provided by Yorick Wilks) illustrates the lexical interactions required to analyze an interesting fragment of text.

4. Joanie washes the hundred patterned dishes up.

The difficulty with this fragment is in determining that the word *dishes* contributes to the meaning of the fragment through interactions with the three words to its left, but that the word *up* contributes by association with the word *washes*, which precedes *up* by many intervening words. The reason that I am avoiding the use of traditional linguistic jargon for describing this phenomenon is the following belief: An understanding of WEP requires the viewing of language interpretation from the vantage point of the individual word and its interactions. An important way to achieve this is to describe the analysis process with reference to the very notions (not the traditional ones) around which it is organized.

In the analysis of the example fragment, WEP would find the referent of *Joanie* and then proceed as follows. The *wash* expert would begin executing, trying to determine its own meaning role in some lexical fragment, and at the same time, trying to provide information to other lexical agents to permit them to do the same. The meaning of *wash* in context depends on a number of factors, including the nature of the words succeeding it, and their own actions in determining their meaning and role contributions in context. The *wash* expert must thus prepare for a number of contingencies, or different things that could happen in the text, and then wait to see if any of them actually occur. If the word *up* appears to the right of *wash*, for example, the words could choose to pair up into a meaningful fragment (as in *throw in* above). Under certain conditions, the word *up* could appear later on in the text, and still pair up with *wash* (as must occur for correct interpretation of the example sentence).

What are the contextual conditions that would permit this? One of the contingencies that wash anticipates is the grouping of the words to its right into a meaningful fragment of their own (i.e. a *concept structure*). The *wash* expert knows that *(a)* the nature of this concept structure may be important for its own sense disambiguation, and *(b)* that the word immediately following the meaningful fragment could pair up with it. In the jargon of WEP, one of the experts in such a meaningful fragment *reports* a concept structure. It is this report that can trigger some new processing by a word expert (by the *wash* expert in the example).

Let us now examine the step by step actions of WEP in reading the given fragment. The word expert for *wash* attempts an interaction with the word to its right, *the*, to determine whether or not a lexical pairing is appropriate. The *wash* expert sends a control signal to the expert on its right, saying 'are you the expert for *up*, *away*, or for some other word that might pair up with me?' Since the the expert knows nothing of such pairings, the *wash* receives no response to its request. However, the *wash* expert prepares for the other possibilities, and waits for the report of a concept structure. The *wash* expert can now do nothing until later. The *the* expert executes, and interacts with the expert to its right, *hundred*, signalling its desire to form a cohesive sequence. The *hundred* expert executes, interacting with *patterned* and continuing the process of mutual agreement on the construction of a coherent lexical sequence. Finally *dishes*[2] executes, and interacts in the same way with *up*. However, the *up* expert does not reply to *dishes* with an acceptable message, putting an end to the lexical grouping activity.

At this stage, the *dishes* expert initiates the process of constructing and reporting the concept structure to represent the fragment under analysis, i.e. *the hundred patterned dishes*. The report of this concept is constantly interrupted as each expert participating in the fragment augments it with meaning information. The control flow of the parsing process thus appears to proceed from right to left, passing from *dishes* to *patterned* to *hundred* and finally to *the*. Finally the *the* expert interacts with the model processes concerned with finding referents for unknown individual concepts, to determine if the fragment just analyzed refers to a particular, already known, set of patterned dishes. In either case, the *the* expert reports a concept structure, and the *wash* expert gets what it was waiting for, and continues its processing. One important note: The reason that control passed in the way it did within the sequence is due to the constraints imposed by the experts themselves on the report of the concept structure they built, not by any central stack mechanism. Sometimes, this kind of reporting is desirable, other times not; as always in WEP, the lexical agents themselves decide.

The rest of the analysis takes place predictably. The *wash* expert interacts with *up* as if up occurred to its immediate right in the text. The pairing up of the two words results from mutual accord, and the *wash* expert creates a concept structure to represent the meaning of the washing up of dishes. Next *wash* organizes the conceptual object, *the hundred patterned dishes*, into the overall meaning of the sentence, and again waits for things to happen. This time, the word expert for the period at the end of the sentence executes, and transmits an appropriate message. The *wash* expert again executes, cleans up its business, and reports the concept structure representing the meaning, in context, of the entire fragment, *Joanie washed the hundred patterned dishes up.*

3.2.2 Passives and relative clauses. Sentences in the passive voice and those containing relative clauses are similar in being complex structural phenomena in natural language, and often suggestive of sentence-level rules as linguistic explanation. Furthermore, the understanding of such constructions by the distributed word-based approach of WEP may be far from evident, especially considering my claim that no explicit notions of structure are referenced by the computer system or used in the theory. Interpretation of textual fragments containing complex syntactic structures takes place through complex patterns of lexical interactions among the appropriate word experts. The words that normally cue a reader about the presence of such structural relations in a fragment are the ones in WEP that coordinate the process of understanding them.

The analysis of a passive sentence involves linguistic interactions among the word experts for the suffix *en*, the word *by*, and the other words composing it. The following sentence has been parsed by the existing WEP system, and discussed at length in Small (1980).

5. The case was thrown out by federal court.

The *en* expert begins executing before *throw*, and the normal attempts by the *throw* expert to coordinate the analysis of the fragment in which it participates are intercepted by *en*. The actions of *en* allow *throw* to pair up with *out*, as outlined above for *throw in* and *wash up*, but its lexical interactions to determine the nature of the object being 'thrown out', and the agent doing the 'throwing' are all intercepted by the *en* expert, which provides *throw* with the correct replies to its queries. Please refer to Small (1980) and Small and Rieger (1982) for a fuller discussion.

Relative clauses beginning with the word *who* are analyzed by WEP through the interactions among the *who* word expert and the experts for the other words in the clause and the larger fragment containing it. The following sentence is an example of such a fragment.

6. The man who throws the game likes to lose.

The *who* expert in this sentence has the responsibility for interacting with the word expert for *likes* to inform *likes* about the *man* doing the 'liking'. Ordinarily, this expert would expect to find a meaningful lexical sequence to its left representing the needed concept. However, the particular structure of the fragment means that *who* must be at the other end of the relevant linguistic interactions of *likes*, rather than the expert for the word to its immediate left, which would normally perform the needed service.

The WEP interpretation of the example fragment proceeds as follows. The word experts for *the* and *man* agree to form a meaningful sequence and construct a concept structure to represent its meaning. The *who* expert begins executing, gets hold of this concept, and waits for the *throw* expert to start exploring the nature of the lexical sequence on its left. In addition, the *who* expert anticipates that another word expert further down the line (in the example, the expert for *likes*) will also seek out information about the sequence to its left, in exactly the way that *throw* does. The *who* expert, like every word expert in WEP, plans a strategy to interact with the experts involved in both its prior context and its subsequent context, cooperatively to interpret fragments of text.

The *throw* expert begins executing and investigates the nature of the lexical sequence to its left. The *who* expert provides the appropriate information, i.e., the concept structure representing the *man*, and *throw* begins to disambiguate its meaning in context. The experts for *a* and *game* mutually agree on their local meaning, and through linguistic and idiosyncratic interactions with *throw* help it determine its meaning as the 'throwing of a contest'. The *likes* expert starts executing, and its messages in search of the person doing the 'liking' are intercepted by the *who* expert, which has been on the lookout for such interactions since the beginning. Since the *who* expert knows the unique name of the concept structure representing the *man*, it sends this concept to *likes*, which proceeds normally, knowing nothing of the structural complexities preceeding it.

The word experts for both *throw* and for *likes* can be expected to explore the underlying meaning of the lexical sequences preceding them. Note the way that WEP applies this linguistic knowledge to the interpretation of fragments of natural language text containing these words. Rather than saying that *throw* and *likes* act as finite verbs in certain contexts (which are described in some relational representational scheme, such as grammar rules or logic), we say instead that these words carry on linguistic interactions with the active processes modelling the other words making up the (local linguistic) context to arrive at a mutually acceptable characterization of their individual contributions to textual meaning. The advantage of this perspective comes from the fact that linguistic interactions constitute but a portion of all possible lexical interactions that represent in WEP the process of understanding.

3.3 Discourse interactions

While it is clear that certain lexical sequences cannot be understood solely through recourse to syntax and semantics, namely those fragments for which idiosyncratic interactions are required (i.e., specific remembered contexts), why do we need other kinds of general knowledge? We have already seen examples suggesting the answer to this question. In trying to understand the meaning of *throw in the towel*, the relevant word experts must find out some things about the person performing the described action, before knowing what action he is in effect performing.

If the discourse describes some sort of competition between two people (or teams), for example, *throw in the towel* could indicate a concession of defeat by one of them. The following fragment illustrates such a contextual situation.

7. Rick and Joanie play chess. Rick throws in the towel.

On the other hand, if the discourse has recently made reference to a place where one might dispose of a towel, *throw in the towel* might be signifying the putting of some towel in that place. The following example illustrates this case.

8. Joanie drops a penny in the pit. Rick throws in the towel.

I am not claiming that knowledge of the discourse context is sufficient to disambiguate the meanings of the example sentence, but rather, that such knowledge is required to understand it.

The discourse interactions required to interpret the above example take place *(a)* between the *throw* expert and a higher order process modelling the *activity context*, and *(b)* between the *in* expert and a process modelling the discourse *focus of attention*.[3] There are two aspects to the processing of the activity mechanism, the unsolicited sending of control signals to indicate the anticipation of certain actions in the text and concept structures to represent them, and the more data-directed interactions with word experts (and other understanding processes) to determine the nature of the actions that actually do occur. The *throw* expert must carry on *activity context interactions* to determine if the discourse could be seen as discussing some competitive activity. If so, the 'concession of defeat' interpretation of the example sentence is plausible. The *in* expert carries on *focus of attention interactions* to find out if some location has recently been described in the text *in which* something might be thrown.

While the WEP system has been directed toward the understanding of fragments of text occurring in textual discourse, the issues arising in the interpretation of dialogue are very similar. The difference between the two tasks involves the nature of discourse interactions. In interpreting fragments of dialogue from the vantage point of one of the participants, word experts must interact with model processes monitoring the goals of the other participant. The following example (provided by James Allen) illustrates the question.

9. When is the Windsor train?

In trying to understand this question from the perspective of the person at the information desk of a train station, the question could be directed at eliciting either of two pieces of information (Allen 1978), i.e., the time of the next arrival from Windsor, or the time of the next departure to Windsor.

By saying that the *Windsor train* is a 'noun-noun pair', we get nowhere in trying to understand it. In WEP, the word experts for *Windsor* and *train* would interact locally and determine the range of possible interpretations for the fragment. In the case of textual discourse, the *train* expert would carry on discourse interactions with the activity process to find out if discussion of some particular train were anticipated in the text. In the case of dialogue, these interactions would occur between *train* and an *intention mechanism*, which might determine that the speaker in the dialogue is concerned with the trains coming from Windsor, and not with the trains leaving for Windsor. If the processes modelling the activity context or the speaker intentions cannot provide help to the *train* expert, the word experts for the sequence would construct a concept structure to represent the disjunct of the two possibilities, but continue to await the information that would decide between them.

3.4 Logical interactions

The understanding of fragments of natural language text *by a particular individual* (or computer program) often requires knowledge of the beliefs of that individual. How can this be true given the fact that, even when the discourse context has not been made to render a particular fragment unambiguous, the majority of readers still interpret it the same way? The answer lies in the common experience brought to understanding by readers from the same culture. This notion carries over to the common experiences of people in all sorts of sub-cultures as well, such as scientific communities (e.g. linguists, psychologists), religious groups, age and class groups (e.g., college students, ghetto youth), and so forth. There are pieces of text that would be understood in common by members of these groups and not by people outside these groups, and other fragments that would be understood in common by almost everyone.

A psychological experiment at Stanford University (Smith, Rips and Shoben 1974), described in the paper by Bolinger (1979) that I have made such extensive use of here, tested the meaning of various words in terms of class membership. Subjects were asked to judge the truth or falsity of certain sentences, such as *A robin is a bird* and *A chicken is a bird*. The fact that it generally takes longer to judge the latter true than the former led the researchers to conclude that there are degrees of birdiness. Clearly, different people with different conceptions of notions like birdiness would understand the same sentence in different ways. Furthermore, the data of these psychologists, when interpreted in terms of language understanding, suggests that a lexical sequence could be viewed as representing, *to a greater or lesser degree*, some particular conceptual notion.

It is my belief that the understanding of many sequences of words takes place through a process of comparing new sequences to already interpreted ones. Since the linguistic experience of each individual is different, language comprehension must necessarily take place in a person-specific manner. Examine the following sentence for an example of what I mean.

10. Joanie Caucus throws a seminar.

Most people reading this sentence will understand the notion of *throwing a seminar* by comparison with the other kinds of things they have (linguistically) seen thrown. When someone *throws a party*, for example, he is organizing a social event. When someone *throws a chess match*, he is losing the match on purpose. My claim is that by comparing *throwing a seminar* with other fragments involving *throwing*, people come up with the intended interpretation of the fragment.

3.4.1 Multiple choice perspectives. This notion of comparison with already known concepts is a fundamental method of interpretation in the Word Expert Parser. Individual word experts interact with a memory of real-world knowledge to determine whether certain conceptual notions can be perceived as other ones. The paradigm for these interactions is based on multiple choice: of all the fragments of text that have already been understood (the finite choice), which most closely resembles the one now being examined? For the example sentence above, the question in WEP would be put forth by the *throw* expert and would be some variation on the following (depending on the knowledge of *throw* stored in the *throw* word expert): 'Is a seminar better viewed as a party, a tantrum, a chess game, a legal case, or a baseball?'[4]

This type of logical interaction (interaction between a word expert and a process modelling beliefs about the world) has a fundamental role in WEP language understanding. The queries like the example are called (*multiple choice*) *VIEW interactions*. It is important to note that these multiple choice queries often take place without including a 'none of the above' option. The understanding process must be directed toward the goal of providing some interpretation on each portion of input text. This means that a reader must do the best that he can to understand it, whether or not he has sufficient linguistic and cultural experience to come to the correct (intended) interpretation. Sometimes we make mistakes.

3.4.2 Plausibility of propositions. The multiple choice view interactions allow word experts to use general knowledge about conceptual items in the world to understand fragments of natural language text. Another kind of general knowledge concerns structures more complex than single items, namely relations among several such conceptual items. When we perceive such a relation as being convertible into some sort of truth value, we call it a *proposition*. In WEP, propositions may have truth values along a wide range, from something we might call *completely disbelieved* to the opposite extreme we could call *completely believed*. I say that propositions in WEP work like this not because of the existence of a computer program to operate on them, but rather, because such a program must exist for language understanding within the WEP framework.

The reason involves one class of logical interactions, those between individual word experts and a process maintaining beliefs about the world. A word expert may interact with this belief modelling process to determine the *relative plausibility* of two propositions. Consider the following sentences, both of which have been successfully interpreted by the existing WEP system (with the user acting as the belief modelling process).

11. The man eating tiger growls.

12. The man eating shrimp growls.

The difference between these two fragments from the perspective of WEP involves the relative plausibility of *tigers that eat men* and *men who eat tigers* in the first case, and of *shrimp that eat men* and *men who eat shrimp* in the second. Of course, in certain contexts, the problem is resolved through discourse interactions; the activity context or focus of attention could make clear the appropriate meaning of the sentences without any need at all for more general knowledge. Clearly, however, we can understand these fragments perfectly well without any guiding discourse context.

The understanding of these fragments is coordinated in WEP by the word expert for the affix *ing*. The ing expert interacts linguistically with the experts for the words around it, helping them form meaningful sequences, and carries on logical interactions with the belief modelling process to determine the relative plausibility of the two propositions possibly signified by the larger sequence. In the first case above, the *ing* expert begins executing after *the* and *man* have already started constructing a concept structure to represent the meaning of *the man*. It awaits the report of this concept structure, as well as the one to be reported by the *tiger* word expert. Furthermore, *ing* carries on linguistic interactions with *eat* to arrive cooperatively at a concept structure representing its meaning. The *ing* expert then has a *plausibility interaction* with the belief modeller, and coordinates the remainder of the understanding process based on this important knowledge. See Small (1980) for a computer trace of the analyses of example sentences 11 and 12.

4. EXAMPLE: 'THE MAN THROWS IN THE TOWEL'

The following example trace of the Word Expert Parser was made at the University of Rochester with a version of WEP very similar to that described in Small (1980) and Small and Rieger (1982). The text which follows was altered only in the following trivial ways from the exact output of the parsing program:

A) All data typed by the user have been set in bold face;
B) all simulated interactions with parallel inference modules (i.e., queries to the user about such topics as focus of attention) have been set in italics; and
C) the spacing and indentation were changed to facilitate the commentary in the right hand column.

Each part of the trace separated by a line of asterisks represents an execution of a word expert. Since these are coroutines simulating parallel processes, a particular expert may execute several times before finally terminating. Each expert has a name indicated on the first line of the trace; for example, the first occurrence of the word *the* is called e00009 by the model. The next line of the trace for a particular execution of some word expert contains *(a)* the name of the entry point (the modular subpiece of an expert) where execution resumes; and *(b)* the name of the word expert responsible for sending its input data (on the next line). This data includes a *concept structure* and a *control signal* (as described in a previous section of this paper). Note that sometimes one or both of these inputs are empty.

The rest of the trace shows the execution of each entry point. Most of the word expert actions and model events are left out of this short execution trace, as the details of the WEP theory have not been described in this paper. The important aspects of the trace for the current purposes are *(a)* the general flow of activity in the model, including the suspension and resumption of experts; and *(b)* the interactions of word experts with each other and with external knowledge sources. These latter lexical interactions are easily spotted in the example by their appeal to the user for input. Recall that the parallel comprehension processes required by WEP are currently simulated by the user.

Script started on Thu Oct 1 18:32:35 1981

$ ipclisp
/usr/lisp/ipclisp 11/16/80.

1.(loadwep)
Word Expert Parser loaded
t

2.(w%wep)
Word Expert Parser
Micro-WEP 5.2
IRCAM/Paris VIII/Rochester/Maryland

[wep] **trace 5**

[wep] **parse**

This is a version of Franz Lisp running on the VAX-780 at the University of Rochester. All WEP research is now being conducted with this system. Other versions of WEP include one running in VLISP on the PDP-10 at *IRCAM* in Paris and one running in Maryland Lisp at the University of Maryland.

Version 5.2 of WEP has been developed at IRCAM, the Universite de Paris VIII (Vincennes), the University of Rochester, and the University of Maryland.

The trace is set at level 5 (the highest setting is level 20) to print just the minimum of information.

WORD EXPERT PARSER

text» **The man throws in the towel.**
»◄─
reading: the
initializing: the/e00009

****

*e00009 **entry/initentry *expert/nil
*the **concept/nil *signal/break
»entry: initentry
»entry: e0

****

The WEP reader requires more text. The parser does not work on whole sentences at a time, but rather on individual words and phrases as they are read. Textual analysis completes only when the user explicitly states that there will be no additional input.

The *the* expert executes first, receiving no concept structure as input, but receiving the BREAK control signal, which indicates a preceding sentence break. The expert starts the construction of a concept structure (to represent the mapping of the recognized noun phrase), and then pauses execution.

```
*e00009 **entry/e1 *expert/wep
*the **concept/nil *signal/pause
»entry: e1
reading: man
initializing: man/e00023
```

The pause allows any suspended experts to resume execution on the basis of the new information just broadcast by the expert. When WEP becomes fully parallel (i.e., experts as processes rather than as coroutines), certain details of this control will change. The *the* expert finally suspends its execution and awaits the report of the anticipated conceptual entity.

****

```
*e00023 **entry/initentry *expert/e00009
*man **concept/nil *signal/entity-construction
»entry: initentry
»entry: e0
»entry: e1
```

The word expert for *man* begins executing with the ENTITY-CONSTRUCTION control signal reflecting the inference from the *the* expert about the processing state of the parser. The *man* expert determines immediately that *man* denotes a human adult male (this word is not currently disambiguated), and reports the concept structure representing this to the rest of the system.

****

```
*e00009 **entry/e2 *expert/e00023
*the **concept/c00037 *signal/nil
»entry: e2
q»*******» Discourse Focus «*******
q»
q»c00037: c#human-adult-male c#/#man
   c#anything
q»**lexical: the man
q»
q»Is such a concept in focus? no

reading: throws
initializing: s/e00055
initializing: throw/e00056
```

Only a single word expert was awaiting this concept report, the *the* expert, and it now continues its processing. It must now determine, in consultation with the focus of attention process, whether or not the new description has a referent in the existing context. If so, *the* reports this referent concept to the rest of the model; otherwise it sends along the concept just constructed. In the example, we assume that there is no previous referent (or we shall have to provide it!) and answer no to the query.

****

```
*e00055 **entry/initentry *expert/e00023
*s **concept/nil *signal/complete-entity
»entry: initentry
»entry: e0
```

The next word expert to execute is that for the suffix *s*. Experts for suffixes always execute before the root words to which they are attached. Context analysis by the *s* expert determines that the input is starting to describe an action, and thus it broadcasts the relevant control signal, the ACTION-CONSTRUCTION signal, to the rest of the system.

```
*************************************************
```

```
*e00056 **entry/initentry *expert/e00009
*throw **concept/nil *signal/action-construction
»entry: initentry
»entry: e0
»entry: e2

q»*******» Multiple Perspective «*******
q»
q»c00037: c‡human-adult-male c‡/‡man
   c‡anything
q»**lexical: the man
q»
q»c00079: c‡anything
q»
q»Can the former be viewed as the latter? yes

»entry: e1
```

The *throw* expert is the most important process involved in the analysis of the example fragment. It consists of many entry points (subprocesses) and executes several times. On this first execution, *throw* starts the construction of an action concept, and then attempts to refine its meaning to be as precise as possible given the existing discourse context and surrounding lexical constraints. Its first action toward this goal is to search the local active memory for a concept structure potentially representing the agent of the designated action. The system queries the user as part of the matching process, after *throw* finds a prospective match. Next, *throw* uses this prospective agent to begin its disambiguation. The conceptual relationship between the concept in the subject position and various known agents (i.e., machines, people, horses, and organizations) leads to inferences by *throw* about its meaning. In this case, we tell WEP that a man is more like a person than like the other possibilities.

```
q»*******» Conceptual Proximity «*******
q»
q»c00037: c‡human-adult-male c‡/‡man
   c‡anything
q»**lexical: the man
q»
q»view concepts:
   c‡machine c‡horse c‡person c‡organization
q»Which views apply (best first)? c‡person
```

The *throw* expert asks that the next word be read, since often its immediate successor affects fundamentally its meaning (as in this case). The *in* expert thus begins executing with the PARTICLE control signal. This signal requests that *in* decide if it plays the role as verb particle. The incoming concept

»entry: e70
»entry: e50
»entry: e3
reading: in
initializing: in/e00137

gives *in* the advice of *throw* about the decision. Note that the system is robust enough that a non-response by *in* within a certain time is treated as a rejection.

****

*e00137 **entry/initentry *expert/e00056
*in **concept/c00145 *signal/particle
»entry: initentry
»entry: e0
reading: the
initializing: the/e00169

The *in* expert must await the execution of subsequent experts. If the next expert begins construction of an entity concept structure (i.e., representing a noun phrase), *in* awaits the report of that structure. If the next expert does anything else, *in* continues its processing.

****

*e00169 **entry/initentry *expert/e00015
*the **concept/nil *signal/setting
»entry: initentry
»entry: e0

In this example, the *the* expert immediately broadcasts the awaited ENTITY-CONSTRUCTION signal, and then pauses. Note that the pause is significant here, as the *in* expert resumes execution.

****

*e00137 **entry/e1 *expert/e00169
*in **concept/nil *signal/entity-construction
»entry: e1

The *in* expert prepares to receive the forthcoming concept structure and suspends itself once again.

****

*e00169 **entry/e1 *expert/wep
*the **concept/nil *signal/pause
»entry: e1
reading: towel
initializing: towel/e00191

The pausing *the* expert now continues its processing, and begins the construction of the new concept structure (representing the meaning of the noun phrase). The reader examines the next word, *towel*, and initializes its expert.

****

*e00191 **entry/initentry *expert/e00137
*towel **concept/nil *signal/entity-construction
»entry: initentry
»entry: e0
»entry: e1

The word expert for *towel* builds the very much awaited concept structure, which it reports to the model as a whole. This particular broadcast causes great fireworks in the system, as many suspended word experts await the concept.

****

*e00169 **entry/e2 *expert/e00191
*the **concept/c00205 *signal/nil
»entry: e2

q»*******» *Discourse Focus* «*******
q»
q»c00205: c‡towel c‡/‡towel c‡anything
q»**lexical: the towel
q»
q»*Is such a concept in focus?* **no

The *the* expert resumes execution, and along with the reference mechanism, tries to find a referent for the towel description. Again playing the part of this mechanism, we answer that there is no matching description in the focus of attention of the system. This causes the just created structure (intercepted by *the*) to be sent along to other awaiting experts.

****

The *in* expert resumes, now equipped to determine whether or not it plays the role of verb particle to *throw*. The process it goes through to determine this involves comparing the expectations of *throw* in the existing context with those normally associated with *in*. Thus, *in the morning* would cause *in* to reject a role as particle, while *in the tractor* would lead to acceptance of that role. The query to a simulated knowledge base mechanism asks whether the reported concept more closely resembles a physical object, an idea, a gear, a machine, a time, a state, or a volume. The first four cases cause acceptance of the particle role; the latter three cause rejection. We answer that indeed towels can be viewed as physical objects better than as times, states, or volumes.

*e00137 **entry/e41 *expert/e00169
*in **concept/c00205 *signal/nil
»entry: e41
»entry: e2

q»*******» *Multiple Perspective* «*******
q»
q»c00205: c‡towel c‡/‡towel c‡anything
q»**lexical: the towel
q»
q»c00145: c‡anything
q»** *oneof:* c‡physobj c‡idea c‡gear c‡machine
q»** *noneof:* c‡time c‡state c‡volume
q»
q»*Can the former be viewed as the latter?* **yes

****

*e00056 **entry/e4 *expert/e00137
*throw **concept/c00205 *signal/accept
»entry: e4

****

*e00056 **entry/e5 *expert/wep
*throw **concept/nil *signal/pause
»entry: e5

q»*******» *Conceptual Proximity* «*******
q»
q»c00205: c#*towel* c#/#*towel* c#*anything*
q»***lexical: the towel*
q»
q»view concepts:
  c#*physobj* c#*idea*
q» *Which views apply (best first)?* c#**physobj**

q»*******» *Discourse Focus* «*******
q»
q»c00259: c#*anything*
q»** *oneof*: c#*area* c#*volume*
q»
q»*Is such a concept in focus?* **no**

q»*******» *Conceptual Proximity* «*******
q»
q»c00205: c#*physobj* c#*towel* c#/#*towel*
  c#*anything*
q»***lexical: the towel*
q»
q»view concepts:
  c#*physobj* c#*gear* c#*machine*
q» *Which views apply (best first)?* c#**physobj**

The broadcast of the ACCEPT signal thus causes resumption of the *throw* expert, which can now continue its own disambiguation task. After pausing with no intermediate resumptions, *throw* now pursues its complex task of deciding among the various possible meanings of *throw in the towel* in the current context. The first step, shown in the first user query, decides between *throwing in ideas* and *throwing objects into places*. The second query actually determines, without a particular volume or area specified for the *throwing in* action, whether or not one can be located within the focus of attention (e.g., *Rick jumps in the pool. Joanie throws in the towel.*). Thirdly, *throw* asks about the concept to see if it can be some kind of machine being put into operation (e.g., *Rick threw in the tractor*). And lastly, the throw expert tests whether or not some bargaining action (e.g., *Rick and Joanie are bargaining over the price. Rick throws in a dollar*) or some charitable action (e.g. *Rick receives the plate in Church. He throws in a dollar*) are within the focus of attention. Since the results of all these external lexical interactions, both discourse and logical interactions, came out the way they did, the *throw* expert chooses the idiomatic meaning of *throw in the towel*, as can be seen below in the structures built to represent the meaning of the fragment.

q»*******» *Discourse Expectation* «*******
q»
q»c00271: c#*anyaction*
q»** *oneof*: c#*charitable-action*
  c#*bargaining-action*
q»
q»*Concept not expected locally.*
q»*Is such a concept expected?* **no**
reading: *period*
initializing: *period*/e00287

****

*e00287 **entry/initentry *expert/e00056
**period* **concept/nil *signal/complete-entity
»entry: initentry
»entry: e0

Lastly, the word expert for the period ending the sentence executes, sending a sentence BREAK signal to the rest of the model. This signal often causes some final bookkeeping to be done within certain experts.

WORD EXPERT PARSER

text»◄─

We provide the system with no more text, and after executing any spontaneous expert resumptions (none in the example), the parsing process terminates.

[wep] **memory**

The active memory contains the constructed meaning representations. Note that WEP is a process model, and the trace of its execution contains far more relevant information about WEP and its value than do these fairly ad hoc case frameworks.

*** *Active Memory* ***

concept: c#anyaction

The concept representing the most general action in the knowledge hierarchy.

concept: c00075
  value: c#/#throw
  isa: c#anyaction
  type: action
  lexical: (s throw)
  aspects: ((agent . c00037))

The concept underlying the linguistic entity throw.

concept: c00101
  value: c#person-throw
  isa: c00075
  type: action

A concept structure representing the action of a person throwing.

concept: c00241
  value: c#/#throwin
  isa: c00101
  type: action
  aspects: ((object . c00205))

A concept structure to represent the linguistic fragment *throw in* in the knowledge hierarchy.

concept: c00203
  value: c#/#towel
  isa: c#anything
  type: entity

An underlying conceptual representation of the lexical item *towel*.

concept: c#anything

The most general conceptual entity (e.g., as opposed to action) in the hierarchy of system knowledge.

concept: c00035
  value: c#/#man
  isa: c#anything
  type: entity

The conceptual entity represented by the word *man* in the lexicon.

concept: c00283
  value: c#give-up
  isa: c00241
  type: action

The representation of the conceptual notion of conceding defeat in a competitive situation. This is the underlying representation for the idiomatic meaning of *throw in the towel*.

concept: c00205
  value: c#towel
  isa: c00203
  type: entity
  lexical: (the towel)
  roles: ((object . c00241))
  role: object
  allof: (c#physobj)

The structure representing the conceptual notion of a towel.

concept: c00037
  value: c#human-adult-male
  isa: c00035
  type: entity
  lexical: (the man)
  roles: ((agent . c00075))
  role: agent
  allof: (c#person)

The concept structure representing a human adult male, and hence, the person underlying the syntactic subject of the example sentence.

[wep] **exit**
WEP

3.(exit)
$

script done on Thu Oct 1 18:35:00 1981

5. SUMMARY

Word Expert Parsing is a psycholinguistic and computational theory of parsing based on a lexical organization of linguistic knowledge represented procedurally in word experts. The comprehension of fragments of natural language text is viewed as a process of word interactions, where active lexical agents cooperate to form meaningful sequences of interrelated lexical items. Lexical interactions are of four types, *idiosyncratic*, *linguistic*, *discourse*, and *logical*. Idiosyncratic interactions allow WEP to explain the understanding of idiomatic (more or less idiomatic) lexical sequences, by comparing new sequences with explicitly remembered ones (called *prefabs* by Bolinger (1979)). Linguistic interactions enable the use of syntactic and semantic generalizations to interpret fragments, and discourse interactions provide word experts with knowledge of discourse activities and foci of attention. Logical interactions allow word experts to use knowledge about the real world, especially about the multiple perspectives of individual conceptual objects within it and the relative plausibility of propositions about it.

ACKNOWLEDGEMENTS

The research described in this report has been supported for several years by Grant NSG-7253 from the National Aeronautics and Space Administration to the University of Maryland. During the writing of this paper, the author was supported by a Fulbright-Hays Lectureship in Artificial Intelligence at the Universite de Paris, and computer facilities were provided by the Institut de Recherche et Coordination Acoustique/Musique. The support of NASA, the Fulbright-Hays program, and IRCAM are gratefully acknowledged. A much abbreviated version of this paper appeared in the Proceedings of the Seventh International Joint Conference on Artificial Intelligence, Vancouver, British Columbia, 1981.

NOTES

1. The fabrication of a proper contextual setting in which this would occur truly requires imagination. Perhaps (?) two people could toss baseballs back and forth while wrapped (together) in a towel. Note the underlying view that any context is possible if improbable, and that a theory of understanding must account for all of them.

2. Actually, an *ed* expert begins executing first and interacts with pattern to determine its role in the local context. This takes place before *hundred* receives an answer to its query. The same would hold true later, when the *s* expert must interact with *dish*. The notion of suffix experts, and the fact that they execute before the root words to which they are attached, is discussed in Small (1980).

3. The term activity context describes a notion similar to the scripts of Schank and Abelson (1975) and to the frames of Charniak (1977). The notion of focus of attention has been taken directly from the work of Grosz (1977).

4. Note the important effect such logical interactions have on motivating general inference processes in understanding. The augmentation of a real-world knowledge base depends on making appropriate inferences, and WEP motivates these by forcing the system to find relationships between previously unrelated notions. For example, by asking to relate seminar and party, the parser instigates the construction of a new concept to represent 'an organized activity of people'.

BIBLIOGRAPHY

Aho, A.V. and Ullman, J.D. (1972).
'The Theory of Parsing, Translation and Compiling. Volume 1: Parsing'. Prentice-Hall, Englewood Cliffs, New Jersey.

Airenti, G., Bara, B.G. and Colombetti, M. (1980).
A semantic memory model as a basis for a problem solving system. *Giornale Italiano di Psicologia* 7, no. 2.

Allen, J. (1978).
Recognizing Intention in Dialogue. Technical Report, Department of Computer Science, University of Toronto.

Allen, J.F. and Small, S.L. (1982).
The Rochester discourse comprehension project. *To appear in* SIGART Newsletter.

Bach, E. and Harms, R. (1968).
'Universals in Linguistic Theory'. Holt, Rinehart and Winston, New York.

Baker, H.G. (1975).
The meat hook parser. Mimeo. MIT, Cambridge, Mass.

Bates, M. (1978).
The theory and practice of augmented transition network grammars. *In* 'Natural Language Communication with Computers'. (Ed. L. Bolc), pp. 191-259. Springer Verlag, Berlin.

Becker, J. (1975).
The phrasal lexicon. *In* 'Proceedings of the Workshop on Theoretical Issues in Natural Language Processing'. (Eds. R.C. Schank and B.L.

Nash-Webber), pp. 70-73. Bolt, Beranek and Newman, Cambridge, Mass.

Bever, T.G. (1971).
Integrated study of linguistic behaviour. *In* 'Biological and Social Factors in Psycholinguistics'. (Ed. J. Morton). Logos Press, London.

Bever, T.G. (1975).
Functional explanations require independently motivated functional theories. *In* 'CLS Parasession on Functionalism'. (Eds. R.E. Grossman, L.J. San and T.J. Vance), pp. 580-609. University of Chicago, Chicago.

Bever, T.G. and Hurtig, R. (1975).
Detection of a non-linguistic stimulus is poorest at the end of a clause. *Journal of Psycholinguistic Research* 4, 1-7.

Bien, J.S. (1976).
Multiple environments approach to natural language. *American Journal of Computational Linguistics* 3, microfiche 54.

Birnbaum, L. and Selfridge, M. (1979).
Problems in the Conceptual Analysis of Natural Language. Computer Science Department Technical Report no. 168, University of Yale.

Bobrow, D.G. and Collins, A. (1975).
'Representation and Understanding'. Academic Press, London and New York.

Bobrow, D.G. and Fraser, J.B. (1969).
An augmented state transition network analysis. *In* 'Proceedings of the First International Joint Conference on Artificial Intelligence', pp. 557-567.

Bobrow, R.J. and Webber, B.L. (1980a).
Psi-Klone: parsing and semantic interpretation in the BBN natural language understanding system. *In* 'Proceedings of the Third Biennial Conference of the Canadian Society for Computational Studies of Intelligence', pp. 131-142. University of Victoria, Victoria.

Bobrow, R.J. and Webber, B.L. (1980b).
Knowledge representation for syntactic/semantic processing. *In* 'Proceedings of the 1st. Annual Conference of the American Association for Artificial Intelligence'. pp. 316-323, Stanford University, Stanford.

Boguraev, B.K. (1980).
Resolution of Linguistic Ambiguities. Technical Report no. 11, Computer Laboratory, University of Cambridge, Cambridge.

Bolc, L. (1978).
'Natural Language Communication with Computers'. Springer Verlag, Berlin.

Bolinger, D. (1975).
'Aspects of Language'. Harcourt, Brace, Jovanovich, New York.

Bolinger, D. (1979).
Meaning and memory. *In* 'Experience Forms. their Cultural and Individual Place and Function'. (Ed. G.G. Haydu). Mouton, The Hague.

Bower, G.H. (Ed.) (1974).
'The Psychology of Learning and Motivation'. Vol. 8. Academic Press, New York.

Bransford, J.D., McCarrell, N.S., Franks, J.J. and Nitsch, K.E. (1978).
Towards unexplaining memory: towards an ecological psychology. *In* 'Perceiving, Acting and Knowing'. (Eds. R. Shaw and J.D. Bransford), pp. 431-466. Lawrence Erlbaum Associates, Hillside, New Jersey.

Bresnan, J. (1977).
Variables in the theory of transformations. *In* 'Formal Syntax'. (Eds. P. Culicover, T. Wasow and A. Akmajian), pp. 157-196. Academic Press, New York.

Bresnan, J. (1978).
A realistic transformational grammar. *In* 'Linguistic Theory and Psychological Reality'. (Eds. M. Halle, J. Bresnan and G. Miller), pp. 1-59. MIT Press, Cambridge, Mass.

Brooks, L. (1978).
Non-analytic concept formation and memory for instances. *In* 'Cognition and Categorization'. (Eds. E. Rosch and B. B. Lloyd). Lawrence Erlbaum Associates, Hillside, New Jersey.

Bundy, A., Byrd, L., Luger, G., Mellish, C. and Palmer, M. (1979).
Solving mechanics problems using meta-level inference. *In* 'Proceedings of the Sixth International Conference on Artificial Intelligence', pp. 1017-1027. Tokyo.

Burton, R. (1976).
Semantic Grammar: An Engineering Technique for Constructing Natural Language Understanding Systems. Technical Report 3453. Bolt, Beranek and Newman, Cambridge, Mass.

Catell, R. (1976).
Constraints on movement rules. *Language* 52, 18-50.

Charniak, E. (1977).
Ms. Malaprop, a language comprehension program. *In* 'Proceedings of the Fifth International Joint Conference on Artificial Intelligence', pp. 91-97. Tbilisi.

Charniak, E. and Wilks, Y. (1975).
'Computational Semantics'. North Holland, Amsterdam.

Chase, W.G. (Ed.) (1973).
'Visual Information Processing'. Academic Press, New York.

Chomsky, N. (1957).
'Syntactic Structures'. Mouton, The Hague.

Chomsky, N. (1963).
Formal properties of grammars. *In* 'Handbook of Mathematical Psychology'. (Eds. R.D. Luce, R.R. Bush and E. Galanter), Vol. 2, pp. 323-418. Wiley, New York.

Chomsky, N. (1964).
Current issues in linguistic theory. *In* 'The Structure of Language'. (Eds. J.A. Fodor and J.J. Katz), pp. 50-118. Prentice-Hall, Englewood Cliffs, New Jersey.

Chomsky, N. (1965).
'Aspects of the Theory of Syntax'. MIT Press, Cambridge, Mass.

Chomsky, N. (1966).
'Topics in the Theory of Generative Grammar'. Mouton, The Hague.

Chomsky, N. (1972).
'Language and Mind'. 2nd edition. Harcourt, Brace, Jovanovich, New York.

Chomsky, N. (1979).
On markedness and core grammar. *To appear in* 'Proceedings of the III Glow Conference'. (Eds. A. Belleti, L. Brandi and L. Rizzi). Annali della Scuola Normale Superiore di Pisa, Pisa.

Chomsky, N. (1980).
On the representation of form and function. *To appear in* 'Proceedings of the 1980 CNRS Conference on the Cognitive Sciences, Paris'. (Ed. J. Mehler).

Chomsky, N. (1981).
'Lectures on Government and Binding'. Foris Publications, Dordrecht, Holland.

Chomsky, N. and Halle, M. (1968).
'The Sound Pattern of English'. Harper and Row, New York.

Chomsky, N. and Lasnik, H. (1977).
Filters and control. *Linguistic Inquiry* 8, 425-504.

Chomsky, N. and Miller, G.A. (1963).
Introduction to the formal analysis of natural languages. *In* 'Handbook

of Mathematical Psychology'. (Eds. R.D. Luce, R.R. Bush and E. Galanter), Vol. 2, pp. 269-321. Wiley, New York.

Colby, K. (1975).
'Artificial Paranoia'. Pergamon Press, Oxford.

Colmerauer, A. (1970).
Les Systèmes Q. Publication interne nr. 43, TAUM. Université de Montréal.

Colmerauer, A. (1975).
Les Grammaires de Métamorphose. Groupe d'Intelligence Artificielle, Université de Marseille-Luminy. *Reprinted as* Metamorphosis grammars *in* 'Natural Language Communication with Computers'. (Ed. L. Bolc). Springer-Verlag, Berlin.

Conway, N.E. (1963).
Design of a separable transition-diagram compiler. *Communications of the ACM 6/7*, 396-408.

Davies, D.J.M. and Isard, S.D. (1972).
Utterances as programs. *In* 'Machine Intelligence 7'. (Ed. D. Michie). Edinburgh University Press, Edinburgh.

Davis, R. (1977).
Generalised procedure calling and content directed inference. Proceedings of the Symposium on Artificial Intelligence and Programming Languages. SIGART/SIGPLAN.

Davis, R. (1980a).
Reasoning about control. *Artificial Intelligence* 15, 179-222.

Davis, R. (1980b).
Content reference: reasoning about rules. *Artificial Intelligence* 15, 223-239.

Davis, R. and Buchanan, B.G. (1977).
Meta-level knowledge: an overview and applications. *In* 'Proceedings of the Fifth International Joint Conference on Artificial Intelligence', pp. 920-927. MIT, Cambridge, Mass.

Davis, R. and King, J. (1977).
An overview of production systems. *In* 'Machine Intelligence 8'. (Eds. E.W. Elcock and D. Michie), pp. 300-304. Edinburgh University Press, Edinburgh.

De Jong, G. (1979).
Prediction and substantiation: a new approach to natural language processing. *Cognitive Science*, Vol. 3, 251-273.

Dingwall, W.O. (1976).
'A Survey of Linguistic Science'. Greylock Publishers, Stamford, Connecticut.

Dresher, E. and Hornstein, N. (1976).
On some supposed contributions of artificial intelligence to the scientific study of language. *Cognition* 4, 321-378.

Dyer, M. (1981).
Integrated parsing in the context of narratives. Mimeo. Computer Science Department, Yale University.

Earley, J. (1970).
An efficient context-free parsing algorithm. *Communications of the ACM* 13, 94-102.

Eisenstadt, M. (1979).
Alternative parsers for conceptual dependency. *In* 'Proceedings of the 6th International Joint Conference on Artificial Intelligence', pp. 238-240. Tokyo.

Elcock, E.W. and Michie, D. (Eds.) (1977).
'Machine Intelligence 8'. Edinburgh University Press, Edinburgh.

Erman, L.D., Hayes-Roth, F., Lesser, V.R. and Reddy, D.R. (1980).
The Hearsay-II speech understanding system: integrating knowledge to resolve uncertainty. *Computing Surveys* 12 (2), 213-253.

Fahlman, S.A. (1979).
'NETL: a System for Representation and Use of Real World Knowledge'. MIT Press, Cambridge, Mass.

Feigenbaum, E.A., Buchanan, B.G. and Lederbury, J. (1971).
On generality and problem solving:a case study using the Dendral program. *In* 'Machine Intelligence 6'. (Eds. B. Meltzer and D. Michie), pp. 165-190. Edinburgh University Press, Edinburgh.

Feigenbaum, E. and Feldman, J. (Eds.) (1963).
'Computers and Thought'.McGraw-Hill, New York.

Feldman, J.A. and Ballard, D. (1982).
Connection networks and their properties. *Cognitive Science* 6. (to appear).

Fikes, R.E. and Nilsson, N.J. (1971).
STRIPS: a new approach to the application of theorem proving to problem solving. *Artificial Intelligence* 2, no. 3/4, 189-208.

Fillmore, C.J. (1968).
The case for case. *In* 'Universals of Linguistic Theory'. (Eds. E. Bach and R. Harms), pp. 1-88. Holt, Rinehart and Winston, New York.

Findler, N.V. (1979).
'Associative Networks'. Academic Press, New York.

Foderaro, J.K. and Hirst, G. (1980).
FRANZ LISP... The Manual. Department of Computer Science, Brown University, Providence, Rhode Island.

Fodor, J.D. (1978).
Parsing strategies and constraints on transformations. *Linguistic Inquiry* 9, 427-473.

Fodor, J.D. (1980).
Parsing, Constraints and Freedom of Expression. Mimeo. University of Connecticut.

Fodor, J.D. (1981).
'Does Performance Shape Competence'. *Published as* Philosophical Transactions of the Royal Society, Series B, Vol. 295.

Fodor, J.D., Bever, T.G. and Garrett, M.F. (1974).
'The Psychology of Language'. Mc Graw-Hill, New York.

Fodor, J.D. and Frazier, L. (1980).
Is the human sentence parsing mechanism an ATN? *Cognition* 8, 417-459.

Fodor, J.A. and Katz, J.J. (Eds.) (1964).
'The Structure of Language'. Prentice-Hall, Englewood Cliffs, New Jersey.

Frazier, L. and Fodor, J.D. (1978).
The sausage machine: a new two-stage parsing model. *Cognition* 6, 291-325.

Gazdar, G. (1980a).
A phrase structure syntax for comparative clauses. *In* 'Lexical Grammar'. (Eds. T. Hoekstra, H. van der Hulst and M. Moortgat). Foris, Dordrecht.

Gazdar, G. (1980b).
A cross-categorial semantics for co-ordination. *Linguistics and Philosophy*, Vol. 3, 407-409.

Gazdar, G. (1981).
Unbounded dependencies and co-ordinate structure. *Linguistic Inquiry* 12, 155-184.

Gazdar, G. (1982).
Phrase structure grammar. *In* 'The Nature of Syntactic Representation'. (Eds. P.I. Jacobsen and G.K. Pullum). pp. 131-186. Reidel Publishing Co., Dordrecht.

Geach, P. and Black, M. (1960).
'Translations from the Philosophical Writings of Gottlob Frege'.
Blackwell, Oxford.

Georgeff, M.P. (1979).
A framework for control in production systems. Stanford AI Memo
AIM 322. Stanford University.

Georgeff, M.P. (1982).
Procedural control in production systems. *Artificial Intelligence* 18,
2, 175-201.

Gershman, A. (1979).
Knowledge Based Parsing. Computer Science Department Technical
Report No. 156, Yale University.

Gries, D. (1971).
'Compiler Construction for Digital Computers'. Wiley, New York.

Grimes, J. (Ed.) (1975).
Network Grammars. Summer Institute of Linguistics Publications
in Linguistic and Related Fields no. 45.

Grishman, R. (1976).
A survey of syntactic analysis procedures for natural language.
American Journal of Computational Linguistics, microfiche no. 47.

Grishman, R. and Hirschman, L. (1978).
Question answering from natural language medical data bases.
Artificial Intelligence, Vol. 11, nos. 1, 2, 25-43.

Grosz, B. (1977).
The Representation and Use of Focus in Dialogue Understanding.
Technical Note No. 151, Stanford Research Institute.

Halle, M., Bresnan, J.W. and Miller, G.A. (1978).
'Linguistic Theory and Psychological Reality'. MIT Press, Cambridge,
Mass.

Harman, G. (Ed.) (1967).
'On Noam Chomsky'. Anchor Books, New York.

Harman, G. and Davidson, D. (Eds.) (1972).
'Semantics of Natural Language'. Reidel, Dordrecht.

Haydu, G.G. (Ed.) (1979).
'Experience Forms: their Cultural and Individual Place and Function'.
Mouton, The Hague.

Hayes, Patrick J. (1977).
In defence of logic. *In* 'Proceedings of the Fifth International Joint Conference on Artificial Intelligence'. pp. 559-565. MIT, Cambridge, Mass.

Hayes, Patrick J. (1978).
The Naive Physics Manifesto. Working paper No. 34, ISSCO, Geneva.

Hayes, Philip J. (1975).
Semantic markers and selectional restrictions. *In* 'Computational Semantics'. (Eds. E. Charniak and Y. Wilks). pp. 41-54. North-Holland, Amsterdam.

Hayes-Roth, F. and Lesser, V.R. (1977).
Focus of Attention in the HEARSAY II Speech Understanding System. Carnegie Mellon Computer Science Department Report. Carnegie Mellon University.

Hewitt, C. (1971).
Description and Theoretical Analysis (Using Schemata) for PLAN-NER: A Language for Proving Theorems and Manipulating Models in a Robot. MIT Artificial Intelligence Laboratory Report AI-TR-258. MIT, Cambridge, Mass.

Hoekstra, T., van der Hulst, H. and Moortgat, M. (Eds.).
'Lexical Grammar'. Foris, Dordrecht.

Hopcroft, J.E. and Ullman, J.D. (1969).
'Formal Languages and their Relation to Automata'. Addison-Wesley, Reading, Mass.

Hornstein, N. and Weinberg, A. (1981).
Case theory and preposition stranding. *Linguistic Inquiry* 12, 55-91.

Hudson, R. (1980).
Constituency and dependency. *Linguistics*, vol. 1, 179-198.

Isard, S.D. (1974).
What would you have done if ...? *Theoretical Linguistics* 1, no. 3, 233-255.

Jackendoff, R. (1977).
X-bar Syntax: A Study of Phrase-Structure. Linguistic Inquiry Monographs 2. MIT Press, Cambridge, Mass.

Jacobsen, B. (1978).
'Transformational Generative Grammar'. North-Holland, Amsterdam.

Jacobsen, P.I. and Pullum, G.K. (1982).
'The Nature of Syntactic Representation'. Reidel Publishing Co., Dordrecht.

Johnson, D.E. and Postal, P.M. (1980).
'Arc Pair Grammar'. Princeton University Press, Princeton.

Kaplan, R.M. (1970).
'The MIND System: a Grammar Rule Language'. The Rand
Corporation, Santa Monica.

Kaplan, R.M. (1972).
Augmented transition networks as psychological models of sentence
comprehension. *Artificial Intelligence* 3, 77-100.

Kaplan, R.M. (1973).
A general syntactic processor. *In* 'Natural Language Processing'. (Ed.
R. Rustin), pp. 193-241. Algorithmics Press, New York.

Kaplan, R.M. (1975).
On process models for sentence analysis. *In* 'Explorations in Cognition'.
(Eds. D.A. Norman and D.E. Rummelhart), pp. 117-135. Freeman,
San Francisco.

Kaplan, R.M. and Bresnan, J.W. (1980).
Lexical-Functional Grammar: A Formal System for Grammatical
Representatoin. Occasional Paper no. 13, MIT Center for Cognitive
Science, MIT, Cambridge, Mass.

Katz, J.J. and Fodor, J.A. (1963).
The structure of a semantic theory. *Language* 39, no. 2, 170-210.
Reprinted in 'The Structure of Language'. (Eds. J.A. Fodor and J.J.
Katz). Prentice-Hall, Englewood Cliffs, New Jersey.

Kay, M. (1973).
The MIND system. *In* 'Natural Language Processing'. (Ed. R. Rustin).
Algorithmics Press, New York.

Kay, M. (1975).
Syntactic processing and functional sentence perspective. *In* 'Proceed-
ings of the Workshop on Theoretical Issues in Natural Language
Processing'. (Eds. R.C. Schank and B.L. Nash-Webber), pp. 6-9.
Bolt, Beranek and Newman, Cambridge, Mass.

Kay, M. (1976).
Experiments with a powerful parser. *American Journal of Computational Linguistics*, microfiche no. 43.

Kay, M. (1977).
Morphological and syntactic analysis. *In* 'Linguistic Structures

Processing'. (Ed. A. Zampolli), pp. 131-234. North Holland, Amsterdam.

Kay, M. (1980).
Algorithmic schemata and data structures in syntactic processing. Nobel Symposium on Text Processing, Stockholm.

Kayne, R. (1981).
ECP extensions. *Linguistic Inquiry* 12, 93-133.

Keenan, E. (Ed.) (1975).
'Formal Semantics of Natural Language'. Cambridge University Press, Cambridge.

Kimball, J. (1973).
Seven principles of surface structure parsing in natural language. *Cognition* 2, 15-47.

Kimball, J. (1975).
Predictive analysis and over-the-top parsing. *In* 'Syntax and Semantics'. (Ed. J. Kimball), Vol. 4, pp. 155-179. Academic Press, New York.

Knuth, D. (1971).
'The Art of Computer Programming'. Vol. 1. Addison Wesley, Reading, Mass.

Koster, J. (1978).
'Locality Principles in Syntax'. Foris Publications, Dordrecht, Holland.

Kuno, S. (1965).
The predictive analyser and a path elimination technique. *Communications of the ACM* 8, 687-698.

Lakoff, G. and Peters, S. (1966).
Phrasal conjunction and symmetric predicates. *Reprinted in* 'Modern Studies in English'. (Eds. D.A. Reibel and S.A. Schane). Prentice-Hall, Englewood Cliffs, New Jersey.

Lehnert, W., Dyer, M.G.,Johnson, P.N., Yang, C.J. and Harley, S. (1981).
BORIS, an experiment in in-depth understanding of narratives. Computer Science Department Memo No. 188. Yale University.

Lenat, D.B. (1977).
Automated theory formation in mathematics. *In* 'Proceedings of the Fifth International Joint Conference on Artificial Intelligence', pp. 833-842. MIT, Cambridge, Mass.

Levrat, D.B. and McDermott, J. (1977).
Less than general production system architectures. *In* 'Proceedings of the Fifth International Joint Conference on Artificial Intelligence'. MIT, Cambridge, Mass.

Lightfoot, D.W. (1980).
Trace theory and explanation. *In* 'Syntax and Semantics'. (Eds. E.A. Moravcsik and J.R. Wirth), Vol. 13, pp. 137-166. Academic Press, New York.

Luce, R.D., Bush, R.R. and Galanter, E. (1963).
'Handbook of Mathematical Psychology', vol. 2. Wiley, New York.

McCarthy, J. (1963).
A basis for a mathematical theory of computation. *In* 'Computer Programming and Formal Systems'. (Eds. P. Braffort and D. Hirschberg), pp. 33-70. North-Holland, Amsterdam.

McCawley, J.D. (1968).
The role of semantics in a grammar. *In* 'Universals in Linguistic Theory'. (Eds. E. Bach and R. Harms), pp. 125-169. Holt, Rinehart and Winston, New York.

McDermott, D. (1977).
Flexibility and Efficiency in a Computer Program for Designing Circuits. AI Technical Report 402, Artificial Intelligence Laboratory, MIT, Cambridge, Mass.

McDermott, D. and Forgy, C. (1978).
Production system conflict resolution strategies. *In* 'Pattern-directed Inference Systems'. (Eds. D. Waterman and F. Hayes-Roth), pp. 177-203. Academic Press, London.

Marcus, M.P. (1975).
Wait and See Strategies for Parsing Natural Language. Working Paper 75. Artificial Intelligence Laboratory, MIT, Cambridge.

Marcus, M.P. (1978).
A computational account of some constraints on language. *In* 'Theoretical Issues in Natural Language Processing 2'. (Ed. D. Waltz), pp. 236-246. Illinois.

Marcus, M.P. (1979).
An Overview of a Theory of Syntactic Recognition for Natural Language. AI Memo no. 531, Artificial Intelligence Laboratory, MIT, Cambridge, Mass.

Marcus, M.P. (1980).
'A Theory of Syntactic Recognition for Natural Language'. MIT Press, Cambridge, Mass. and London.

Markov, A. (1954).
'A Theory of Algorithms'. National Academy of Sciences, U.S.S.R.

Marslen-Wilson, W.D. (1975).
Sentence perception as an interactive parallel process. *Science*, Vol. 189, 226-228.

Marslen-Wilson, W.D. (1976).
Linguistic descriptions and psychological assumptions in the study of sentence perception. *In* 'New Approaches to Language Mechanisms'. (Eds. R.J. Wales and E. Walker). North-Holland, Amsterdam.

Marslen-Wilson, W.D. and Tyler,L.K. (1980).
The temporal structure of spoken language understanding. *Cognition* Vol. 8, 1-71.

Marslen-Wilson, W.D. and Welsh, A. (1978).
Processing interactions and lexical access during word recognition in continuous speech. *Cognitive Psychology*, Vol. 10, 29-63.

Mellish, C.S. (1980).
Some problems in early noun phrase interpretation. Proceedings of AISB Conference, Amsterdam, July 1980. (*Available from* Cognitive Studies Programme, University of Sussex, Sussex.)

Mellish, C.S. (1981).
Coping with Uncertainty – Noun Phrase Interpretation and Early Semantic Analysis. Ph.D. Thesis, Department of Artificial Intelligence, University of Edinburgh, Edinburgh.

Meltzer, B. and Michie, D. (1971).
'Machine Intelligence 6'. Edinburgh University Press, Edinburgh.

Michie, D. (Ed.) (1968).
'Machine Intelligence 3'. Edinburgh University Press, Edinburgh.

Michie, D. (Ed.) (1972).
'Machine Intelligence 7'. Edinburgh University Press, Edinburgh.

Miller, G.A. (1956).
The magical number seven, plus or minus two. *Psychological Review* 63, 81-97.

Miller, G.A. (1962).
Decision units in the perception of speech. *IRE Transactions on Information Theory*, IT-8, 81-83.

Miller, G.A. (1978).
Semantic relations among words. *In* 'Linguistic Theory and Psychological Reality'. (Eds. M. Halle, J.W. Bresnan and G.A. Miller). MIT Press, Cambridge, Mass.

Milne, R. (1980a).
Using Determinism to Predict Garden Paths. Department of Artificial Intelligence Research Paper no. 142, University of Edinburgh.

Milne, R. (1980b).
Parsing against Lexical Ambiguity. Department of Artificial Intelligence Research Paper no. 144, University of Edinburgh.

Mitchell, T.F. (1971).
Linguistic 'goings on'; collocations and other lexical matters arising on the syntactic record. *Archivum Linguisticum*, Vol. 2.

Montague, R. (1968).
Pragmatics. *In* 'Contemporary Philosophy: A Survey'. (Ed. Klibansky), pp. 102-122. La Nuova Italia Editrice, Florence.

Montague, R. (1972).
Pragmatics and intensional logic. *In* 'Semantics of Natural Language'. (Eds. G. Harman and D. Davidson). Reidel, Dordrecht.

Moran, T.P. (1973).
The Symbolic Imagery Hypothesis: A Production System Model. Computer Science Department Report, Carnegie Mellon University.

Nelson, R.J. (1968a).
Toward a realistic model of transformational grammar. *In* 'Linguistic Theory and Psychological Reality'. (Eds. M. Halle, J.W. Bresnan and G.A. Miller). MIT Press, Cambridge, Mass.

Nelson, R.J. (1968b).
'Introduction to Automata'. Wiley, New York.

Newell, A. (1973).
Production systems, models of control structures. *In* 'Visual Information Processing'. (Ed. W.G. Chase), pp. 463-526. Academic Press, New York.

Newell, A. (1980).
Physical symbol systems. *Cognitive Science* 4, no. 2, 135-183.

Newell, A., Shaw, J.C. and Simon, H.A. (1963).
GPS, a program that simulates human thought. *In* 'Computers and Thought'. (Eds. E. Feigenbaum and J. Feldman), pp. 279-296. McGraw-Hill, New York.

Nilsson, N. (1980).
'Principles of Artificial Intelligence'. Tioga Publishing Co., Palo Alto.

Norman, D.A. and Rumelhart, D.E. (1975).
'Explorations in Cognition'. Freeman, San Francisco.

Parisi, D. and Giorgi, A. (1981).
'A Procedure for the Production of Sentences'. Istituto di Psicologia del Consiglio Nazionale di Ricerche, Rome.

Pereira, F.C. and Warren, D.H. (1980).
Definite Clause Grammars Compared with Augmented Transition Networks. DAI Research Paper no. 116. Department of Artificial Intelligence, University of Edinburgh.

Perlmutter, D.M. (1971).
'Deep and Surface Structure Constraints in Syntax'. Holt, Rinehart and Winston, New York.

Petrick, S.R. (1965).
A Recognition Procedure for Transformational Grammars. Ph.D. Thesis, MIT, Cambridge, Mass.

Petrick, S.R. (1966).
A Program for Transformational Syntactic Analysis. Airforce Cambridge Research Laboratories Report AFCRL-66-698. Cambridge, Mass.

Petrick, S.R. (1973).
Transformational analysis. *In* 'Natural Language Processing'. (Ed. R. Rustin), pp. 27-41. Algorithmics Press, New York.

Plath, W.J. (1973).
Transformational grammar and transformational parsing in the REQUEST system. *In* 'Computational and Mathematical Linguistics', vol. 2. (Eds. A. Zampolli and N. Calzolari), pp. 367-384. Leo S. Olschki, Florence.

Post, E. (1943).
Formal reductions of the general combinatorial decision problem. *American Journal of Mathematics* 65, 197-268.

Postal, P.M. (1964).
Constituent structure. *International Journal of American Linguistics*, Part II, Vol. 30, no. 1.

Reich, P.A. (1969).
The finiteness of natural language. *Language* 45, 831-843.

Rieger, C. (1976).
Viewing parsing as word sense discrimination. *In* 'A Survey of Linguistic Science'. (Ed. W.O. Dingwall), Greylock Publishers, Stamford, Connecticut.

Rieger, C. and Small, S. (1979).
Word expert parsing. *In* 'Proceedings of the Sixth International Joint Conference on Artificial intelligence', pp. 723-728. Tokyo.

Riesbeck, C.K. (1974).
Computational Understanding: Analysis of Sentences and Context.
Ph.D. Thesis, Department of Computer Science, Stanford University.

Riesbeck, C.K. (1975a).
Computational understanding. *In* 'Proceedings of the Workshop on
Theoretical Issues in Natural Language Processing'. (Eds. R.C. Schank
and B.L. Nash-Webber), pp. 15-20. Bolt, Beranek and Newman,
Cambridge, Mass.

Riesbeck, C.K. (1975b).
Conceptual analysis. *In* 'Conceptual Information Processing'. (Ed.
R.C. Schank), pp. 83-156. North-Holland, Amsterdam.

Riesbeck, C.K. and Schank, R.C. (1976).
Comprehension by Computer: Expectation-Based Analysis of Sen-
tences in Context. Research Report no. 78, Department of Computer
Science, Yale University.

Ritchie, G.D. (1976).
Problems in local semantic processing. *In* 'Proceedings of the AISB
Conference', pp. 234-241. Edinburgh.

Ritchie, G.D. (1977).
Computer Modelling of English Grammar. Thesis CST-1-77, Department of Computer Science, University of Edinburgh.

Ritchie, G.D. (1978a).
Augmented Transition Network Grammars and Semantics Processing.
Report CSR-20-78, Department of Computer Science, University of
Edinburgh.

Ritchie, G.D. (1978b).
Predictions and procedures in semantically based grammar. *In*
'Proceedings of the AISB/GI Conference, Hamburg'. (Available from
Cognitive Studies Programme, University of Sussex).

Ritchie, G.D. (1980).
'Computational Grammar'. The Harvester Press, Sussex and Barnes
and Noble Books, New Jersey.

Rosch, E. and Lloyd B.B. (Eds) (1978).
'Cognition and Concepts'. Lawrence Erlbaum Associates, Hillside,
New Jersey.

Ross, J.R. (1967).
Constraints on variables in syntax. *Excerpted in* 'On Noam Chomsky'.
(Ed. G. Harman). Anchor Books, New York.

Roussel, P. (1975).
PROLOG: Manuel de Référence et d'Utilisation. Groupe d'Intelligence Artificielle, Université de Marseille-Luminy.

Rustin, R. (Ed.) (1973).
'Natural Language Processing'. Courant Computer Science Symposium 8. Algorithmics Press, New York.

Rychener, M. (1977).
Control requirements for the design of production system architectures. *SIGART/SIGPLAN Newsletter*, Vol. 12, No. 8.

Sacerdoti, E.D. (1975).
The non-linear nature of plans. *In* 'Proceedings of the Fourth International Joint Conference on Artificial Intelligence', pp. 206-214. Tbilisi.

Sag, I.A. (1976).
A logical theory of VP-deletion. *In* 'Papers from the 12th Regional Meeting of the Chicago Linguistic Society'. (Eds. S. Mufwene, C. Walker and S. Steever). University of Chicago, Chicago.

Sager, N. (1973).
The string parser for scientific literature. *In* 'Natural Language Processing'. (Ed. R. Rustin), pp. 61-87. Algorithmics Press, New York.

Sampson, G.R. (1979).
What was transformational grammar? *Lingua* 48, 355-378.

Sampson, G.R. (1980).
'Making Sense'. Oxford University Press, Oxford.

Schank, R.C. (1972).
Conceptual dependency: a theory of natural language understanding. *Cognitive Psychology* 3, no. 4, 552-630.

Schank, R.C. (1975).
'Conceptual Information Processing'. North-Holland, Amsterdam and American Elsevier, New York.

Schank, R.C. and Abelson, R.P. (1975).
Scripts, plans and knowledge. *In* 'Proceedings of the Fourth Joint International Conference on Artificial Intelligence', pp. 151-157. Tbilisi.

Schank, R., Leobowitz, M. and Birnbaum, L. (1978).
Integrated Partial Parsing. Computer Science Department Technical Report No. 189. Yale University.

Schank, R.C. and Nash-Webber, B.L. (Eds.) (1975).
'Proceedings of the Workshop on Theoretical Issues in Natural Language Processing'. Bolt, Beranek and Newman, Cambridge, Mass.

Schank, R. and Riesbeck, C. (Eds.) (1981).
'Inside Computer Understanding: five programs plus miniatures'.
Lawrence Erlbaum Associates, Hillside, New Jersey.

Shaw, R. and Bransford, J.D. (1978).
'Perceiving, Acting and Knowing'. Lawrence Erlbaum Associates,
Hillside, New Jersey.

Sheil, B.A. (1976).
Observations on context-free parsing. *Statistical Methods in Linguistics*
7, 71-109.

Shipman, D.W. (1979).
Phrase Structure Rules for Parsifal. Working Paper no. 182, Artificial
Intelligence Laboratory, MIT, Cambridge, Mass.

Shortliffe, E.H., Davis, R., Axline, S.G., Buchanan, B.G. Green, C.C.
and Cohen, S.N. (1975).
Computer based consultations in clinical therapeutics: explanation
and rule acquisition capabilities in the MYCIN system. *Computers
and Biomedical Research* 8, 303-320.

Simon, H.A. (1973).
The structure of ill-structured problems. *Artificial Intelligence* 4,
181-201.

Slobin, D.I. (1966).
Grammatical transformations and sentence comprehension in child-
hood and adulthood. *Journal of Verbal Learning and Verbal Behaviour*
5, 219-227.

Slocum, J. (1981).
A practical comparison of parsing strategies for machine translation
and other natural language processing purposes. Doctoral Dissertation.
University of Texas at Austin.

Small, S. (1980).
Word Expert Parsing. A Theory of Distributed Word-based Natural
Language Understanding. Technical Report no. 954, Department of
Computer Science, University of Maryland.

Small, S. (1981).
Demon timeouts: limiting the life spans of spontaneous computations
in cognitive models. *In* 'Proceedings of the Third Annual Meeting
of the Cognitive Science Society', Berkeley.

Small, S. and Rieger, C. (1982).
Parsing and comprehending with word experts: (a theory and its
realization). *In* 'Strategies for Natural Language Processing'. (Eds.
M.D. Ringle and W. Lenhert). Lawrence Erlbaum Associates, Hillside,
New Jersey.

Smith, E.E., Rips, L.J. and Shoben, E.J. (1974).
Semantic memory and psychological semantics. *In* 'The Psychology of Learning and Motivation'. (Ed. G.H. Bower). Academic Press, New York.

Smith, N. and Wilson, D. (1979).
'Modern Linguistics: the results of Chomsky's revolution'. Penguin Books, Harmondsworth.

Sow, T. (1972).
Anaphoric Relations in English. Ph.D. Dissertation, MIT, Cambridge, Mass.

Sparck Jones, K. and Kay, M. (1973).
'Linguistics and Information Science'. Academic Press, New York.

Steedman, M. and Johnson-Laird, P.N. (1976).
A programmatic theory of linguistic performance. University of Sussex.

Stefik, M., Aikins, J., Balzer, R., Benoit, J., Birnbaum, L., Hayes-Roth, F. and Sacerdoti, E. (1982).
The organization of expert systems: a tutorial. *Artificial Intelligence* 18, 2, 135-173.

Stevens, A.L. and Rumelhart, D.E. (1975).
Errors in reading: analysis using an augmented transition network model of grammar. *In* 'Explorations in Cognition'. (Eds. D.A. Norman and D.E. Rumelhart), pp. 136-155. Freeman, San Francisco.

Sussman, G.J. (1975).
'A Computer Model of Skill Acquisition'. Elsevier, New York.

Sussman, G.J. and McDermott, D. (1972).
Why Conniving is Better than Planning. Memo 255A, Artificial Intelligence Laboratory, MIT, Cambridge, Mass.

Swartout, W.R. (1978).
A Comparison of PARSIFAL with ATNs. Artificial Intelligence Laboratory Memo no. 462, MIT, Cambridge, Mass.

Swinney, D.A. (1979).
Lexical access during sentence comprehension: (re)consideration of contextual effects. *Journal of Verbal Learning and Verbal Behaviour* 18, 645-659.

Thorne, J.P., Bratley, P. and Dewar, H. (1968).
The syntactic analysis of English by machine. *In* 'Machine Intelligence 3'. (Ed. D. Michie), pp. 281-309. Edinburgh University Press, Edinburgh.

Valiant, L.G. (1975).
General context-free recognition in less than cubic time. *Journal of Computer and Systems Sciences*, Vol. 10, 308-315.

Waldinger, R.J. (1977).
Achieving several goals simultaneously. *In* 'Machine Intelligence 8' (Eds. E. Elcock and D. Michie), pp. 94-109. Edinburgh University Press, Edinburgh.

Wales, R.J. and Walker, E. (1976).
'New Approaches to Language Mechanisms'. North-Holland, Amsterdam.

Walker, D. (1966).
Recent Developments in the MITRE Syntactic Analysis Procedure. MITRE Report, MTP-11, The MITRE Corporation, Bedford, Mass.

Wall, R. (1972).
'Introduction to Mathematical Linguistics'. Prentice-Hall, Englewood Cliffs, New Jersey.

Waltz, D.L. (1975).
Understanding line drawings of scenes with shadows. *In* 'The Psychology of Computer Vision'. (Ed. P.H. Winston), pp. 19-92. McGraw-Hill, New York.

Waltz, D.L. (1978).
An English language question answering system for a large relational data base. *Communications of the ACM* 21/7, 526-539.

Wanner, E. (1980).
The ATN and the sausage machine: which one is baloney? *Cognition* 8, 209-225.

Wasow, T. (1972).
Anaphoric Relations in English. Ph.D. Dissertation, MIT, Cambridge, Mass.

Waterman, D. and Hayes-Roth, F. (1978).
'Pattern-directed Inference Systems'. Academic Press, London.

Weischedel, R.M. and Black, J.E. (1980).
Responding intelligently to unparsable inputs. *American Journal of Computational Linguistics*, Vol. 6, no. 2, 97-109.

Weizenbaum, J. (1966).
ELIZA - a computer program for the study of natural language communication between man and machine. *Communications of the ACM* 9, 36-45.

Weizenbaum, J. (1967).
Contextual understanding by computers. *Communications of the ACM* 10, 474-480.

Wilensky, R. and Arens, Y. (1980).
PHRAN: a knowledge based approach to natural language analysis. Berkeley Electronics Research Laboratory, Memo No. UCB/ERL/M80/34.

Wilks, Y. (1973a).
The Stanford machine translation project. *In* 'Natural Language Processing'. (Ed. R. Rustin), pp. 243-290. Algorithmics Press, New York.

Wilks, Y. (1973b).
An artificial intelligence approach to machine translation. *In* 'Computer Models of Thought and Language'. (Eds. R.C. Schank and K. Colby), pp. 114-151. Freeman, San Francisco.

Wilks, Y. (1975a).
Parsing English II. *In* 'Computational Semantics'. (Eds. E. Charniak and Y. Wilks), pp. 155-184, North-Holland, Amsterdam.

Wilks, Y. (1975b).
Preference semantics. *In* 'Formal Semantics of Natural Language'. (Ed. E. Keenan), pp. 329-348. Cambridge University Press, Cambridge.

Wilks, Y. (1975c).
An intelligent analyzer and understander of English. *Communications of the ACM* 18 (5), 264-274.

Wilks, Y. (1975d).
A preferential pattern-making semantics for natural language inference. *Artificial Intelligence*, Vol. 6, 53-74.

Wilks, Y. (1975e).
Primitives and words. *In* 'Proceedings of the Workshop on Theoretical Issues in Natural Language Processing'. (Eds. R.C. Schank and B.L. Nash-Webber), pp. 42-44. Bolt, Beranek and Newman, Cambridge, Mass.

Wilks, Y. (1977a).
Frames, scripts, stories and fantasies. *Pragmatics Microfiche* ....

Wilks, Y. (1977b).
Good and bad arguments about semantic primitives. *Communication and Cognition*. Vol. 10, No. 3/4, 181-221.

Wilks, Y. (1978).
Making preferences more active. *Artificial Intelligence* XI, 197-223.

Wilks, Y. (1980).
Some Thoughts on Procedural Semantics. Cognitive Studies Centre
Report no. 1, University of Essex.

Wilks, Y. and Bien, J. (In press).
Beliefs, environments and points of view. *To appear in Cognitive
Science.*

Williams, E. (1977).
Discourse and logical form. *Linguistic Inquiry* 8, 101-137.

Winograd, T. (1972).
'Understanding Natural Language'. Edinburgh University Press,
Edinburgh.

Winograd, T. (1975a).
Frame representations and the declarative-procedural controversy.
In 'Representation and Understanding'. (Eds. D.G. Bobrow and A.
Collins), pp. 185-210. Academic Press, New York.

Winograd, T. (1975b).
Five lectures on artificial intelligence. *In* 'The Psychology of Computer
Vision'. (Ed. P.H. Winston). McGraw-Hill, New York.

Winograd, T. (1976).
Towards a procedural understanding of semantics. *Revue Intern-
ationale de Philosophie* 3-4, no. 117-118, 260-303.

Winston, P.H. (1975).
'The Psychology of Computer Vision'. McGraw-Hill, New York.

Woods, W.A. (1970).
Transition network grammars for natural language analysis. *Communications of the ACM* 13, 591-606.

Woods, W.A., Bates, M., Brown, G., Bruce, B., Cook, C., Clovstad,
Machoul, J., Nash-Webber, B., Schwartz, R., Wolf, J. and Zue, V. (1976).
Speech Understanding Systems-Final Report; Vol. IV. Technical
Report 3438, Bolt, Beranek and Newman, Cambridge, Mass.

Woods, W.A., Kaplan, R.M. and Nash-Webber, B. (1972).
The Lunar Sciences Natural Language Information System. BBN
Report no. 2378, Bolt, Beranek and Newman, Cambridge. Mass.
Also available as publication N72-28984 of the US National Technical
Information Service.

Woods, W.A. (1973).
An experimental parsing system for transition network grammars.
In 'Natural Language Processing'. (Ed. R. Rustin), pp. 112-154.
Algorithmics Press, New York.

Woods, W.A. (1977).
Lunar rocks in natural English: explorations in natural language question-answering. *In* 'Linguistic Structures Processing'. (Ed. A. Zampolli), pp. 521-568. North-Holland, Amsterdam.

Woods, W.A. (1980).
Cascaded ATN grammars. *American Journal of Computational Linguistics* 6, no. 1, 1-12.

Zampolli, A. (Ed.) (1977).
'Linguistic Structures Processing'. Fundamental Studies in Computer Science 5. North-Holland, Amsterdam.

Zwicky, A., Friedman, J., Hall, B.C., and Walker, D.E. (1965).
The MITRE analysis procedure for transformational grammars. *In* 'Proceedings of the 1965 Fall Joint Computer Conference'. Thompson Books, Washington,D.C.

INDEX

action: 36, 200
  speech action: 251
active node stack: 96, 98, 99, 107, 120f.
activity context interactions: 261, 264
algorithm: 16, 151
'and so did' construction: 163
attention: 228, 248
attention-shifting rules: 123
augmented transition network: 51, 59, 66ff., 86, 92, 93ff., 99, 118, 119, 125, 129, 135, 138, 204f. 213, 214, 221, 239
automata: 60ff.
  finite state automata: 60, 223
  push down automata: 61
  linear bounded automata: 61
aux-inversion: 122

backtrack: 12, 44, 45, 69, 86, 92, 93ff., 119, 129, 192, 200, 228, 229
base component: 20, 127, 157
  base tree: 20
belief structure: 246, 248, 262
binding: 175f.
bottom-up: 9, 67, 96, 239
bracketed string: 6
breadth-first: 10, 15, 69, 229
buffer: 96, 98f. 102f., 120f., 236

case: 174f.
case frame: 206, 213, 215, 228, 239

case inference: 225
case ambiguity: 230
C-command: 174f., 186
chart: 52, 73ff.
collocation: 253, 255
combinatorial explosion: 23, 44
commutativity: 42
complex NP constraint: 110ff., 179f., 182, 183
competence: 182, 221, 223
complex symbols: 164
concept structure: 252, 253, 254, 257, 258, 260, 261, 264
conceptual dependency: 201, 206, 225, 234, 235, 239
conceptual object: 258
conceptual templates: 236, 237, 238
concrete syntax: 206
condition: 37
conflict resolution: 47, 55f.
  conflict set 45
  conflict resolution strategy 55
constraints: 172f., 174, 181f.
constraint satisfaction: 215
context: 202, 212, 241, 247ff., 250f., 252, 254, 257, 260
context-free grammar (rules): 5ff., 22, 30, 151ff., 187
context-sensitive grammar (rules): 67, 156, 161
control: 174, 258
control language: 46, 47
  context-free control language: 57
control signals: 252, 253, 254, 261
control strategy: 39
  irrevocable control: 42
  tentative control: 45
controlled production system: 45, 57
co-ordinate structures: 159, 168
  co-ordinate structure constraint: 182, 183
cyclic rules: 31, 108
cycling: 27, 32

database: 36, 37, 52
dative movement: 136, 138
decidability: 16, 62
deep abstract syntax: 206
deep parsing: 219ff., 225ff., 229ff.
deep-structure: 155, 200, 221, 222
deep syntactic structure: 220
deletion: 25, 31, 159

dependencies: 162, 169, 184
depth-first: 10, 45, 69, 225, 228, 229
derivation: 9, 20
  direct derivation: 9, 40
  indirect derivation: 9
derivation tree: 14
determinism, non-determinism: 12, 42f., 44, 47, 49, 91ff., 119, 152, 252
D-structure: 173
discourse interaction: 253, 260, 264
discourse process: 255
discourse structure: 248
distributed system: 250, 251
  distributed process: 252

Earley's algorithm: 159, 168
embedding: 31, 184, 223
empty category principle: 175, 178, 181, 186, 187, 189,192
environment: 210
episodic facts: 240
equi-np deletion: 136
equivalence: 7
expectation: 222, 225, 228, 229, 236, 241, 256
expert systems. 221ff.
expressor: 184
extraction: 238

feedback: 251, 252
fillers: 185f., 187f.
filters: 172f., 174, 178
focus of attention interactions: 261, 264
focus of discourse: 255
formal grammar: 5, 53
fragmentation: 204, 224, 232, 233, 236, 256
frame: 220, 228, 239, 240, 241, 245
function words: 250

gaps: 185f.
garden path sentence. 92, 101ff., 136, 160
generalized phrase structure grammar: 161f., 187
goals: 251, 252
goal-directed production system: 47
  goal-directed invocation: 57
goodness-rating: 123
government: 174f., 186

grammars: 3ff., 60, 98
  length increasing grammars: 62
  constituent structure grammar: 67

heterarchical organization: 154
heuristics: 225, 236
heuristic search: 46
hierarchical structure: 213,220, 233
homogeneous sentence analysers. 199, 201

identity condition: 25
idioms: 249, 253, 254
idiosyncratic interaction: 253, 254, 255, 260
indirect object construction: 234
inference rules: 169, 212, 225, 229, 230, 233, 239, 244
  inferential processes: 247
interleaved semantic processing: 199, 206f., 213f.
intermediate structure: 228, 234
interpreter: 36, 38
issue skeleton. 244, 245

key words: 224

left branch constraint: 180
  generalised left branch constraint: 190, 192
left parse: 13
lexical interaction: 253
lexical knowledge: 248
linguistic interaction: 253, 256, 260, 264
linguistic universals: 91, 110ff., 174, 183, 221, 222
logical form: 104, 105, 160, 161, 167, 169, 172
logical interaction: 253, 262, 263, 264
lookahead: 95, 101

machine translation: 203, 223, 230, 251
macro-semantic analyser: 220, 243
Markov algorithm: 35
means-end analysis: 57
memory processes: 247
meta-level knowledge: 55
metarule: 167, 190
micro-semantic analyser: 220, 239
minimal parsing procedure: 224
move α : 173ff., 177
multiple choice perspective: 263

noun phrases: 205, 207, 216, 226, 239, 253, 256f.

object semantic structure: 207, 210.
optional transformation: 24, 30

parallel search: 44
parallel processing: 93ff., 117, 123, 134, 158, 248, 252
parsing strategy: 9
paraplate: 204
passive: 169, 258
patterns: 236
percolation-projection (p-projection): 178f.
performance: 182, 221
phrasal analyser: 236
phrasal lexicon: 223
phrase structure grammar (rules): 126, 155ff., 172
planning: 252
plausability interaction: 264
post decision hypothesis: 251
prediction and substantiation: 244
preference semantics: 203f., 234f.,
prepositional phrase: 226, 228, 232
primitive act: 226
prior decision hypothesis: 250
priorities: 122
procedure: 7
   basic procedure: 48
   complex procedure: 48
procedural-declarative issue: 71
procedural programming language: 48, 66, 251
process interactions: 249, 250, 252
production: 36
   production set: 37, 53
   partitioned production set: 56
   uninterpreted production: 37
   production conditions: 56
   production sequencing: 56
   production rules: 236
production system: 35ff., 66, 76, 223, 225, 234, 239
projection (from pseudo-texts): 242
pronoun disambiguation: 212, 216, 230, 233
pseudo-text: 241
psychological reality: 92, 101, 140, 152ff., 223, 235, 250

Q-systems: 56, 83

raising: 131, 177
recogniser: 7
recursion: 6
  recursive: 17
  recursively enumerable: 17
  recursively solveable: 17
recursive transition networks: 60, 62ff.
reference evaluation: 210, 215f., 248
referential semantics: 206, 208f., 210
regular language: 60
  regular expression: 168
rejection rules: 29
relation mapping rules: 215
relative plausibility: 264
relevant generalization: 118, 125f.
  (see also significant generalization)
requests: 201f., 203, 225, 226, 229, 236, 239
respectively: 162
rewrite rule: 37
right parse: 13
rule ordering: 26
rule-packet: 98
  active rule packet: 99, 109, 121f.

script: 220, 239, 240, 241
  sketchy script: 244
selectional restriction: 204, 240
selective modifier placement: 201
semantics: 129f., 134, 155, 160, 161, 191, 199ff., 219ff., 251
semantic ATN: 204f.
semantic anomaly: 204, 207, 210
semantic block: 233, 241, 242
semantic consistency: 208
semantic density: 233, 235
semantic feed-back: 200, 201, 204, 208, 209, 212
semantic formula: 203, 230, 232, 234, 245
semantic grammar: 205, 220
semantic head: 232
semantic interpretive rules: 213, 214
semantic marker: 223
semantic parser: 245
semantic predictions: 202, 205, 206
semantic preference: 233
semantic primitive: 204, 230, 238, 239, 243
semantic representation: 219, 229, 238

semi-grammaticality: 117, 119
sense and reference: 208, 210
sentence-final semantic interpretation: 199, 200
sentential subject constraint: 190
serial processing: 153ff.
shadowing: 152ff.
significant linguistic generalisation: 53, 165ff., 223, 228, 234, 245
  (see also relevant generalization)
slashed categories: 187
solution set: 43
  computable solution set: 46, 47f.
solution space: 43
solution state: 41
specified subject constraint: 105
S-structure: 173
state: 60
  state diagram: 61
state of the world: 210
strong generative capacity: 4
structural ambiguity: 200, 211
subcategorisation (restrictions): 173, 188
subjacency constraint: 115
subject gaps: 191f., 193
subject-verb agreement: 124, 138
superficial parsing: 219ff., 223ff.
surface abstract syntax: 206
surface grammar: 21, 22, 29, 160
surface sentence (surface text): 20, 21, 219, 229
surface structure trees: 21, 213
surface syntax: 199, 204, 213
symbol structures: 250

template: 230, 232, 233, 235, 237, 241, 242, 243
  bare template: 232, 237, 238
tensed S constraint: 105
text-skimmer: 244
there-deletion: 128
there-insertion: 125
top-down: 9, 66, 67, 69, 96, 206, 225, 239, 244
trace: 104ff., 112f., 158, 171ff.
transducer: 8, 19
transformational grammar (rules): 3ff., 104, 106, 118, 125, 140, 155ff., 172, 221
transition networks: 59ff.
Turing machine: 62

understanding: 248
ungrammaticality: 118, 124f., 137f.
uniform coding: 235
unrestricted rewrite system: 62

view interactions: 263
VP-deletion: 171f.

wait-and-see parser: 221
weak generative capacity: 4, 165
well-formed (sub)string: 4, 74
   well-formed symbol table: 70
word-based system: 236, 247ff.
word expert parsing: 247, 252ff.
word-sense ambiguity: 202, 204, 212, 230, 233, 248ff., 250, 252, 254
   word-sense discrimination: 248
world-knowledge: 222, 260, 263
wh-movement: 126, 128f., 136, 178, 189

$\overline{X}$-theory: 178

yes-no questions: 166